Praise for *Permission Granted*

"If you've ever wondered how you can love and show courage even when things are not going your way, wonder no more. Regina Louise has you covered — in style and with engrossing storytelling and encouraging words."
— **Susie Moore**, author of *Stop Checking Your Likes*

"You will be completely captivated by this book."
— from the foreword by **Dr. Margaret Paul**,
bestselling author of *Inner Bonding*

"Anyone who has read and loved Regina Louise's luminous self-revelations in her memoirs will need to have this book. Whether she's talking about power, loyalty, integrity, or of course love, Regina is sharp, witty, clear-eyed but never self-pitying, and frequently hilarious. This is a book that every woman should have. Her words will lift you up!"
— **Jane Ganahl**, author of *Naked on the Page*
and cofounder of Litquake festival

"There is no one better suited than Regina Louise to show us that we have the power to make our dreams come true. Her personal stories of thriving in the face of trauma, paired with her no-nonsense, practical advice, will motivate you to be inspired by your challenges and to embrace your best self with kindness and kick-ass courage."
— **Richard Dry**, author of *Leaving* and professor of English
and creative writing, Las Positas College

"This is the kind of book that changes lives. Regina Louise not only gives us permission to live our best lives, she also offers chapter-by-chapter strategies for granting that permission to ourselves. Regina Louise is sassy, insightful, compassionate, wickedly funny, and a born storyteller. I guarantee: once you start reading this book, you won't be able to stop. It's that f**king brilliant."

— **Hope Edelman**, author of *Motherless Daughters* and *The AfterGrief*

"Regina Louise has created an owner's manual for personal empowerment and self-love. Ever met someone so fierce and fabulous that you wanted to know how to capture that light for yourself? That is how I felt when I heard Regina reading her last book. With *Permission Granted* she shares pages of strategies to find your own light source. During times like these, what could be more valuable?"

— **Kari Byron**, TV personality, producer, and author of *Crash Test Girl*

"Regina Louise reminds us that self-love is the foundation of freeing our minds and souls from the binds that we place on ourselves. Granting yourself permission to love and appreciate who you are can be one of the hardest trials of your life."

— **Ashley Blank**, founder of Adventures in Literature

"Wow, wow, wow! Regina Louise is the real deal, a ray of sunshine in the self-help field! She has 'done the work' of emotional mastery. Her audacity to love herself and give you strategies to do the same is genius."

— **Maureen Healy**, author of *The Emotionally Healthy Child*

"Part memoir, part 'speak up for yourself' manifesto, *Permission Granted* provides a powerful blueprint for how to love yourself, love your voice, and use your one precious life to live your legacy. Regina Louise will help you heal from self-doubt and step into the life you were born to lead."

— Alexia Vernon, author of *Step into Your Moxie*

"Regina Louise takes us on a warrior's journey and bares all in daring to share the anguish, pain, and ecstasy of her path to self-acceptance and self-love. She invites us to do the same with her handbook of tools to navigate that uncharted wilderness in each of us — the interior of our own souls. Her words are an invitation and a challenge to be all that we can be and a celebration of the exultant triumph of manifesting our dreams. *Permission Granted* is a searing firebrand of a book, and even if you never practice one technique, to spend time here is to feel something unforgettable — Regina's love."

— Yvonne Chotzen, film producer, corporate trainer, and founder of Chotzen Communications

"No matter what, a voice of truth and love will be heard above the din and noise of ordinary life. That's why Regina Louise stands out as an authentic voice of intention and positive action. She has discovered and given herself permission to live the 'kick-ass strategies' of self-love and courageous possibility. Now, with a desire to empower whoever seeks to know, she generously shares her strategies with us."

— Liza Ingrasci and Raz Ingrasci, Hoffman Institute Foundation

"In *Permission Granted*, Regina Louise relates the journey of her lessons learned and puts them right at your fingertips. You'll put this book down inspired, moved, and armed with practical strategies that will allow you to live your life in a fuller way!"

— Steve Pemberton, author of *A Chance in the World* and *The Lighthouse Effect*

"Regina Louise is the real deal. She is the wise, irreverent, loving, funny aunt you always wanted. This book has so much wisdom packed into it, but unlike other self-help books, she offers real, accessible tools to make her wisdom your own. This is the permission slip we all need to live with unapologetic boldness."

— **Laura McKowen**, author of *We Are the Luckiest*

PERMISSION
Granted

Also by Regina Louise

Somebody's Someone

Someone Has Led This Child to Believe

PERMISSION *Granted*

KICK-ASS STRATEGIES
TO BOOTSTRAP YOUR WAY
TO UNCONDITIONAL
SELF-LOVE

Regina Louise

Foreword by Margaret Paul

New World Library
Novato, California

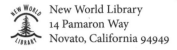 New World Library
14 Pamaron Way
Novato, California 94949

Text design by Tona Pearce Myers

Library of Congress Cataloging-in-Publication Data

Names: Louise, Regina, author.
Title: Permission granted : kick-ass strategies to bootstrap your way to unconditional self-love / Regina Louise ; foreword by Margaret Paul.
Description: Novato, California : New World Library, [2021] | Includes bibliographical references and index. | Summary: "Real-deal ways to defy expectations and love oneself into a high-performing life, from a fabulous and fierce Black woman, speaker, teacher, and coach"-- Provided by publisher.
Identifiers: LCCN 2021007445 (print) | LCCN 2021007446 (ebook) | ISBN 9781608687268 (paperback) | ISBN 9781608687275 (epub)
Subjects: LCSH: Self-acceptance. | Self-esteem. | Self-actualization (Psychology)
Classification: LCC BF575.S37 L678 2021 (print) | LCC BF575.S37 (ebook) | DDC 158.1--dc23
LC record available at https://lccn.loc.gov/2021007445
LC ebook record available at https://lccn.loc.gov/2021007446

First printing, June 2021
ISBN 978-1-60868-726-8
Ebook ISBN 978-1-60868-727-5
Printed in the United States on 30% postconsumer-waste recycled paper

 New World Library is proud to be a Gold Certified Environmentally Responsible Publisher. Publisher certification awarded by Green Press Initiative.

10   9   8   7   6   5   4   3   2   1

Dedicated to Spirit, for always showing up and showing out on behalf of what is true about each of us: we are worthy of this One life.

Also dedicated to those of you seeking your own permission to, in the words of Alonzo King, founder and artistic director of LINES Ballet, "live the idea" of your best life. Do it unapologetically, fearlessly, and as fabulously as all get-out!

And to my biological mother, who transitioned during the last few days of my final rewrite, in January 2021. You were the most unpretentious, unapologetic, life-on-your-own-terms human I've ever met. Your terms were so fierce they taught me to be the wild thing that could not afford to feel sorry for herself for too long, and for this I am truly grateful. Thank you for giving me a life worth living, worth examining, and worth transforming into something to write about. Where the hurting ends, the healing begins — here's to healing the world's hearts!

Contents

Foreword

I first met Regina Louise when she attended one of my Inner Bonding five-day intensives. I was immediately drawn to the power of her energy, and I knew, just from being in her presence that first moment of meeting her, that she was an extraordinary human being, so connected to her inner child. In addition, I sensed in Regina a very deep ancient wisdom — an ancient wisdom that our world desperately needs right now. I am delighted to discover in this book more of what I discovered in that intensive — more about the depth of her ancient wisdom, the depth of her inner and higher knowing.

Regina is an incredible writer — and you will be completely captivated by this book — as well as a powerfully loving and vulnerable role model for what it means to move beyond fear and fully manifest yourself. The challenging journey that she has been on, and what she has been able to do, may seem to many of you to be miraculous. But by reading this book, you will be given a pathway for creating your own miracles for yourself, through learning to trust the gifts that you've been given — the gifts that each of us have been given — and to trust your own inner and higher guidance.

Our spiritual guidance is always here for each of us, but many of us learned not to listen to or trust our own knowing. Regina had to stay connected to her intuition and higher guidance in order to survive, and throughout this book she lets us in on how powerful that inner and higher guidance has been for her.

Learning to access and trust my own guidance has been a huge part of my journey toward love and wholeness. Having been brought up with no spiritual background, I had to find my own way. At this point, everything I say and do comes through me from my higher guidance, and I was thrilled to read that this is also true for Regina.

Regina is one of those incredibly one-of-a-kind people, so hard to describe in words. Sometimes quiet. Sometimes totally out there. Sometimes funny and sometimes unbelievably wise. She is a unique expression of the Divine. She is so brilliant, so beautiful, such a big, compelling presence. What's most powerful about her is how connected she is to her inner and higher truths.

She has found the path to embracing who she is and expressing it in the world. Her kick-ass strategies are so powerful. This is not a superficial book. This is a book of depth, a journey into the soul — a journey into discovering who you truly are and giving yourself permission to be all that you came here to this planet to be.

I didn't have that permission growing up, and neither did Regina. I would guess that most of you did not have that permission. Instead, I was told over and over to be less than I am. I was too intense and too smart and too sensitive and too perceptive for my narcissistic parents, and I grew up believing that these intrinsic qualities were bad.

Now, I fully love these qualities. I've given myself full permission to be as intense, as smart, as sensitive, as perceptive, and as connected with my source of truth as I am, and when I meet another person who embraces their beautiful intrinsic qualities, I deeply connect with them, heart to heart. Which is what happened with Regina: we connected heart to heart in the intensive.

Regina was a threat to one of the men in the intensive who projected his own self-judgments and resulting self-loathing onto her. I was appalled and asked him to leave the room until he could come back in a more regulated state and apologize to her, which he did. But this was an example of how men are often threatened by the beautiful, powerful, brilliant, gifted, and talented woman you're going to learn about and read about in this book. It is so sad to me than anybody would be threatened by Regina, but as you will see, not only men but also women have been threatened by her magnificent gifts. I find this heartbreaking. We need Regina. We need who she is and what she offers in this beautiful book — a way of moving beyond our programming that keeps us limited, that keeps us believing we're not good enough, and into embracing the beauty that we are.

I'm so grateful to Regina for writing this book to lead the way for each of us to embrace all that we are. We came to this planet to evolve in our ability to love, which has to start with learning to love ourselves, and to fully manifest the gifts we've been given. We cannot do this when we don't know who we are and haven't given ourselves permission to be all that we are.

You will receive this permission in this book. I hope you stay open to all that Regina is offering you and do the exercises that will take you deeper and deeper into yourself. Allow

Regina to incite you to give yourself permission to evolve in your ability to love yourself and share your love with others, and to manifest all that you are. In our world today, each of us needs to step up to the plate to be the love that we are and to offer it to each other and to the planet.

This book offers you a powerful way to learn to see, love, and value who you truly are, and also to let go of the projections of others and the false beliefs that you've absorbed about yourself over the years. This book is for anyone who has been holding themselves back from fully manifesting their God-given gifts.

As you will see, Regina is an unbelievably courageous woman. Nothing was going to stop her from learning to love and value herself. Nothing was going to stop her from taking the risks she needed to take. She was courageous enough to be willing to be hurt — to be willing to have her heart broken over and over.

Many years ago, I made two decisions that changed my life. One, that I was willing to be hurt rather than continue to try to protect myself from pain. And two, that I was willing to lose others rather than lose myself. These are obviously the same decisions that this incredibly courageous woman also made.

Regina, I honor you for all that you've done and all that you offer us.

— **Dr. Margaret Paul**, bestselling author of
Inner Bonding, relationship expert,
and cocreator of the Inner Bonding® self-healing process

Introduction

Welcome, Dear Reader

Thank you for allowing me to share just how excited I am to begin this journey with you! I've spent the better part of three decades accumulating a plethora of life experiences. Choosing to observe, examine, and make meaning out of the actions I've taken to be my own (s)hero has become my joy, has been what makes my life worth living. Being courageous enough to take a look at the consequences of our actions, examining what did and did not work, and committing to transforming our learnings into empowering new beliefs, well, I want in on that! My hope is to offer you a fresh perspective on how to navigate a life of choice, clarity, and courage.

Throughout this permission manifesto, I will lavishly reiterate the importance of having a life on *your* terms. Your life is yours to decide how you want to live it. The way I see it is: if I'm not living from the standpoint that my life is just as meaningful as that of every other human being on the planet, then I'm nowhere in the vicinity of living my best life; I may as well be on the bleachers, on the sidelines, in the attic peering out through the dormer window. If I'm not aware that I have the right to recognize that my existence is *all about me*, then I may as well be doomed to make it all about everyone else (and believe me when I say I have a lot of tenure in that department). If I'm not willing to take my life into my own hands and fashion it into some semblance of excellence, the same as I would encourage those I love and support to do, I may as well assign myself to perpetually asking the question, *What about me?* Again, been there, and nearly drowned in that. And sometimes we may find ourselves as both the swimmer in distress and the lifeguard we need to become in order to save ourselves.

For much of my journey, I have found myself in situations where I've had to defend my dignity, or in a few extreme cases, my right to be alive. In other words, I've spent a lot of time advocating, campaigning for, and reimagining what life could be not only for myself but for the tens of thousands of people I've had the honor to address, coach, and engage with virtually, by telephone, via satellite, and face-to-face. Some of whom, like me, were not supposed to beat the odds, be them large or small. But that's the catch. I've chosen to examine the voices who cheered me on to my demise, putting them in check, poking and testing their logic, and releasing what didn't ring true, and I am here to encourage you to do the same.

The prologue of my most recent memoir, *Someone Has Led This Child to Believe*, opens this way: "This *is* the task of anyone who carries the burden of his or her own 'unworthiness': to learn to give one's own self merciful favor while standing in the blistering heat of a primal wound; to seek refuge within one's own heart; and to wipe someone else's fatalistic narrative of what their life *will be* from their consciousness, hand it back to the disbeliever, and say: 'I believe this belongs to you.'" I will say this up front: often we need to awaken to the fact that we may have unwittingly given our power to others, and we need to make moves to take it back. As I will say several times along this journey: your life need not be as dramatic and or chock-full of adverse childhood experiences as mine in order for you to recognize that you deserve better and to accept that changes need to happen. No matter our walk of life, in my experience we always have the opportunity to expand our consciousness, come into awareness of our full potential, and grow ourselves up to fill our own shoes. Doing so, becoming the champions of our own permission, helps us follow our dreams, connect with our deepest desires, and realign with our dampened passions and purpose.

What began as a suspicion has grown into a full-blown belief: I don't have the luxury to take my personal challenges, well, personally, and I don't have the inclination to buy into the myths of my limitations. Too much has happened. I've experienced a succession of childhood-into-adulthood events that have threatened to disrupt all my dreams and aspirations. Instead of folding from the pressure, I've been more likely to take out my scepter and wave it to indicate that X marks the spot where I begin and where the naysayers end. I hereby grant you permission to mark the spot where you begin and where that which no longer serves you ends. Gaslighting extinguished!

Self-preservation by way of setting loving boundaries is a must-have for all beings, and this is especially true for artists, empaths, and those of us who tend to be more porous in our spirit and in our emotional signatures, meaning that we feel *everything* more lastingly and more deeply. If you know what I'm saying, go ahead and shout it out: *I know that's right!* Drawing that line in the sand, establishing my boundaries, claiming my birthright of personal empowerment has made all the difference in ending up a victor instead of a self-assigned victim.

Making the decision, not so long ago, to stop running, hiding, and lowballing my self-worth, which meant breaking up with my worst fixations and fears and instead turning toward myself in a homecoming kind of way, was the beginning of *Permission Granted*.

It's a continual process, giving ourselves permission to become the compass needle that orients us back to who we really are, again and again: self-determining beings with the deep capacity to love and connect with ourselves and others. With every opportunity we step into, we experience a new level of personal achievement. Perhaps we're enticed to want more, and if so, it is our own consent that will either propel us forward or signal us to drop it and move on entirely. To know when to pivot is the gift of discernment. However we decide to play it, the choice is ours.

As the subtitle of this book suggests, not only have I discovered and claimed some kick-ass and bootstrapping strategies for myself, but I have also used every inner resource imaginable to hack the limited and uninspiring narrative I was unwittingly born into. Offering myself an alternative way to live on my own terms, I've taught myself to *kick* my disenfranchisement's *ass* all the way back to where it came from. Who says that being born a woman of African descent, poor, supposedly unwanted, neglected, marginalized, stigmatized, and labeled batshit-cray means that's all life will *ever* be? For some, all those adversities are the gateway to a life of disastrous results, one in which more of the same is surely to be lived out. Okay. Absolutely. If you agree to the terms of that kind of contract, of your most certainly utterly awful future, then indubitably the outcome will match it.

As far as I am concerned, we live in a generous Universe

that is indifferent to what we manifest. Whether we manifest chaos or gifts of goodness is purely up to us. Positive manifestation has everything to do with what I believe to be true, not only about myself but also about every other human being: the power to make our lives our own on our own terms is an inside job, and all we need do is align with what is true for each of us. That is what gets manifested, the truth of who we believe ourselves to be and what it is that we desire.

What do you know to be true about the Universe in which you live? No pressure. No judgment. Your insights are between you, yourself, and, well, the Universe.

I am not here to talk anyone out of underperforming their life. My only hope is to be a go-to for you, a friend, a mentor, a confidante or coach, someone to support you in realizing what is written on the walls of your heart, and to help you compose a new reality if what is written no longer serves you. I know what it feels like to want something deeply but not to have enough opportunities or support to broker those wants into reality; and that's pretty much everything I've ever wanted. One of the biggest potential pitfalls for the parentless and for those who have no family is not having a safety net to catch us when we fall. We don't get to benefit from our parents' privileges of social class, economic success, or generational successes. Many of us are left to live the life of the archetypal orphan, a life where we decide to either make it on our own terms or fail as the result of permitting our circumstances to decree our future.

I've learned over time to be wary of anything intended — unconsciously or otherwise — to invite me to feel completely excluded or alienated from myself. And yes, I definitely had moments that tested my resolve. Haven't we all? I still do. I mean, let's keep it real. How does anyone feel successful if they're taught to feel disqualified from the life they're entering at the moment of their birth? The mere fact of the skin color you were born into can make it feel as if your potential to live your best life has already been determined and that the prospects are limited to few to none. It's like starting the race for your life, and when the gun goes off, you're stuck in your starting blocks, running nowhere. Fast. And by the time you finally get going — if you ever do — the rest of society has had a several-hundred-year head start. It's exhausting. Terrifying. Who in their right mind would want such a life for themselves, or for any other human being? I don't know about anybody else, but I've never been intent on staying too long in misfortune's company. Out comes that scepter: permission *not* granted. Facts!

I am now grateful to have committed to winning by determination, hard work, reframing, and faith. As a result of going the distance and staying the course of my highest good, I became inspired by my challenges to spend the past three decades writing, speaking, shouting, acting (in a mausoleum), singing, and advocating for what's possible when we honor the sacred within us: our own love, our own acceptance, our own dignity, our own bodies as a place of refuge. Unconditional love permits me to know what is true about me: *I am right to be here! I am right to love myself! By grace alone, I am worthy.* And if it is true for me, it is true for you too, because when we strip down all the variables separating us into the unfavorable classifications of less and more, we all become united in our common humanity. We all suffer, grieve, experience loss, and we are all resilient and built to forgive, to love, and to lead joyful lives.

Let's explore the axiom "Your wound is your gold." I did not understand the strength of these words until I acknowledged, held, and ultimately began the journey of healing my wounds in order to earn bragging rights for myself, my own permission. Healing is often a start, then stop, then start, then repeat-again process. I've gone forward a hundred miles and backslid double that right into habits that did not serve me. Instead of viewing myself as broken or unfixable, as damaged goods, I slowed down and developed a practice of personal inquiry. It took me years of cultivating a safe-enough relationship with my therapist to eventually recognize there was actually *nothing* wrong with me. It was like an overnight success story for enlightenment. LOL. Although the truth is that I'd worked most of my life to arrive at that epiphany. Like many of us, I'd never really had the chance to be who I've always been: a loving and kind person deserving of reciprocal love, acceptance, and belonging. Instead, like so many humans, I was tasked with responsibilities so far and above my capacity to understand as a child, that naturally whenever my efforts fell short, I thought it meant there was something wrong with me. I carried that lie around like a "You Ain't Sh*t Express" Black card with unlimited access to feeling worthless. How does anyone recover from that? From doing the work of rewiring the truth as an adult, I have learned that we are all deserving of love on our terms. I recently read an article proclaiming that we humans are born with the God-given inalienable qualities of joy, love, and beauty. These are factory installed, so to speak, potential ways of being for us to revel in as we see fit. I hope this is a discovery you will come to repeatedly on our journey together.

And what I've learned from standing before those tens of thousands of people I've spent my career addressing, people from all walks of life, is that I'm not alone in my quest to live a more meaningful life. I am betting that the reason you're holding this book right now is that you want to know not only how to traverse the challenges you've encountered but also how to give yourself permission to transform those adversities into opportunities to stand in your own sense of self-worth and to access your own unconditional love.

Enter *Permission Granted: Kick-Ass Strategies to Bootstrap Your Way to Unconditional Self-Love.* Think Beyoncé takes center stage at Coachella. Snap. Or Lizzo storms Las Vegas in a sequined batwing swimsuit, complete with cape, flute, and mad vocal chops. Unapologetically being the joy, love, and beauty that are their trademarks. Permission. Granted! These women sought to express the truth of who they are. In the 2020 presidential election more votes were cast than ever before in the history of our country. The presidential race ran on and on, and it felt at times as though we were collectively hanging over a fire by a fraying rope. In the end, democracy manifested herself in the first woman ever chosen as our vice president. Not only is Kamala Harris the first woman, the first Black person, and the first person of South Asian descent to be vice president, but she is also a person who at one time was a patron of Ketér, my hair salon in Berkeley, California. My salon was the first ever Black-owned and Black-operated business on trendy Fourth Street, and to have the district attorney of San Francisco as a patron of my small business felt like democracy in action. Her mother, Shyamala, would at times accompany her daughter and sing her praises, like a proud mama does. One day her stylist, Joachim, let it be known that "she, Kamala, will be president. Watch what I tell you," and Shyamala shook her head and beamed with pride.

On November 7, 2020, donning a white suit finished off with a pussy bow, Vice President-Elect Harris took to the stage to thank those who had supported her, especially the person she believed was responsible for her success: her mother. Having witnessed firsthand the bond between the two, I have no doubt that Harris's mother fostered a fierce degree of agency and permission in her daughter. In her closing words, Harris thanked her running mate, Joe Biden, for his "audacity" in breaking a historical and substantial barrier of choosing the first woman in the second most powerful position of leadership. "While I may be the first woman in this office, I will not be the last."

And so, I say, while you might be the first person in your friend group, your family, your relationships, or your work environment audacious enough to stand courageously at the threshold of your growth edge, you are also capable of changing your history. The time to heal is now, your time to shine is now, and should you choose to cast your vote for yourself, there will not be a ceiling strong or high enough to prevent you from shattering someone else's expectations of what is true for you.

I hope you will grant yourself the kind of permission the women mentioned above give themselves, fully.

User's Manual for This Book

Allow me to throw in one more good reason why this book will be a fun foray into personal growth: I've searched through my speaking, teaching, and coaching archives for festive ways to serve all these permission strategies up to you, so that all you're being invited to do is to languish in the joy of you, the beauty of you, the She-EO of you, the *boss bish* of you, to grant yourself permission to *be* whoever you are, wherever you are, and to have the courage to meet yourself on your terms. Remember, it's all about *you*, *you*, and, yes, *you*, and, oh, did I forget to mention this is also for, well, *you*?!

I've gathered stories from everyday kinds of people. People like you and me. People who have defined success on their own terms. People who have worked or are working their asses off to get off the bleachers of their lives and onto the court of their dreams. In this book I offer a surplus of kick-ass strategies that are intended to be highly accessible, applicable, playful, engaging, and provocative. You'll have opportunities to explore your experiences and come out the other side with a better understanding of who you are and what you've been through, as well as ways to transform your devastations into your motivations. You'll learn to shift from blaming to reclaiming. You'll have a chance to provide yourself with the proof of just how staggeringly efficient you are by walking through the fire of what is true for you. *Permission Granted* is an example of a heuristic approach to learning: it places the possibilities of self-discovery and problem-solving in your hands. In this way, you have the ultimate say in how you engage with the inner you. The choice to exercise your agency, to embolden your sense of self-efficacy, rests in your hands. This personal-growth journey offers you the opportunity to arrive at whatever you are willing to experience. I am all about the adage "If it's meant to be, it's up to me!" Let's go forth and kick some ass!

This book is replete with self-awareness and compassion exercises, meditations, and a host of other ways to engage with yourself. I invite you to participate in these experiences. Decide what you want your takeaway to be, intrapersonally and professionally, interpersonally and communally. My website, www.iamreginalouise.com, offers meditations and visualizations that will provide you with a chance to become intimate with yourself as you step into transformative and deep learning. There you will also have a chance to peruse a selection of permission slips, journals, and other inspirational offerings intended to support you on your journey of personal discovery.

Permission Granted is a self-directed avenue of healing, an opportunity for you to give yourself permission to be the best version of yourself in any situation. Whether you are in the privacy of your own home, on the front lines of defending and preserving democracy, front and center at the podium, or in the boardroom, it will offer you tools you can use to permit yourself to begin again and again, right where you are. Think of it as a journey toward your own inner assets of self-worth and dignity.

With this book you get to better understand what it means to "dust yourself off and try again." My intention is for you to have a say in what is best for you, on your terms. And for anyone who lives in doubt about what it means to be human and struggles to be accepted on those terms, this book is an opportunity to build a bridge to a renewed sense of belonging to and with yourself. As I mentioned, a homecoming.

Though we sometimes lose ourselves in our trauma and pain by going into the survival mode we learned as children, here in these pages we find our way back, through our self-understanding, our self acceptance, our unconditional self-love, and the courage to be our own best caregivers, our own good-enough mothers. This book promotes self-care in ways both realistic and understandable; you'll have many opportunities to self-parent in the ways that suit your particular nature.

When I was eleven years old, my life careened out of control. I saw no other option but to take the wheel and steer myself back onto a road of possibility. Therefore, as someone who was tasked with the responsibility of raising myself, I've needed to invent some *seriously* creative ways to get through life. Can you imagine an eleven-year-old at the helm of repurposing chaos into something more meaningful, into her life's purpose, which is to be right here writing this for you now? Hell, at one time or another the child in many of us has had to pull off some straight-up Oscar-worthy adultification moves in order to make it to this exact moment. Especially young Black girls. According to a 2017 study conducted by Georgetown Law Center on Poverty and Inequality titled "Girlhood Interrupted," adults view young Black girls between the ages of five and fourteen as more adultlike and less innocent than white girls and thus less worthy of protection. It is beyond humbling to recognize that I have been pulling my life back from the effects of what that study discovered.

I, like many of you, whether you identify as Black, brown, indigenous, Asian American, or white, have imagined openings in places where there were none, tore through seams that were sewn tight. Double-stitched. I, like some of you, have had to fight my way toward taking my seat at the table of democracy, have searched for the mirrors of possibility that reflect my dreams as an inevitable reality back to me, have swallowed back, without chasers, my resistance to haggling over my self-worth with untutored hearts who dared not see me for fear of having to tolerate me. Like you, I too am from an ancestral line of folk who have embraced the hardscrabble means of making a way where there was none. And it is from this meandering, sashaying, navigating, and imagining that I share my lessons and passion for the power of creating our own privilege(s). There is no need to wait for someone to grant us entry into our best selves and our best lives. I am here to cocreate with Spirit to save myself. I invite you to do the same.

Who Am I, Regina Louise, to Write This Book?

It's no secret to anyone who has traveled alongside me as I've written about how I've gone from a childhood of marginalization, solitary confinement, and time in a level-fourteen residential treatment center to college and the creation of several successful small businesses, that I am all for self-efficacy and believing in *being* the way when the path forward isn't clear. In 1981, at age eighteen, I walked out of a residential treatment center with everything I owned in a garbage bag: a fur coat, a bottle of wine, a set of sheets, and an iron. I took a taxi to San Francisco State University. Bag in hand, I stepped out of that taxi in front of hundreds of students, their families tagging alongside them as they moved into their first home away from home. My self-respect in tow, I strode through what could have been a most shameful moment for many but for me was record empowering and dignified action. I'd achieved a dream that I'd been led to believe was impossible: I got accepted into a university after being freshly released from solitary confinement and cramming four years of high school academics into a year and a half. I hit the ground running all around San Francisco, stitching together bits of this and pieces of that, a never-ending hustle that brought me face-to-face with what would be one of my many destinies. Rising above all the incredibly low prospects people held for me was *epic*! It was my moment, something I'd worked for like nothing ever before, and I was hell-bent from then on to belong to every dream (no matter how long it took or how hard it might be) I'd go on to manifest.

Since that day, I have walked, jogged, skipped, and sauntered up on stage after stage, in thousands of cities across twenty-eight states, and counting. Not only do I show up confident (meaning that I trust I can rely on my previous experiences to help me through whatever I am showing up to do), but I work to support myself to be fully in my power, to be at home within myself. The best part is when I get to ask the audience questions, interviewing every willing participant about what brings them to such an event, and always, always, always they respond: *I want to walk away feeling as if the work I do matters.* What I know for sure is this: each of us is the only person qualified to make that so. Gratefully, I recognize that in the work I am blessed enough to get to do, I engage with people who are bound and determined to validate for themselves the thirst for their own … permission. My journey now is to support others, be they dog walkers or billionaires, social workers or entrepreneurs: we can all benefit from a cleared-out heart. I am eager to walk alongside you, to encourage you to dream and be who you are, *no matter what*. I look forward to hearing from you. I look forward to being here for and with you. I am here for this journey, and I hope you are here for it too.

And so it is!

Lovefirmations

Allow Me to Introduce You to the Grand-Mère of Unconditional Love

How often have you heard the bumper-sticker-worthy adage "You must love yourself before you can love anybody else"? How many times have you nodded your head in agreement, making silent promises to do just that, to love yourself first? That is, until you meet your next crush, and off you go, once again convinced that *this time* they will meet your needs and fulfill your wants and desires, and you'll feel just the way you did when you were about five years old: totally innocent and the apple of someone's eye. Well, you're not alone. I too have been there and done that and longed for that paradisiacal feeling.

And that is where Lovefirmations come in. Love provides a sacred place to return to inside ourselves when other doors of refuge may be closed to us. Lovefirmations make us less reliant on outside sources for self-acceptance, empowerment, and permission. By placing Lovefirmations at the front of your journey, you can choose your allies, front-load your resources. For me, you see, love is my ally, an always willing collaborator. Continuously there. Love will never leave me stranded and on my own, confused and alone. When I remember this and am able to connect with the truth of it, I am never unaided, and you don't have to be either.

For those of you who actually bought the bumper sticker and affixed it to your Honda, Tesla, or Jeep, or have worn it on that favorite oversize hoodie as a reminder, know this: I get it. I've been there too. But love isn't something I can drive any more than I can wear it in the hopes of benefiting from its qualities. Unconditional self-love originates from within. It's an internal resource that generates and regenerates from connecting to what's true about each of us and to the larger mystery that we are good and worthy and enough, that we come wired with the qualities of joy, love, and beauty. I consider Lovefirmations the grand-mère of unconditional love because of their power to connect us back through the generational truth of love's depth, grace, and presence. No matter what, love is the prevailing essence that holds us and binds our common humanity across space and time.

We each have our own capacity to love, and we express it in ways that reflect who we are.

Pause to Consider

- What is it to love?
- What does it mean to be loved?
- How do you know love when you see it? Feel it?
- What distinguishes love for you from any other emotion?

How, then, do we take the prescription off the bumper sticker and the sweatshirt and give it legs? How do we connect with our inner love, giving it to ourselves first, the same way we would to a lover, child, or friend?

- How would you know that you have loved yourself?
- How would you know that you haven't?

Without Further Ado

Drumroll, please. Down the red carpet they come, donning the qualities of intimacy, tenderness, kindness and permission, adoration and affection, possessing the ability to meet us where we are. Please allow me the pleasure to introduce to you: Lovefirmations.

You know the moment. You're in a full-fledged doubt spiral, and all you can come up with is more self-recrimination, bringing on even *more* doubt. That's when, instead of contracting with a hypertensive no, you lean in and say yes to your own awareness. You soften. You slow down and turn toward the inner disturbance with the goal to listen. With tenderness you ask the doubt or confusion what it needs, and with your highest intention you move toward ameliorating your distress. It might look something like this:

Hello there, doubt. I feel you here, tugging at the hem of my consciousness; I see you. You are a valuable resource for me, albeit in small doses. I know you want what's best for me: thank you. I am available to listen to you. I am willing, and fully present. What would you like me to know about you? Listening with an open heart and intentionally making room for what *is* allows us to respond to our vulnerabilities not with impatience or violence but with love. As a facilitator of sacred circles, spaces curated for listening in a loving and conscientious manner to the voices of historically underrepresented peoples, I have learned over time the value of slowing down, tuning, and turning in. Lovefirmations, such as the ones above — *I am available to listen to you. I am willing, and fully present* — are a natural accompaniment to this practice.

Lovefirmations, a mash-up of the words *love* and *affirmations*, are statements generated from within you and intended to be expressed toward yourself as an act of unconditional love, as an act of rooting in your own goodness. They invite you to value your own appreciation, tenderness, and encouragement. With love being the equivalent of life itself, Lovefirmations offer a doorway to unlimited, unconditional self-love and freedom from emotional entanglements. The more you believe, the more you will receive that which you believe. All you need to do right now is stop and consider for a moment all you have and value in your life. How did you make this so? What did you believe about yourself that manifested as the life you are living?

I can't tell you how often in my coaching practice I am tasked with leading clients back from the edge of microshaming themselves. By *microshaming* I mean the verbally abusive digs we make on ourselves such as "I suck!" or "I can't f**king believe I'm so stupid!" Although they may feel innocuous, too often we don't recognize how we might be unconsciously reinforcing shame messages, untruths that underscore how we secretly feel about ourselves. What if in place of microshaming ourselves we instead reached for an affirmative love statement that reflects what is true about us? And if we find it difficult to believe that our own love is enough, what's the harm in having the pure intention of acting as if our love messages matter? From my experience, taking on the qualities of whatever I want to experience in my life has proven fruitful. Acting *as if* allows us to embody the qualities of what we aspire to experience. As we move through this journey together, you will read one example after another that attests to this dynamic.

Pause to Consider

Was there a moment, perhaps recently, when you were harsher with yourself than you might have been with a friend, pet, or loved one? If so, go back to that incident. What occurred? Allow the scene to play out. If your response to yourself wasn't thoughtful, considerate, or kind, rephrase what you said to yourself as a Lovefirmation. Pay attention to how your inner essence responds to your newer offering. Breathe into the space that may open up to and for you. Consider this a new baseline to work from when this or a similar situation should arise.

Unconditional Self-Love

I have learned that the less I take out on myself those outmoded beliefs that live inside me, the more I can stay with what is happening in the moment. This gives me the patience I need to better understand my experiences, which in turn supports my ability to accept myself as I am, warts, scars, flaws, and all. The result is that I benefit from my own love, unconditionally. In other words, the more I choose to accept my suffering as real, my pain as my own, and my hurts for what they are, the more I acknowledge a tear in the connection I have with myself or others, the more real I become to myself. The more real I become to my own suffering, and the longer I choose to stay with myself in a moment of distress, the less likely it is that I will project it on to another to hold and fix. No matter where we are, no matter how small or simple the efforts we are making, I believe that we are all capable of moving the needle from the groove of our discontent over to the melody of our highest potential.

One of my clients said to me, "I tried to launch a business

and *of course* I failed." Hidden within this not-so-disguised dig is the energy of a microshame. This message suggests to that tender child within that success was never an option. Not only is communicating ideas like this potentially toxic, because the loss of confidence from the message builds up over time, but also the negative energy creates deep discouragement as opposed to reassurance and understanding. What if, in the face of recognizing our dissatisfaction with the outcome of an endeavor, we were to say something like this: "I tried to launch a business, I gave it my best, and although it didn't go the way I'd hoped this time, I'm so proud that I tried." That right there — "I tried ... I gave ... I'm proud" — is an example of a Lovefirmation in action. Acknowledging the truth of your own efforts is the pure and honest way to disrupt a feeling of failure and instead bootstrap kindness, which builds over time into resilience and offers a soft touch to the suffering parts of ourselves.

Whether I am coaching executives, county human services workers, or a ten-year-old girl living inside her forty-year-old adult self while she tries to understand why her older brother still bullies her, what it comes down to time and time again — after the proper boundaries have been set and reinforced for our psychological safety — is that, while standing in the face of the most intense experiences, we need to accept all of who we are with unconditional self-love. Periodt! Self-love is a motivator for drawing the line and holding it. Self-love places our inner sanctuary and well-being at the forefront of our intention to meet our needs and desires. By returning to our inner sanctum of self-love, over time we build new neural pathways from which to choose when under stress. The better able we are to meet our own needs with satisfaction and consistency, the more likely we are to recognize and therefore experience a fresh sense of what is true and lovable about us.

Allow me to add the following journaling practice to your unconditional-love toolbox.

Using Lovefirmations in Journaling Practice

One of the many rituals I love performing each day is waking up and writing in my spiritual journal. I'll have my cup of coffee and play my favorite song by Tasha Cobbs Leonard, either "Gracefully Broken" or "You Know My Name," and if I'm not in the mood for words I pick the same Paul Cardall song, "Redeemer." Whichever music accompaniment I choose, I set it on repeat. Intentionally, I check in with myself to see what Lovefirmation I want or need to hear. I bang whatever it is out on the computer keys no fewer than a hundred times each day. Here are some examples:

I love you, sweet child of mine.
There is a gift in my feeling doubtful.
I have the power to turn toward myself and meet myself
*   and my suffering with love.*
Nothing in this world can stop me from loving me.
I am my own permission.
Love is wherever I am.
I was born on purpose.
I am kick-ass.
I live my life as the answer to a question not yet asked.
I am lovable.
I am beyond capable.
I am worthy of my spirit.
I am intentional.
I am allowed to make mistakes.

A mistake doesn't define me.
I am as tough as I need to be.
I am never too much.
I am just right as I am.
I know how to meet my needs.
I want to meet my needs.
Everywhere I am, possibility is present.
I deserve to reach out to a friend for support.
I am delighted to hold space for myself.
I have a right to all my feelings.
All of me is welcome wherever I am.

Sometimes, depending on what's going on with me, I might break my Lovefirmations into themes and write fifty of one and fifty of the other. For instance, if I want to connect with the energy of becoming a bit quieter and a bit more tender, I will write fifty times each:

I deserve my own tenderness.
It is okay for me to be softer.

This act empowers me to have quietude on my terms. Most of my life I've been accused of showing up as loud and aggressive. To say that these words trigger me straight into someone's face would be an understatement. However, over time, practicing my own permission, allowing myself to slow down, step back, and become intimate with the silence and tenderness within, has provided me with a more balanced awareness of the volume of my voice. The result is that I am more mindful of how I want to be in a situation. With practice, I'm better able to understand how to wield my presence consciously instead of reactively.

What once was a source of an immediate reaction fueled by anger, historical traumas, and drama is now a superpower, a result of my Lovefirmations practice. Transforming my triggers into opportunities to respond instead of react has benefited me professionally in exciting ways; I am able to connect with my own tenderness, allowing me to better deliver keynote speaking presentations, as well as lead visualizations that are required of me as a performance coach and teacher of the Hoffman Process, a personal growth experience I'll talk more about later. Also, I am better able to hold sacred space not only for myself but also for others in coaching situations, group facilitations, and personal relationships. Lovefirmations also lay the groundwork for emboldening the soft skills of emotional regulation, resourcefulness, maturity, conscientiousness, and perseverance. These skills and many more are necessary in your relationship with yourself and can also be scaled into your professional and interpersonal relationships. Everyone can benefit from engaging with someone who assumes 100 percent responsibility for themselves. Not only is it attractive, but it's also a thoughtful way to engage with others and self.

Here are some other ways I've used Lovefirmations:

- Self-soothing practices
- De-escalation practices
- Mindful practices

Let's take a look at each of these in detail.

Self-Soothing Practices

If anyone had told me that every time I intuitively hugged my knee extra close to my heart when it was scuffed, spoke softly to the place of hurt, and rocked myself into a tender calm that I was giving myself love, I would have thought they were weird or full of Bay Area woo-woo, or both. (Note: I live in Northern California, and apparently, we're about as woo-woo as it gets.) No, seriously, it was just what I did. Intuitively, I knew the value of turning to my own kindheartedness and using loving action on my own behalf as a way to mitigate my distress.

As an adult, if I wanted to be held and a hug wasn't available:

- I hugged a pillow. Sometimes, by spraying it with the perfume scent of the person I missed or loved, or with musk oil or cucumber — my favorite scents — I could make the holding that much more satisfying. In my life, people frequently disappeared without notice or a trace. Holding on to the pillow and letting them go on my terms helped me heal the hurt caused by abandonment and loss. I guess you could say that having closure is a big deal for me, as I imagine it is for many humans.

- I hugged myself until whatever was troubling me vanished. Being loving to myself, taking as long as I needed, aided me in metabolizing my sadness. This way of loving, holding, and being with myself helped ground me in space and time, a dynamic so often hijacked during a traumatic situation. It's an essential act of self-care for anyone recovering from traumas large and small.

I could go on and on about the ways I've loved myself without *knowing* that's what I was doing. Oh, oh, oh, I will share with you how useful my portable compact disc players have been (although now they have been replaced with my iPhone). I know, it's really old-school. Don't hate.

- I recorded my own voice over soft music while saying soothing and encouraging things to my inner child. I've used this technique for encouragement as needed.
- I have sung and recorded bedtime lullabies for my sweet self.
- And then there are the letters I have written and re-corded, validating my hard work and my earnest attempts to be my best, no matter what.

It was natural for me to act as if my actions mattered, as if they held value for me. Of course, it would take decades before I understood that what I thought to do for myself was consid-ered a form of self-love.

Although I've developed ways to respond to my needs with loving awareness and tenderness, from time to time I slip, I forget, and next thing I know I'm up to my tricks of seeking validation from a friend or partner, from shopping, from over-indulging, and from overextending myself in terrifyingly co-dependent ways. Oh, the conscious awareness I've had to bring to that pattern is enormous. So instead of trying to force or manipulate someone to give me what I know I can give myself, I slow down, turn my attention to whatever is going on inside me, and connect to my inner child, Little Red. (You'll get to know more about her later.) I'm a grown-ass woman who has a vibrant five-year-old inside who at times wants to return to the paradise of childhood no matter the expense to my adult self. Over time, however, and with the intention to live my life on my terms, the adult in me has come to know that it's my job to assist the youngest, most vulnerable part of me. It is no joke to confront the places within me that are fixated in the traumas of my childhood. However, what I know to be true is that if we want to live a life on our terms, as opposed to being bullied through life by beliefs that no longer serve us; if we want to individuate as adults, we must remain diligent in growing ourselves up. To nurture the smallest parts of ourselves without abandon. For this, I am grateful for Lovefirmations.

De-escalation Practices

In my world of supporting people who have experienced little to no trauma as well as those who have suffered varying degrees of vicarious and compounded traumas, I have learned that emotional escalation happens quickly, often unconsciously. Who hasn't shouted at a driver on a crowded rush-hour road at the end of a long day? Or turned on themselves at some point?

That gush of stress energy you hurled against that person, who hopefully didn't hear you curse them down to the ground and back again, is called adrenaline. And those of us who are quick on the draw need to prepare ourselves for that extra dose of life force moving through us. Its burst is short and fast and increases your heart rate and raises your blood pressure. Cortisol, a stress hormone, kicks in as well and has the power to sustain this little outburst over a longer period of time. Having a de-escalation plan in your unconditional-love tool kit is essential in protecting your heart from stress responses. Lovefirmations are a great resource for driving while under stress:

- Record your voice on your phone over soft music while saying soothing and encouraging things to your inner teenager. I use this method for encouragement as needed, and it's designed specifically for when we get stressed out while driving.

- Have a list of Lovefirmations printed onto a small plac-ard and hang it over your rearview mirror.
- Create a wallpaper of Lovefirmations for your mobile phone, and attach your phone to your dashboard with a hands-free driving device.

Driving under stressful conditions is only one of the situations for which you can use these de-escalation techniques. What are some other techniques you can use in the face of situations you know you have a history of going into combat with? You know how to care for yourself already. Trust what you know. Lovefirmations are always available for you to fortify the practices you already use — or they can provide you with an alternative to reacting stressfully in triggering situations.

Mindful Practices

As many of you already know, mindfulness is the go-to for slowing down and turning your attention inward, without judgment or condemnation. This seemingly simple practice packs a power-punch opportunity to reconnect with yourself in the moment. Mindfulness aids in cultivating empathy and self-compassion toward yourself and others. It is an ancient practice, yet its benefits continue to unfold. Mindfulness and Lovefirmations can be perfectly paired to invite an inner sense of calm.

- While sitting in *siddhasana* (an ancient seated yoga pose in which the legs are crossed, with the ankle bones touching and the heels above one another), or in a position that is most comfortable for you and your body, repeat your Lovefirmation until your body begins to respond with an inner sense of peace and calm.

- Each time the mind wanders into the wild, wild west of distraction, lovingly and without judgment bring your attention back to your Lovefirmation and begin again.
- Ask yourself what you need to hear in order to get unstuck from a way of thinking that isn't serving you in the moment. Sense the Lovefirmation that speaks best to what you're needing.
- Practice liberally throughout the day and evening. Use this technique as a calming practice to set the stage for bedtime.

You can interchange any and all of these practices. Think of these offerings as if they were listed on a menu, as part and parcel of your kick-ass, bootstrapping unconditional-love toolbox. Throughout this book, you will have chance after chance to build your Lovefirmation muscles. From my heart to yours, go forward and be kick-ass!

Bootstrapping Takeaways

- Practice Lovefirmations.
- Create your own Lovefirmations.
- Engage in self-soothing exercises.
- Cultivate de-escalation techniques.
- Build your unconditional self-love toolbox.
- Permit yourself to self-fully love yourself.

Now that you've had a chance to learn more about Lovefirmations, allow yourself to indulge and immerse in the beauty of what's good about you. Make loving yourself an act of resistance, a practice of resilience, an artful and powerful foray into the mysteries of what takes your breath away about being alive. Imagine you are your own mother, the mother of your dreams. You are a reservoir of tenderness and kindness because after all, aren't these the qualities you'd administer to a loved one in need?

Pause to Consider

- How often have you given everything you have to an other person: lover, family member, or friend?
- Who have you given chance after chance to show you some form of reciprocity?
- What will it take for you to be for yourself the kind of person you've been for others?

Empathy is the ability to walk in someone else's shoes, to drop down into the foxhole with them if needed. Empathy allows you to imagine what another person has endured along their journey and to get in touch with the depth of tenderness, understanding, and patience within you, all qualities that you can cultivate by embodying them. This book asks you to walk in your *own* shoes, to remember what it was like to have your *own* experiences, and to foster the compassionate desire to be with and ameliorate your *own* suffering, using Lovefirmations as your ally.

With the awareness you will cultivate as a result of sojourning in these pages, you will begin to pour into yourself all the things you wish someone else would give you. It might feel odd at first, but stick with it, the same way you would for another person. In time you will begin to notice the subtle changes in what you will and will not tolerate. Ultimately, loving ourselves helps us balance the scales of giving and receiving.

Kick-Ass Strategy #1

Bring Your Own Permission

*We are all meant to shine, as children do. We were born to make
manifest the glory of God that is within us. It's not just in
some of us; it's in everyone. And as we let our own light shine,
we unconsciously give other people permission to do the same.
As we are liberated from our fear, our presence
automatically liberates others.*

— Marianne Williamson, *A Return to Love*

In the introduction I mentioned several iconic people who ask
for no one's permission but their own to paint their fabulosity
all over the globe and back again as many times as they like
Vice President-Elect Kamala Harris gave her unprecedented
acceptance speech, and every other action she will make or take
on behalf of all Americans will be just as unprecedented. Rais
ing the bar of what's possible for future generations of women,
and especially of Black and South Asian American girls, is as
high an aspiration as one could hope to achieve. What these
women's fearless, devil-may-care self-expression seems to suggest, without their having to say anything other than what they

feel called to speak or sing on, gets you up out of your chair to vote or to shake that groove thang! *Hey, now, who knows what I'm talking about?*

Zoom in: If anywhere in these pages you don't know what I'm talking 'bout, don't fret. I'm no pop-culture icon either. It's fun, though, to work toward staying relevant. I usually end up calling on one of the millennials in my life to help keep me up on what's "lit," what's "Gucci," and all things "for real for real." And thanks to the younger Kardashians for prefacing their spoken truths with "Bible," making the most sold and revered book in history relevant to keeping the truth, well, true. *Bible.* Whether through norm-shattering speeches or pop songs, how someone shows up as who they are is about granting oneself permission to be "extra" or "snatched" or "on fleek" (thank you, Peaches Monroee), or to simply express yourself without any concern for the creative twist on linguistics it might take to do so!

Recently, while in quarantine, and on a day when I can admit I was close to being bored in the motherf**king house, I decided to circle back around and give the show *The Good Fight* some attention. I dug Christine Baranski in *The Good Wife* and thought, *Why not?* And between you and me, I still had it bad for Chris Noth from when he played the role of Mr. Big in *Sex and the City. Shut up, right? I know, I know.* I know he was not always so gentlemanly with our girl Carrie Bradshaw, but damn, those eyes, that height, the size of those hands. I digress. Back to my new favorite series. Okay, so I immediately fell in love with all the kick-ass chicks on *The Good Fight.* Tell me, who names their daughter Cush Jumbo without expecting her to stop the world in its tracks? Cush's mama or whoever named her had no qualms about expressing their

originality and setting her up to either go big or go home whenever she heard her named called. I'm just saying. Whether or
not they intended to, they gave that child something to courageously grow into. And when Cush's character, Lucca Quinn,
walks into the room, the molecules change, baby. Without her
saying a word, you already know that she is here for it, kicking
that ass and taking their names. Talk about bringing permission to be who you are, everywhere you go. Talk about inspiring. Talk to the hand, all you common-names folks, 'cause
Cush Jumbo is in the house! Granting yourself permission by
bringing your own permission is powerful and courageous, allowing you to hack uncertainty by inviting what's unknown to
become known. And if you didn't know before, now you know
that I love the power of originality in names. Okay, let's move on.

BYOP

In this first strategy, I'd like you to consider how not only to *be*
your own permission but also to *bring* it. As that old-school
saying by the Buffalo Soldiers goes, "You have to bring ass to
get some ass." To win anything, you must be willing to fight for
it. Therefore, you have to bring your own permission in order
to get permission to get the job of being you done! Here's another way to consider this strategy. You know how when you're
invited to a party, a cookout, a tailgating shindig, and the invite
reads "BYOB," as in bring your own beer, bottle, bae, booty,
and whatever else begins with *B* that you'd want to tote to the
party in order to have that turnt-up time you were hoping to
have? Well, here, I invite you to BYOP, and yes, you guessed
it, as in Bring Your Own Permission everywhere you go. Remember that fly old-school slogan from American Express

Travelers Checks back in the day? There he was, Karl Malden, all earnest sounding with that voice of his commanding us: "Don't leave home without it." This strategy invites you to establish your relationship with and to grow your definition of bringing your own:

- Permission
- Power
- Prettiness
- Passion
- Purpose
- Preemptive moves

Can you imagine the impact of taking all of you everywhere you go? Bringing your own permission every time you go to the office, on a luncheon date, to the grocery store, to the gym, and all the other places you'd likely venture to on any given day ensures that you are putting yourself in the position to have agency and power at the ready. You might think of bringing your permission with you the way you would that favorite shade of Fenty lipstick you'd slide into your evening bag for that touch-up you're likely to need at some point after dinner, drinks, and oh, yes, that passionate kiss you were holding out for. Perhaps you'll write yourself a permission slip to remind yourself that you're pretty enough and powerful enough, that whatever name your mama or whoever gave you is perfect just the way it is. You can place your permission slip in that same handbag and have it at your fingertips in case you need a reminder of just how close your self-approval is at any moment. To have access to your own permission is all a part of having a voice, having your say.

Make a PACT with Personal Freedom

It is no secret by now that my childhood was bushwhacked, hijacked, and left to wither by the side of the road as a result of profound neglect, abuse, and incessant chaos. Beatings and insults were the means of engagement in my family system. If you've read either of my memoirs, *Somebody's Someone* or *Someone Has Led This Child to Believe*, you know that I lived in the same foster home my biological mother had grown up in. Because my mother was a child having a child, she was unprepared to be a parent and therefore abandoned me with her caregivers. Very early on, when I was around eleven years old, I decided that I would not allow my life to be defined by the ill-fated actions of my traumatized and unprotected young mother. Like anyone of sound mind, I wanted more. I needed more. My desire for freedom and personal expression were calling from deep within my spirit. I wanted a life devoid of judgment and shame. My dreams were in part stoked by the only books available for me to read at that time, *Nancy Drew, The Hardy Boys, and Pippi Longstocking*. Within these pages lay a world beyond the one I awoke to every morning. A world where I constantly hoped to find the hidden door that would lead me to the *real* world, the one I was convinced I'd accidentally been locked out of.

If all the children I'd read about could have what felt to me a safe-enough adult to guide their lives, why couldn't I? Never once did I believe that they deserved it and I didn't. More than anything, I believed I could say what I wanted, if only to myself, and that one day I'd get what I'd written on my heart. And somehow, I understood that I must *act* the way I wanted to become. And it was this knowing, this willingness to succumb to the power of imagination, that led me to consider a strategy to flip the script on my circumstances.

I was a child when I first learned to trust my instincts and take the reins of my own permission. (I'll tell you the whole story just below.) I use the word *trust* quite intentionally here. The connection and unity inherent in the word *trust* was brought to my attention recently by my dear friend the poet Susan Wooldridge. Susan is the author of the gem *Poemcrazy: Freeing Your Life with Words.* I'd made a post on Instagram right after speaking to the Council for Leaders in Alabama Schools. I shared that I'd summarized the takeaway of the keynote presentation in the neat little acronym PACT, which stands for Presence, Acceptance, Courage, Trust. That's when my girl chimed in with her comment "Trust. Holds the word *us*," followed by the heart, praying hands, and shining-star emojis. Leave it to the poets to discover words within words. Recognizing the *us* in trust allowed me to see the relational value inherent in the word, the possibility of inclusiveness and belonging. Trust invites us to remain true to who we are, to uphold our integrity in the face of challenges, knowing that we can rely on it at a moment's notice. Trust binds us to like-minded others. Especially if we grant ourselves permission to trust ourselves.

We can heal so much within us when we become willing to make a PACT with ourselves. Whether we are dealing with fear, anxiety, or uncertainty or with a lack of confidence, self-love, or courage, to give to ourselves in ways that support us in showing up as our best selves again and again and again is the definition of self-acceptance and unconditional love. What might it take for you to consider stepping into your presence, acceptance, compassion, and trust as a way forward? What amount of havingness do you imagine might come to you as a result of such acts? This leads me to the day I made my first pact with what I have now come to know as my highest good, the quality in me that is a gift from the realm of the Divine. In other words, it's how what is invisible becomes visible in the way of infinite grace.

Presence

I first became aware of the power of my own presence by way of a dream. Not just once but many times throughout my life, I've experienced the purest sense of my existence during dream states. The first of such dreams occurred when I was around ten. I'd watched my sister braid her own hair and wanted desperately for her to teach me, which she refused to do. I watched her fingers flit in and out of her thick mass of hair, crissing and crossing until a braided pattern appeared. I marveled at what seemed to me to be magic.

Later that night, I took the visual memory of my sister's hair braiding to bed with me. I reenacted her fingers' movements in bullet-time sequence. It was as though I were in a hyper-present state of awareness in which time disappeared and I was in sync with my own finger patterns. Upon awakening, I asked my sister to let me take her hair down and rebraid it. If you know anything about Black women's hair rituals, you know the magnitude of such an ask.

My sister complied. I lay down a set of perfect jailhouse braids (braids beginning at the front hairline and ending at the nape), intuitively mapping out the parts and hair sections so as to not run out of space at the narrowing of her nape. The finished product was exemplary of someone who had years of practice behind them. Needless to say, my sister was dumbfounded. She chided me for tricking her into giving me a chance to "show off." Although I made every attempt possible to convince her that I'd learned what she knew in my dream the night before, I failed to convince her. Soon enough, however, I learned to transfer what happened in my dream state into my waking hours. With practice, I eventually grew my ability to show up, slow down, and get zoned in on whatever I was doing.

This prepared me to *be with* whatever was happening in the moment. I became present to my own presence, my intuitive agency. Becoming this attuned has come in handy in many ways. All I needed was to see something, anything that caught my interest, one time, and with the power and purpose of presence I was able to make the experience my own, with replicable results.

Presence is the ability to show up in the moment with your awareness intact, wide-open to where and who you are; your listening is tuned in, your heart is cleared out, and you are attuned in the moment to what you're doing and how you intend to be. Presence is one of the most powerful states, whether sleeping or awake, I have experienced. Presence is *being with* Spirit, blending with whatever is happening and staying the course for as long as needed. It's matching up our inner world with our outer expression. It's a practice of aligning who we say we are with actually *being* what we believe to be true about us. On our terms.

Acceptance

Acceptance requires our consent. It asks us to be in agreement with what is. By doing so, by giving ourselves permission to accept what is, we are invited not to grasp, not to challenge, but simply to let go and trust in the moment. Have you ever had an experience when you *just knew* that something was off, when the atmosphere didn't feel quite right? I will always remember a particular incident that was wrought with fear and confusion. I was eleven. Sadly, the upshot of coming from an early life of complete chaos was learning to become present on a dime to changes in the atmosphere of wherever I lived. Hypervigilance, I believe it is called. Prior to the day when I was beaten within an inch of my life, I'd made a pact with God. It was clean and simple: *God, should I be beaten one more time, I'll know it's a sign for me to leave.* I was engaged in a battle of wills between myself and my overwhelmed caretaker, Lula Mae. By the time Lula was in charge of caring for me, my mother had already left. I had to face this adult woman on my own terms. Making the pact in the first place meant I was accepting the responsibility not to allow anyone to beat me ever again. It was also the day that I gave my trust over to Spirit and the moment not only when my faith was put to the test but also when my awareness of faith came into being. I felt it, deeply, that I had slowly but surely outgrown the situation over the years and that a change *must come* if I was going to survive to see the light of adulthood.

With acceptance, we permit ourselves to receive a way out. Acceptance also allows us to be received, gives us a new way to belong to something greater than before.

Courage

To assume the risk involved in whatever endeavor we choose to undertake, we need courage. We move from and with our heart, trusting in our ability to face, on our terms, whatever needs facing, whether it be our emotions, our suffering, our desire to be who we want to be in the face of opposition. Courage springs forth from an inner place, from a remembrance of what came before your current need, reminding you how your resilience helps you to understand the risks and to move forward anyway. The audacity of jumping empty-handed into the void, leaning in toward any disturbance in our emotional field, standing firm against social humiliation, doing the right thing when no one else will is courage in action. To move from courage is to be concerned with neither the good nor the bad, the right nor the wrong; it is to show up fully without knowing what the outcome will be. Courage permits us to feel the full spectrum of our emotions without needing to hide from our own vulnerability, our own intimacy. Courage requires us to begin where we are, paving the way for us to face what we fear, befriend it, and come through to the other side, understanding and receiving the learning and growth that come from whatever we were courageous enough to permit.

So the day I received that beating I'd decided would be my last, I left home at age eleven, taking a Greyhound bus to North Carolina to reunite with my mother. That day, armed with courage, I did so knowing it was what both my heart and my spirit insisted on me doing. Although it didn't end up working out for me to live with my mother — my trip there was followed by two years of back and forth between her home and my father's in California, until I finally had to turn myself in at a police department — the fact that I had enough inner trust to save myself was all that mattered.

Trust

To trust another person is to have faith that they will come through for you. It is to rely so much on faith that all lesser beliefs that may try to override our sense of faith such as "I'm not worthy" or "God has failed me" fall by the wayside. You are strengthened by what you believe, you are buoyed, you hold firm to this knowing. You extend your trust to your friends, family members, and lovers with the faith that your intimacies will not be betrayed or exploited, that your vulnerabilities will be respected and therefore protected.

I believe that by grace I can restore my trust each time it has been breached, and so can you. Your permission creates access to this truth. Trust is evergreen in terms of my direct relationship to it and how it holds and keeps me, for trust begins with me. I want to be clear that I am not saying here that even when someone betrays you, you immediately give them access back into your life. I am also a proponent of Maya Angelou's most salient quote — at least for me: "When people show you who they are, believe them." When trust is betrayed it's important to, well, trust the red flags and interior experiences that signal a breach has occurred and to do what's needed to suture that breach. It takes time to heal from a betrayal. My highest recommendation is to do so on your own terms as opposed to the terms negotiated by the person who betrayed you. Trust is not something out there, a destination we can travel to and check out as we like. Trust originates from within our souls. We come from trust, and it comes through us, in us, as us.

I'll say it again. Above all else, we need to trust ourselves. I've earned my own trust as a result of the many times I have remained worthy to my word, remained true to who I believe myself to be, someone who works to make my actions congruent with my words. When we trust ourselves, we learn what qualities to look for before we decide to trust another.

Drawing a Line in the Sand

Sometimes it needs to happen like this. The day I ran away from the kinship home I lived in as a child, my drawing a line in the metaphorical sand, unapologetically, placed me in the position of my own power. I had no idea what lay beyond that line. All I knew was that, along with being beaten, I was done having people talk smack about me to my face. I was done hearing about the sins of my mother who had left and was not there to fight my battles. I was done being on the receiving end of unkept promises, of being the one always left empty-handed. The one who was left to do the work of figuring out why adults couldn't do better by me. I believed I could do better than most of the adults in my life, and also that in time I could become the best person I could possibly be as a result of taking action. It felt good to actually *become* the last word as opposed to being accused of always wanting to have it. No, actually, it felt better than good: it felt *great*!

You might think to yourself, "How can a child *really* know the difference, make these sorts of decisions?" Have you ever witnessed a two-year-old vehemently declare no? It is an affirming act not soon forgotten by the parent on the receiving end. When it comes to establishing her territory, her sense of self, her sense of *not at all* and under no uncertain circumstances, she screams it, scrunchy-faces it, foot-stomps it in a no-means-no type of way. Coming into your no is one of your developmental milestones as a human being. We've all gone through that stage of individuating from those with power over us, those who have what we want and believe to be ours. We've all — I hope — had our chance to yell out, to use our voice to assert where our world ends and everyone else's begins, even if we didn't quite understand what that meant. My point here is to highlight that personal permission lives in us all as our God-given, inalienable right and begins to assert itself early on. I've coached enough young people to know that some can be so doggedly determined and full of conviction that they become nearly impossible for their parents to manage. If you know what I am talking about, nod your head, raise your hand, or go on and say it: *I know that's right!* For my caregivers, I was that child who today is known as precocious, difficult, and yet advanced in the ways I interacted with those around me. Back in the day, it was known as, "Say another word, and watch what happens to you." I felt threatened — constantly — for being the self I was set up to be: adultified or, depending on your point of view, parentified.

So, on the day when that weapon of ass destruction (a cut-off water hose) wielded by Lula Mae thundered onto my tender flesh, not only was I ready to do what I'd said I would do between myself and my highest good, but also, and more important, I *became* my word in action. I literally took the agreement I'd made, stepped inside it, turned on the engine, and reset the trajectory of my life. I may have left that home with lacerations, but I did so with a courageous heart. Given the prognosis I was given on the daily, that I'd have more children than I'd know what to do with by the time I was a teenager, I was happy to do whatever it took to drive that death-of-a-future straight off a cliff. One thing I know for sure is this: whether it be courage, trust, taking action, or power, none of these qualities come *for* us but from *within* us. The fact is, all we have is choice, in each moment of each day. Whether or not we activate that choice can often mean the difference between a life of erasure or one with the chance of living from the best of your abilities. On your terms.

Sometimes You Just Have To...

Have blind faith. I know, I know, you might be thinking, "There is no way I'd willingly jump empty-handed into the void." I hear you. Had it not been for my caretaker's misplaced rage toward me, I might not have felt compelled enough to do anything about my circumstances. And, as I will repeat early and often, your circumstances need not be the makings of a horror story before you take action on your own behalf. A friend who talks unrelenting smack behind your back will eventually need to be dealt with, possibly downgraded to frenemy in order for you to get your power back. A Chatty-Cathy-love-to-distract-you coworker may need to be reminded of your boundaries if you're trying to get your work done. As a child, I had to become calculating in my escape. Never letting anyone know my plan allowed me to stay true to what was written on my heart. I experienced a deep feeling of empowerment once I was certain that leaving was my only hope of having a shot at being who I was born to be: someone worthy of her own consent. Only then would I have a chance to build my budding faith in myself. I believed as a child that God had given his only son so that I could live. I was willing to test that theory, push what I believed to its limit. The result was the beginning of my relationship with my intuition and my trust in myself.

Pause to Consider

- In what ways do you trust yourself?
- What does trust mean to you?
- What interferes with your ability to trust yourself? What happens instead?
- How would you like to be different in this area?
- What is your working definition of *permission*?

What I am asking is for you not to allow anything to get in the way of your happiness. To stave off your unwillingness to be on the cutting edge of your incredible personhood. On that cutting edge of growth is where change happens. Often it feels so much easier to give up, to hand over your power to trust yourself to someone else. This act of self-abandonment and self-sabotage happens all the time. I get it. Many of us have been led to believe that other people's opinions are more valuable than our own. Sometimes on our journeys we (unwittingly) enlist the guidance of our lowest common denominator: our self-deprecation. The tiny voice that is the advocate of all your letdowns, your disappointments, your belief in not being good enough. And in doing so we end up desperately seeking the protection of the queen bee in someone else. We look to her to give us license to be cool, to be on fiyah! We turn on ourselves. We hand over our Divine shine in exchange for standing in the dimly lit shadow of an exalted tormentor. How many Hollywood films are based on this hackneyed trope of using class, privilege, and one-dimensional standards of beauty to hijack unsuspecting victims out of their sense of self-knowing and self-worth? To date, the blockbuster film *Mean Girls* has raked in more than $130 million.

Pause to Consider

- Why do you think we give ourselves away?
- When have you given yourself away, believing you'd receive something better in return?
- What are you *really* hoping to get from a one-sided relationship?
- How do these patterns of self-abnegation show up in your life?

So many of us (especially women) have been primed not to trust ourselves, which translates into not trusting our instincts, which basically adds up to not trusting our own power to be the only permission we need in any given moment.

Faith vs. Trust

Because the two concepts are important in my life, my practice, and this book, I wanted to better understand the differences between trust and faith. I sat down and contemplated these ideas until I found my way to an acceptable answer. I appreciate what came forth and would like to share it here.

Trust is a building block of any healthy relationship, whether it be with yourself or another, and it is also active and alive. It gives us something to believe in, to count on. Trust, if given a chance, shows up as the best friend you want in a pinch, the one who gives that "I wish you would" look that instantly provides order. And if you have a Southern sensibility, then you know trust as something to "swear by." It's unequivocally reliable, trust is, when it's given a chance to shine. Trust promotes a deep sense of consideration for ourselves and others. Trust is built over time, and when there are no breaches in it, it has the chance to prevail and eventually, with practice, morph into a thing called integrity.

Faith, on the other hand, requires something else. Something a bit more robust, more stouthearted. Faith is trust on steroids, all grown up into a full-blown measure of conviction and optimism of restorative proportions. It is by way of faith that we are coaxed to take that leap into the unknown, to shed our hesitations at the threshold of every new venture. Faith requires that we go to that deep place of curiosity and from there, free-fall into the unknown. A cool saying suggests that instead of "faking it till you make it," consider "faithing it till you make it."

The best thing I have ever done for myself is to provide myself with an opportunity to close the gap on my own disadvantage. To have a hand in changing the course of my life. Had I not been bold, had I not dared to imagine a life that was a giant step up from my lowest common denominator at the time — poverty, disenfranchisement, and lack of opportunity — heaven only knows where I, a poor, Black, orphaned girl might have ended up. The permission I gave myself then is the same I give myself now, the result of which allows me to shine bright like a thousand diamonds and to help others grant themselves permission to do the same.

Bootstrapping Takeaways

- Become unwilling to remain complicit with your own demise.
- Have the courage to BYOP.
- Identify what your own permission is.
- Make a PACT with yourself.
- Explore what you are worth to you.
- Define what personal freedom means to you.
- Identify the difference between keeping up with the Joneses and being your own vibe.

───❦───

Let's face it. Most of you reading this book have already experienced ridiculous amounts of success in your own right. Am I right, or am I right? You've done the hard work, the heavy lifting, and have created a life worth living on your own terms.

And given that you know what success feels like, what will it take for you to level up? To go the full distance, to have that peace of mind, to know you're living your life's purpose? What will it take?

Take some time to reflect on where you are right now. If you've been taking mental notes with the intention of coming back to them and figuring out how any of this matters, why not come back to it right now? How did you get here? What did you have to give up in order to be where you are? What will you need to give up in order to get to the next level of achievement? Who will you need to become in order to bring forth what you want?

I'm So Glad We Had This Time Together

Now is the time for me to acknowledge you for pushing through and making it to the end of the first strategy. Hold your hand up, count to three, and say, "I did that!," knowing that I am meeting you where you are and giving you a virtual high five, hand to hand, skin to skin. So now let's take it down a notch. Take a breath and connect with what's going on inside you. As mentioned earlier, mindfulness practices have withstood the test of time in terms of their effectiveness as a means to an end. And the end I'm referring to is kindness toward the self. According to author Kristin Neff, "self-kindness involves more than merely stopping self-judgment. It involves *actively* comforting ourselves."

Go ahead and ask yourself what would make you feel comforted and supported. In what way might you comfort yourself right now? I love the act of swaddling myself in a favorite throw or scarf, preferably cashmere. The wrapping itself feels ritualistic. It's an act of letting myself know that I matter, that I'm worthy of my own attention. Another way is to connect to your breath. That's right. Make it personal, bring it close. For what is actually closer to you than your own breath? I've been a meditator off and on for decades, and I recently transformed this simple act of turning mindfully toward my breath into a daily practice. Connecting with the rhythmic ease of my own breath helps me separate the present moment from the incessant chatter of consciousness. It provides a refuge, a quietude for however long I'm able to stay present to it.

Declaration of Permission

The Declaration of Independence was written to declare our country's right to choose how to be governed. I'd like you to consider making such a declaration for yourself. What is it within you that wants a certain type of justice established? How do you see yourself becoming what you want? How would you use your permission to promote your well-being, your dreams and desires? What forgotten desire is beseeching you to set it free? What needs your blessing in order to blossom? What does your permission legacy look like? From whom or what do you need to declare freedom? What will you allow to fall away in order for you to become your own permission?

Once you've taken some time to ruminate over the questions posed above, try to answer them as best you can. Be generous with your responses. Take them to their limits; don't hold back. I prefer to give myself permission to carve out a specific time during the day, about an hour, to engage with whatever personal growth work I'm involved in. If you have a quiet space you've sanctioned in your place of living — a closet, a "she shed" or a "her hut," a "man cave" or a "dude den" — where you can get away for some downtime, go there now. I am always down with it when it comes to intimacy and quality time with yourself. Meeting your needs is a sure sign of moving toward self-acceptance. Perhaps a useful Lovefirmation here is *I'm worth my own time, love, and care.*

Take some time and think of the ways you will make a PACT with yourself. Write it out. Post it someplace where you have easy access to it. Go back to this PACT of self-permission often. Update it frequently to meet your needs on your terms.

Kick-Ass Strategy #2

Do. Not. Give. Up. Ever.

Ladies and gentlemen, my name is Sally O'Malley.
I'm proud to say that I am fifty years old. I'm not one of
those gals who's afraid to tell her real age, and I like to
[demonstrates] kick! Stretch! And KICK! I'm fifty!

— Sally O'Malley, *Saturday Night Live*

Wake up. Kick ass. Repeat.

— Kendra Lowe

CAUTION! Heavy load of kick-ass ahead. I think we can all safely attest to the fact that 2020 was one heck of a year. It not only kicked our communal asses, but it did so while commandeering us onto one corkscrew, dip-dive, dive-drop sequence of roller-coaster turns after another. Talk about "We're all in this together" being the understatement of the century. Not only has our hair collectively been whipped back and forth (thank you very much, Willow Smith, for the context), but so has our faith in one another, and our get-up-and-go to reinvent ourselves. All of us have been tested to the core, our sense of predictability shattered. We got to where we are today by standing in the eye of the storm of uncertainty, holding steadfastly to our hope for this moment to arrive, moored in our collective faith that we'd get through to the other side. We faithed it on steroids till we made it! *Can I get a witness up in here?!* Let's take a moment and commend ourselves for getting to the other side of 2020, for being willing to be a hope for ourselves and others, for being our own silver lining.

To allow yourself to take the risk and jump empty-handed into the possibility of making a difference not only in your life but in the lives of others is to me the working definition of *kick-ass.* Sure, you may have *heard* stories of others' successes or *witnessed* goals achieved, but it's an entirely different experience to take something intangible and gestate it into a reality for yourself. In other words, to manifest your dreams, desires, ideas, concepts (feel free to use your own terminology here) into the world of the tangible takes a kick-ass attitude. And that's exactly what is being asked of us. To put on our big-girl pants, cowgirl the f**k up, and you guessed it: Kick. Some. Ass. We have a lot to catch up on, ideas to bring into fruition, dreams to manifest, people to see. Places to go! And never, I repeat *never,* allow your mouth to write a check your ass can't cash.

I'm suspecting that as you hold this book the unemployment rate is slowly coming down from numbers as high as they have ever been in our history. Our underlying concerns and fears are enough to make the most stouthearted believers among us question whether *anything's* ever gonna give in a way that suits us all. Eventually. However, the upshot is that we Americans are on the road to bootstrapping ourselves back from a series of calamitous events. We are positioning ourselves to reclaim our agency, our pride, and our sense of humanity. It would be impossible for me to capture what each of you has personally endured. But I would like to applaud you not only for your ability to withstand the storm but also, for those of you who walked right into its eye, for your willingness to support others in enduring these times. Let me hear you say it: *that's kick-ass!*

I want to acknowledge your straight-up efforts by saying this: thank you. You are the definition of bootstrapping and unconditional love. I see you. Kudos for your bravery, for being the poster child for powerful effectiveness in its highest form.

Wake Up!

Are you ready to get this party started? Wait, what's that? I'm sorry, I can't hear you. Oh, you'd like me to repeat myself, get perfectly clear so that you don't miss a single word I'm throwing down? Word! Let's do this: *Are. You. Ready?* That's more like it! How many of you are tired of being tired? Yeah, I bet. (As I'm writing this, it's well into the pandemic, and I'm feeling lazy from the mandate to be lazy for almost a year now. Anyone else?) Who's exhausted from feeling as if you've had to work so hard to get to, well, nowhere fast? I don't know about you, but I feel like an exhausted water polo player endlessly treading water with no one to pass the ball to. Where are my teammates? I'm ready to get busy; how about you? All right then. Let's go!

What are you ready to change about your circumstances? What goal, no matter how large or infinitesimally small, are you interested in accomplishing? Kick the limits off, think so far outside the box it would take a posse of NASA scientists to pull up in the *Millennium Falcon* to find you and bring you back. What conditions do you need to create so that you can initiate change or work with the changes already afoot in your life? If you are a student or recent graduate, or perhaps part of the pandemic unemployed, what are you up to right now? How are you either managing or plotting to get through this time?

Be Here for It

As you're considering the questions I've posed thus far, allow me to share the story of a brilliant man, a friend of mine who along with the rest of the US men's water polo team literally kicked ass all the way to the 1972 Olympic Games. Maybe you're thinking, *1972? Uh, excuse me, but that was a long time ago. Is that even relevant?* Hells to the yes, it is! I don't know how much you know about water polo, but it's a sport that re-lies on resilience, endurance, and straight-up know-how. As far as I know, the rules of the game haven't changed since 1972, so the classic nature of being par excellence bar none is what's relevant here. There are no shortcuts to staying above the bot-tom of the pool anywhere from thirty-two to forty-eight min-utes, depending on time-outs and other official rules, without using your hands to stay afloat. It takes tremendous ability to egg-beat water for an entire game.

Just like the year 2020, the 1972 Olympics went down as one of the most difficult experiences to fathom as a global village. I'm not about to go into a full-on history lesson about it, other than to say eleven world-class athletes lost their lives owing to human cruelty. (You get to feed your curiosity and get your research on.) This is where my friend and former client Jim Slatton comes in.

By September 5, 1972, it had already been forty years since the US men's water polo team had won a medal at the Olympics. Some speculated that it would be the goalie Jim Slatton who'd change the course of this losing streak. Let's find out.

On the day that Jim awoke to the chance to change the course of history, I, on the other hand, was well on my way to a committed smoking habit. I lived in a group home (where the police had brought me after I went to them) and spent my morning rolling tobacco from the butts of half-smoked cigarettes I'd found on the ground onto a tampon wrapper. The tampon was free, and the paper thin enough to get the job done. In the sanctity of my makeshift hideout — a rotted-out tree trunk — I got my smoke on. And Jim Slatton, the goalie for the US men's water polo team, made "Go hard, go strong, go long" look like a strategy worthy of induction into the kickass hall of fame. Here's how Jim tells it:

As a competitor, you want to model yourself on the top people in the profession, from watching TED Talks to reading books like *The Black Swan*, where you learn to prepare for the extraordinary. In preparation for the games, I'd get up each morning and ask myself a simple question: "If I am the Olympic champion, what do I need to do today to prepare myself for that honor?" Perhaps the answer is, "I am going to go swim several miles around the Santa Monica Pier." So I go down to the beach and run between the guard towers in the sand, and if you've never done that, you'd find out fast how darn difficult that is. It feels as if your heart is gonna jump out of your body.

Before Munich, we won the Olympic trials for Tokyo, in 1964. We were very successful at UCLA. We were one of the few teams that ever went undefeated at the time. When we got to the '72 games, we knew how to train. That was never the issue. As the goalie for the water polo team, I had unique training that I would follow every day. I'd take a diver's weight belt — it was thirty-five pounds — and put it around my waist and tread water. The other thing I did was take a kind of square rubber brick, and I'd hold it up above my head. I'd turn the radio on by the side of the pool, get in the water, and just kick lap after lap, back and forth. The trick is to balance yourself. Not only do you train hard for the strength, but also you learn to keep your balance while in the game.

Each person is unique, and everyone's body responds to training in different ways. As you experience a variety of training modalities, you get more creative each day. And preparedness becomes intuitive once you've committed yourself. By the time you've committed yourself, you've also learned to pay the price to get to your goal; therefore, you will eventually learn not to give up. I always looked for excellence. I believed that there was always another level to get to.

Competition is a mirror of life, and you just have to say, yeah, you might get beat up. I've lost many games where things just didn't quite go my way. That's part and parcel of life. Going for the long game is a way to prepare for anything that may come your way. And if you're to be successful, you just have to stay with it. There's no doubt about it. Stumbling blocks along the way are par for the course. There are those people who allow the stumbling blocks to beat them. Once you do that, you've always got an excuse to give yourself.

That day in Munich the sky was blue, with a couple of puffy clouds. The Olympiastadion stadium was built like the Hollywood Bowl. The entrances onto the track made the orchestra visible. They played Beethoven at the opening ceremonies. I could hardly believe I was there, getting to be with all those fabulous people from all over the planet who were having this unique experience. Thinking of it gives me chills even now.

If nothing else, the Olympic Games taught me that no matter what, I could never give up. You may get beaten, that's true. But let the other team beat you because they were better and not because you quit. I believe that you just never, never give up. You have to keep trying. You have to.

With his strength and his excellent balance, the sun glaring in his eyes, and in his persistence to "never, never give up," on that auspicious day in September 1972 Jim blocked an opponent's goal while reeling in the water from a concussion he'd just gotten. He led his team to the bronze medal, turning the page on America's forty-year losing streak. In 1999 Jim Slatton was inducted into the US Water Polo Hall of Fame. That's what I'm talking 'bout, y'all. Regardless of the concussion, the sunlight blinding him, and working under a level of stress unknown to most of us, Jim kept his head, his heart, and most important, his kick in the game. No matter how you view the story, Jim practiced his ability to show up with the contingency plan to not give in. He was there to turn the tides of change.

Bootstrapping Takeaways

- Get up.
- Show up.
- Stay up.
- Put up.
- Pull up.
- Prepare for the long game.
- Ask yourself, *What do I need to do today to prepare myself for success?*

Out of the Mouths of Babes

This strategy of *kicking some ass* showed up in my life when my son was an adolescent. Are you a parent? If so, then you know that kiddos are known for saying the darndest things. My child, who I'd raised to be up-front, was no exception. One day he got up in my face with: "You're going to die if you don't quit smoking, Mommy," a deadpan expression on his face. "That's what my teacher says." *Great*, I remembered thinking. All along, I'd somehow imagined my kid hadn't noticed that every time we turned around, there I was with another ciggie, or "fag," as I so affectionately called my cigarettes, imitating the British hairstylists I worked alongside.

But the truth is that his observations were echoed by nearly every client I had. Repeatedly, clients, friends, and lovers let it be known just how much my hands and clothes reeked of stale cigarette smoke. *Got it!* It was true. Between clients, while my assistant was at work shampooing or blow-drying, I'd run to the laundry room, into the alley alongside Vidal Sassoon salon on Post Street in San Francisco, into the bathroom with the fan blowing full blast, or anywhere else I could light up.

It never dawned on me that I was tethered to smoking in a habit kind of way, although the half pack of Kool Longs soon morphed into an entire pack of Marlboro Reds and eventually grew into two packs a day of Marlboro Lights. Through it all I had left my girlfriend for my boyfriend, married a friend, and had a child. I had quit during pregnancy but started up again the moment I learned my son couldn't nurse.

I was one of those smoking enthusiasts convinced I could *quit anytime I wanted to* and that smoking wasn't so much an addiction as it was an oral fixation. *Oh, how Freudian. Oh, how bourgeois!* It could be worse, right? Oh, sure, I could've been a heroin or sex addict, but I chose nicotine instead. The way I saw it, if smoking was the least of my vices I'd be just fine. Smoking was like being on one of those economy vacays hosted by Carnival Cruise Line. You watch the over-the-top ice sculptures being paraded out, stuff your piehole with all the pretty little canapés and finger foods from the buffet, telling yourself the calories just don't count as much because, after all, it's vacation. Right? Well, because I was in denial about the smoking, I told myself its potential consequences — chronic bronchitis, a shortened life span, lung disease — just didn't count.

So, there I was first thing in the morning and the last thing at night puffing away hard, strong, and long. I was a fiend. Anytime I had a feeling, I'd light up. Stressed, I'd light up. Sad, afraid, lonely, feeling abandoned, I'd light up. And given that back then I pretty much had those feelings all the time, smoking became my way of attempting to escape the feelings. I was terrified to get close to anyone other than my kiddo, to be in my own skin. It took my child to confront me, to give me something to consider in place of my self-absorption.

Kicking the Habit

My son strewn across my shoulder, I bolted through the emergency room doors. He was nearly unconscious, his breathing barely audible. We were just in time. How I carried both our weights at that speed remains a mystery. "What did you do to him?" the white nurse yelled at me. *Judgmental witch.* I didn't know what I had done. One minute we were looking at a pre-divorce two-bedroom apartment, and the next my kiddo was sliding from my side onto the floor. *Unfit mother.*

After both the nurse and doctor interrogated me, we concluded that the brand-new hardwood floors in the apartment had triggered Mike's life-threatening, first-time asthma attack. The hospital considered referring my "case" to a social worker. *This is how it begins … first comes the blame, then they take names, then they come for your children.* As the millennials would say, I finessed my way right out of becoming some

Child Protective Services statistic. Instead of following my impulse and wilding out on the entire emergency room staff, I went code-white and pulled out my "Oh, my God" lexicon. The Valley Girl semantics have saved me many a day. It confused people, made situations that could go either way tip toward a sense of familiarity that lowered the cortisol levels — for those who needed it — in a flash.

I'd sworn that when cigarettes went from $1.75 to more than $3.00 a pack, I'd kick the habit. Instead, I deceived myself by purchasing cartons. After the episode with Michael, however, I pinkie-promised him that I was done smoking. I found all the cartons I'd stashed around our flat and placed them in a cardboard box and dropped them at the corner. I made my peace and walked away without looking back. That's one of the benefits of having an itinerate childhood: the ability to shut it down and walk away, for good. I placed all the beautiful lighters I'd collected in a velvet-lined sachet and sat it alongside the cartons and all the various-degrees-of-empty individual packs.

I kept one cigarette. I'd picked it up from a souvenir shop at Pier 39 while pretending we were tourists, my son and I. Michael hadn't seen me purchase it, nor had he ever been present whenever I procured my sticks. The single cigarette was enclosed in a glass test-tube-like vial. On the outside of the glass, in red ink, was printed: "In case of EMERGENCY break glass." And that's what it would have taken for me to break the glass; a feening (craving, in case you're not in the know) so severe it qualified as an actual emergency. I had to go hard on breaking up with smoking. I had to be willing to take no prisoners. I had to acknowledge that my habit was just that, a habituated response to my longing for connection. Smoking was my mama, my daddy, my sister, and my brothers. It was the loss of childhood, adolescence, and young adulthood all wrapped up in a thin, fragile piece of paper quick to catch fire, quick to go up in smoke. Double entendre intended.

There was only one way to be without smoking, and that was to find a way to be with myself, my feelings, my loneliness, the reality of my circumstances, the depth of the loss and pain. Have you ever felt terrified at the thought that if you were to allow yourself to truly feel your feelings, you'd lose control and not be able to bring yourself back? Yeah, well, that's pretty much how I felt, all the way to my midforties.

I purchased a bottle of chewable herbal nicotine pills and some nicotine gum and got a prescription for a patch. I made contingency plans.

Go Strong

I loved cigarettes most in the morning, with coffee; after a satisfying meal; at bedtime; after sex; but most deliciously before, during, and after drinking cocktails. As a hairstylist, I mostly drank socially right after work after standing all day. Nevertheless, I needed a plan to unmoor the habits from my daily routine. And for me, that's exactly what transforming an addiction into a tolerance came to mean: excavating the impulse from the soul by staring it down, engaging with it, and replacing it with the unconditional attention and love I and it desire. This is what I mean by going strong: having the guts and the grit and enough game to be with the most disowned aspects of ourselves.

My plan was to awaken each morning, mindfully allow the soles of my feet to touch the floor, and to sit, right where I was, until the desire to smoke came a-knocking. And once it did, and it did until it didn't, I'd sit through the sensation for as long as it took to come, entice me to abandon my resolve, and eventually go. In the beginning a moment felt like an eternity. It was the willingness to sit in my own presence and remain calm in the face of temptation that made the difference. I quickly learned to pay close attention to my body, and if I had a scratch, I wouldn't scratch it; if I had a desire to move, pee, or talk, I'd slow everything down, stay with the awareness of what was presenting, and instead of responding I'd turn my attention toward what cried out the loudest and then deny the natural response to alleviate the discomfort. In time this expanded my endurance in sitting with the discomfort of my feelings. Once I had success with that, which took about fifteen minutes each day, I'd remind myself that if all else failed, when the desire to smoke arrived, I had a second, third, fourth, and fifth line of defense:

- *First line:* sitting with my feelings each day.
- *Second line:* the ear seeds from my acupuncturist. I was to push on the seeds when impulse arrived.
- *Third line:* the chewable pills.
- *Fourth line:* the gum.
- *Fifth line:* the emergency cigarette.

Go Long

Jim Slatton was referred to me by another client. As Vidal Sassoon–trained stylists, we were known for the meticulous effort we put into our signature haircuts, especially the men we served. As opposed to barbers, who were noted for using clippers to shape their clients' hair, those of us trained the "Sassoon way," did not. We used a scissor-over-comb method that took years to perfect. Most men who ventured into Sassoon salons did so because of Sassoon's reputation of pursuing excellence.

Soon enough, after learning that Jim was an Olympic swimmer, I'd shared my angst about wanting to give up smoking in favor of working out. "With smoking," Jim said, "it's the sensation you're going for." Curious to know more, I asked him to explain. He assured me that all I needed to do is let go of all the other interventions and make up my mind to simply stop smoking. But then he dropped the mother of all suggestions, the coup de grâce that would forever deliver me, my lungs, and my son from the depths of nicotine stank. "This is what you do," Jim said. "You grab yourself a case of Calistoga water, and every time you get the urge to light up a cigarette, take a sip of water instead. The carbonation is what does the trick; it's the sensation you're looking for, the feeling of having an experience."

Although at the time I wasn't a big fan of carbonated water, I purchased seven cases of it. Jim was correct. Along with sitting in the presence of my own attention and tenderness and willingness to be with myself, popping the cap on the bottled water became my go-to. I continued with the homeopathic ear seeds in conjunction with the carbonated water until the desire to smoke was completely eliminated.

Kicking that habit took the time it took. I was less concerned about time frame and more invested in doing whatever would serve me, on my terms. I was in it for the long game as well as for my son's well-being. So often when we want to change a behavior, we get sidetracked when the results aren't immediate. I have found this to be true not only with habits we want to change but also with relationships that have become stifled and shut down due to blame and a lack of taking 100 percent responsibility for our own behaviors. Intellectually we might recognize that it took years to gain that extra weight or misspend our savings, or pull away from the love we'd hoped would last, but still, the emotional response is to want an immediate experience of change. You must have a deep affinity with possibility in order to commit to changing your behaviors. What are the chances that a Black and orphaned girl would grow herself up to cross paths with a world-class athlete who would share something that his Olympic training coach had shared with him and eventually have what was shared change her life?

One of the many awesome outcomes of kicking the habit was that I had a chance to create something that I valued — not smoking — as a result of my hard work. I felt proud to have my son witness the steps I took to build character and live in integrity with myself. At that time, I may not have had a family to share with my son, but I did have an opportunity to show him what earnestness in action looks like. It is said that trauma expresses itself in our cellular memory, or epigenetically, for five generations. The time had come for me to be the change I wanted to experience in my relationship with my son. It was up to me to offer an alternative to the trope of victimization, that I could only treat myself and others as well as I'd been treated. Letting myself be guided by that narrative felt familiar, and sometimes a known entity feels safer and more comforting than facing the depth of the aloneness that could be a result of taking steps to change. Up to that point I'd believed that I'd rather belong to my loss, to my painful history, than face what I believed to be the terrifying fact that I had nothing in terms of a caring mother or a father to guide me, no active relationships with siblings, grandparents, aunts, uncles, cousins. That isn't by any means to diminish the value of my son, but the way I saw it was I needed to be the best mother I could for him: it was not his job to be anything for me other than his best self.

Being kick-ass is all about taking the chance to achieve what might seem highly improbable at first glance. Quitting smoking was tough. However, I opened up to the prospect of becoming tougher than my addiction. I wanted to reclaim my lungs, my sense of taste, my sense of smell, and my son's respect back from the overinvested minutes and hours and days I'd spent connecting with the only constant I felt I had any control over. Here's the thing. After I committed to kicking the habit on my own behalf and showing up for my feelings instead of dissing them with the smoking, I eventually recognized what my addiction was about. It was a way to stay connected to my biological mother. Kicking the habit was tied to my abandonment narrative: if I let it go, I'd lose my mother. Smoking was all I had left of her.

As a young girl, and in the measly amount of time I spent with my biological mother, I was put in charge of lighting her cigarettes. I loved being useful, feeling seen. Getting to puff on her cigarette in order to light it and then give it over to her was an act as meaningful to me as arriving at the end of the rainbow and grabbing that pot of gold; being in my mother's presence *was* my pot of gold. Because it was in that simple act of feeling seen, if only in service of her getting her need met, that I learned to get my own needs met. That realization led me onto my path of healing. I recognized how I settle for the smallest of crumbs. However, simultaneously, I understood the power of being grateful for the smallest of things. Victim or victor thinking? It's up to you. To this day, twenty-four years later, I have not given up on myself and the freedom I have from smoking two packs of cigarettes a day, not even once. For this accomplishment I am proud.

Zoom in: I allowed myself to believe that smoking was a

way to keep a piece of my mother, no matter how toxic the habit was. It seemed a safe alternative to being with her, which was dangerous in its own right for more reasons than I care to grind out. With smoking, I inhaled the best parts of my mother, her laughter, her bitchiness (yes, I have a penchant for sassy, in-your-face people). Smoking meant we needn't be separated. But it would take the *true* love of my child to make me see the metaphorical and literal toxicity of the love that no longer served me. In choosing to quit smoking, I took the first step in leveling up my paltry expectations for love. It felt scary, of course, but I'd already gained a bit of personal power from the success of kicking the habit, and this in turn bolstered my trust in myself.

Also, due to my particular relationship with abandonment and rejection, there was one thing that fueled my desire to smoke: smoking, unlike my mother, would never leave me. I would have the power to break up with it on my terms. After I had a bit of ex-smoker tenure under my belt, I sought out my biological mother, Mattie. I traveled to Austin, Texas, and hung out with her for as long as my guest card status would allow, about four days. Not only did I have a rule to not stay longer than I felt welcome, but I also knew enough about my mother to know she had a low threshold for tolerating the intimacy my presence promised. During that time, my mother smoked like "there ain't no tomorrow," as she liked to say. You better believe I knew enough to stay away from the heavy topics, the ones that began with "Why did you…?" Instead, I took full responsibility for my feelings and let her know that I was breaking up with wanting her. With wanting her to be a certain way toward me. She laughed and told me I was "crazy as f**k" and wanted to know what California had done to me. Then she offered me a cigarette. I turned it down. And later, when she called out, "Hey, Red, run down to the sto' and get yo' mama a pack of cigarettes," I said … no. That is when my real journey back to myself began.

Bootstrapping Takeaways

- Dare to quit a behavior that no longer serves you, and be willing to seek medical help if necessary.
- Dare to quit someone whose needs no longer serve yours.
- Place a loved one's well-being over your unhealthy choices.
- Make a PACT with yourself first, then with someone you love, and keep it.
- Decide to succeed.
- Find someone exceptional to emulate.
- Develop an intervention plan chock-full of lines of defense.
- Be kind and loving toward yourself.
- Boldly let go of the relationships that no longer serve you.
- Search through *Who's Who* to find a worthy inspirer.

Throughout this chapter I've presented a host of ways to explore where you are in your life. Take some time and thoughtfully consider what you'd like to change about the way you are expressing or experiencing your life. Contemplate something that requires you to employ your will in a way that's strikingly different from how you might normally do it. For instance, if you'd like to eat less sugar, remove all your favorite go-tos from your house entirely. Then make a date with yourself to have that favorite dessert you only allow yourself to have on a special occasion. In other words, make having the dessert the occasion itself. Work up to the sweet treaty-treat instead of feeding the impulse for it ad nauseam (literally).

In the meantime, limit your sugars and consider replacing them with higher-quality and/or organic, sugar-free options, preferably options that aren't as enticing but that if you reached the feening stage, you'd have the healthier alternative to snack on. Go three days, let's say. And on the fourth day allow yourself one third of what you'd typically indulge in. You can do this with anything you want to scale back on. It's all about choice and volition, right? Life, at least for me, is a lot more fun when I feel I have a choice in how I live it. I encourage you to take a moment and consider to whom or what your impulsive way of eating might be attached. Perhaps it's an unrequited love, and if it is, gently and lovingly consider transforming that connection so that it is in service to your best self. Admitting that you've unwittingly settled for the smallest dividend, whether in life or in love, is incredibly empowering. It's a reminder of just how brilliant Spirit is. In other words, there is no place where Spirit doesn't reside, and where Spirit is, possibility is too. I am grateful for the crumbs that stayed me in my time of need. They've become the fish and loaves of bread that have multiplied thousands of times over, sustaining me throughout my life. This same principle of multiplicity is what I am offering you here.

Breaking up with a habit is challenging, no matter the impetus for the breakup. It's so important to remain aware of how you respond to yourself when considering and making significant life changes. A variety of emotions are bound to present themselves, and how you meet your more vulnerable nature will have *everything* to do with how well you succeed. And remember: success gets to be on your terms.

You decide what you want to change, when you plan to change it, and how you'd like to go about it. Take into account the means by which you plan to support yourself along the journey. Journals for writing in are a sure bet. Electronic devices are great for engaging with apps that might assist you with time management. I'm old-school and prefer to write almost everything down in long hand. The prettier the journal, the more face time I tend to have with it. But that's also because my moon is in Venus, and I am all about aesthetics and anything romantic.

Pause to Consider

Take some time for yourself. Get cozy with capturing your thoughts, however you choose to do so. Allow yourself to go into deep praxis with what you've experienced here. Take your time, stay for a while, and consider these questions:

- What are some of the habits you'd like to kick?
- To whom would you like to attribute this gift of changed behavior, including yourself?
- What are some of your takeaways from this chapter's strategy?
- How might you implement what you've learned in your everyday affairs?

Kick-Ass Strategy #3

Stand in Your Dignity

The kind of beauty I want most is the hard-to-get kind
that comes from within — strength, courage, dignity.

— Ruby Dee

No power on this earth can destroy the thirst for human dignity.

— Nelson Mandela

In sharing my own interpretation of the meaning of dignity, I recognize the value we were all born with, the intelligence, the beauty, the God-given inalienable rights of freedom and self-expression, and the fact that our very existence is evidence of our worth. We are all born with built-in attributes of goodness and intuition; we are all worthy of respect. Especially our own. As we grow, we learn that our dignity is inviolable. While there may be moments when we forget who we are, giving our power away and lessening personal agency, our dignity is always present, just waiting for us to remember it. Our dignity stands at the ready to serve us. In other words, to become aware of what is good about you is to work in the realm of the sacred and to consider yourself as no less worthy than the sum of your whole spirit. Doing so allows you to accept yourself as worthiness in action. The transformative process of alchemy allows those who believe in its principles to tap within themselves the power to restore their spirit. Once you've stood in your dignity, you can always restore that state of being for yourself.

Have you ever appeared on location in your dream come true? What do you remember about it? Were you able to take it all in, to celebrate the glory of manifesting your desires with equipoise and dignity? If you've benefited from your own hard work and were able to accept it on your own terms, you're ahead of the rest of us, and we are on your heels, determined to catch up. Although I've had a lifetime of amazing successes, so many have felt rote or not quite right. I've not always understood the *why* behind what I've done, and dignity hasn't always been part of the journey to get there. Perhaps this is true for you too. Take as much time as you wish to ponder the questions posed just above, and when you're ready, let's keep going.

Zoom in: Throughout the strategies presented in each chapter, you might recognize some core themes that repeat themselves. From my experience, core behaviors such as self-abandonment, overextending to others, and giving all of ourselves away tend to be linked to survival fixations leftover from childhood, which we may not even be aware of. Therefore, it is okay to revisit ideas in order to understand them better and extract the learning for yourselves.

Don't Stop Believing

April 17, 2019. There I sat, a nervous wreck. My appointed PR team and I were in the green room at NBC Studios in New

York City. It was a dream-come-true moment. I was on a press junket to promote the Lifetime feature film *I Am Somebody's Child: The Regina Louise Story*, about how I survived thirty foster home failures, a year in a level-fourteen residential treatment center while being administered antipsychotic drugs, and thrown into solitary confinement as a child. Heavy-duty themes, right? I know. Not to worry. We are not heading back down that rabbit hole, so *breathe*.

And that's exactly what I did as I waited. *Inhale through your nose...1...2...3, exhale through your mouth...1...2...3.* For a year I had anticipated the interview, and thanks to one of our executive producers, Andrea Buchanan, the deal was done. And here it was at last, my chance to speak with one of the most trusted broadcasters in America, Robin Roberts. It felt otherworldly the way I was escorted onto the set — the lights, the cameras, the action!

Near the end of our six or so minutes together, Roberts posed a question that later motivated me to more deeply examine what I know to be true about granting ourselves permission. "What would you tell your younger self now, looking back?" she asked. *Oh, dear.* It was fast becoming one of those deer-in-the-headlights situations. Only moments before I'd rehearsed (or so I thought) the answers to the questions her producer, Mark, had said she'd ask. Five million viewers had tuned in that morning, as they had every day, making *Good Morning America* the top-rated morning news and entertainment show. I leaned back in my chair, considered the query, and realized...*rut-roh*...I had nothing.

Then suddenly I launched into my rendition of Steve Perry's "Don't Stop Believin'." (Love you, Journey!) This song was a favorite of mine when I was a teenager. For a moment Robin looked as surprised as I had just moments before, and I side-eyed the live audience as they bopped and clapped. For a few dizzying seconds, everyone was wrapped up in my spontaneous burst of innocent delight to be on Robin's show, sitting across from what I called her from there on out: one of the queens of Black Girl Magic.

"She's an author, she can sing, and her movie airs this —" Robin said, her smile finishing the interview. I literally buzzed from the spectacle of it all.

When I was done, I walked backstage thinking, *What in the hell did I just do?* I had tons of successful media events in the bag, but never had I unexpectedly busted out in rhythm and song. I wasn't sure if I should feel satisfied or horrified. And for a teeny-tiny second, I questioned whether I'd taken up too much space (as I am way too often accused of doing) or violated a copyright agreement by performing someone else's work.

"You were great!" Robin said as she stood and made the effort to connect with me, lessening my anxiety with a hug. "I'm proud of you." I continue to be speechless about those last few words that came out of Robin's mouth, words that every Black girl, woman, person should hear, no matter their age. I'd craved being seen by women who looked like me, women who'd walked through their lives on their own terms in a world that sometimes feels indifferent to those of us known for our Blackness, and those who identify as people of color.

It was only later, in my hotel room, that I put two and two together. Had Robin asked the question differently, as in what I *told* myself as a child, I would have informed her that I was quite accustomed, at that time in my life, to granting myself permission to do whatever needed to be done and to be who I believed myself to be in order to achieve my dreams. It has been said that necessity is the mother of invention. And so it was for me: out of the necessity to parent myself safely into adulthood, against a maelstrom of odds, the permission to do so was mine, and mine alone. And I granted it to myself. Unapologetically. It was dignifying to do so.

As an adult, I've managed to value the gift of my consent, with the result that I'm better able to accept all of me, as in author, speaker, teacher, coach, and yes, at times, singer. I'm also a woman who is very much in touch with her inner child and how she, the little one, felt so free to be who she was in front of Robin. Singing that Journey song shored me up when I was a young Black girl living in remote and mostly white towns listening to KFRC, the only radio station that came through my transistor radio with minimal static.

So perhaps the question I should have asked myself the day I sang my answer to Robin's question wasn't whether or not I was being *too much* but, *What does it feel like to stand in full acceptance of all of me? How was it to be on location of a dream come true?* These, my friends, are but two of the questions I invite you to find the answers to for yourselves by the end of our journey together.

A Little Heart-to-Heart about Dignity

For me life has been about understanding the importance of cultivating a sense of dignity. Another way of saying this is that it's been imperative for me to cultivate a relationship to my own worth. I get it. This may sound like an endeavor in *really* heavy lifting, as in, *Who in their right mind wants to walk around with the Empire State Building on her shoulders?* But strangely enough, it hasn't felt that way. Once I began taking my life back from the horrors of my childhood, the weight of the past lifted, and my self-respect soared. I gained more clarity about what I'd gone through, acknowledged my survival as genius, forgave myself and those I'd held in contempt, and began to thrive.

Acting from a place of self-worth provides us with the strength to acknowledge the wholeness of ourselves. In so doing, we are better able to hold fast to what's true when the outside world threatens our sovereignty, bullies our humanity, or attempts to seduce us into questioning whether or not we matter. We are never alone when we are in alignment with ourselves because *knowing* that our presence on earth is merited navigates us toward right action and is also evidence of our ability to be in sync with our truth, our spirit.

What do you believe to be true about you? Jot down whatever comes to mind. Don't overthink it.

Here are a few more thoughts on the matter that might help you answer the question. Have you ever experienced a feeling of satisfaction or comfort after taking action from the beliefs that guide you? Perhaps you stood up for yourself or someone else. No matter the outcome, you felt great because you knew that you had done the right thing, from a good place, and that your life as well as the other person's would be forever altered. That's what I mean when I invite you to stand in your dignity. It means to be bold in your own way, on your own terms. It's to have a say, to grant yourself permission to make the best choices available to you in any particular moment. Periodt!

To recognize that we matter invites our significance to become our ally, a benevolent accomplice, an authentic representation of our solidarity with ourselves. The more we know ourselves, the more generous we can be with others because we will know what enough feels like; we will better understand the necessity for boundaries.

Employing Your Dignity

A very fine example of someone who demonstrated the power of personal choice and profound self-determination is Nelson Mandela. He was a man who remained sound under pressure while standing behind his thirst for democracy, and he not only withstood but also transformed all the obstacles that blocked his path. Mandela, marshaling his internal resources of resoluteness, integrity, and gall, hustled his way forward, aligning with the powerful objective of actualizing his self-respect. Here's how he bootstrapped a paradigm shift.

On April 20, 1964, at the now infamous Rivonia Trial, the already imprisoned Nelson Mandela was convicted of high treason and sentenced to life in prison for his attempt to overthrow the rule of apartheid, a social system based on skin color and facial features designed to enforce racial discrimination against nonwhites in South Africa. In his defense he gave his impassioned three-hour "I Am Prepared to Die" courtroom speech: "I have cherished the ideal of a democratic and free society in which all persons will live together in harmony and with equal opportunities. It is an ideal which I hope to live for and see realized. But, My Lord, if it needs be, it is an ideal for which I am prepared to die." There was a worldwide call at the time for the release of Mandela and Walter Sisulu, another anti-apartheid activist. Mandela went on to serve twenty-seven years in prison, many of them as forced labor, and was finally released in February 1990. Four years later, apartheid ended with a new South African constitution that enfranchised Blacks and other racial groups.

Anything worth fighting for often starts with the desire to take a stand and defend what is right and true about the human spirit: that we are all born with inalienable, God-given rights.

Courage may have invited Mandela to put himself on the line for what mattered; dignity held him in his power to become the change he wanted to see. It inspirits us in the face of fear, dignity does, strengthening our resolve to stand on our own two feet and know that we are indeed decent and virtuous. A healthy and felt sense of self-understanding and unconditional love supports us in trusting the nature of our own heart.

Although I use Mandela's revolutionizing example of going to extraordinary measures to take action on behalf of a nation, it is not a requirement of *you* to do so as a result of reading this book! And, yes, I understand that at times you may have questioned the very nature of what it means to be human, to be alive, and to be a part of such a complex and diverse global community. Hopefully, your humanity hasn't been threatened to such a degree that you need to offer your life in exchange for an ideal!

What I am asking is that you consider the qualities that already live in you and what you can do to bring about your own bootstrapping moments. So often I have heard clients admit that they are stuck and can't seem to find their way out of a particularly challenging situation. That's when I might ask, "What do you need in order to turn the situation toward a more favorable outcome?" Sometimes I am met with answers suggesting hopelessness or overwhelm. Often people admit that they don't know. Some may offer that they don't have the financial means to move their ideas forward or change their situation, and they therefore give up. I encourage them to reconsider the truth of what they are saying, as I will do here with you.

Zoom in: In the opening of the book, you came across the terms *permission*, *bootstrap*, and *kick-ass*. Let's look at these terms again for a sec. To bootstrap a situation, you can consider self-determination a form of currency, as is hope, as is believing in the possibility that you are worth the struggle it may take to realize your dreams. To bootstrap is to have a hand in changing your circumstances toward a more favorable outcome. It's the opposite of doing nothing. To bootstrap is to take initiative to get something started or rebooted, as in a plan of action. Kicking ass is the energy and attitude it'll take to get things done. Kicking ass and bootstrapping lead you toward your own permission because what it all comes down to is: if it's meant to be, it begins with me. You get to be the arbiter of your highest end, and these strategies become the means by which to realize your dreams.

Take a moment and consider several accomplishments in your life. How have you manifested your successes? What do you attribute these successes to other than pure drive and determination? Below you'll find a few examples of inner resources that I imagine Mandela relied on during his quest. For now, all I'm asking is that you identify three inner resources that you have relied on. Feel free to choose from the list below as well. Make note of what you discover about yourself. Be generous. Practice kindness toward yourself. When we commit to employing our best qualities on our behalf as well as for the greater good of all concerned, we will never be without opportunities to participate in endeavors that require our goodness to lead the way.

Bootstrapping Takeaways

- Face your fear.
- Speak your truth.
- Persevere.

- Be self-determined.
- Hold to your integrity.
- Stand in your dignity.
- Hold true to your value.

Note: I'd love to hear from you. Once you discover your three resources, if they are different from the ones offered, feel free to share them with me on Instagram. Let's make ours a community of healing.

Abandoning My Dignity

In the early '90s, I decided it was time to stop playing small and to face my fear of not being good enough. I began to pursue the career that remained fallow in my heart yet lived brazenly in my mind. Becoming a hairstylist was a dream I'd been encouraged to abandon as an adolescent. "You'll probably end up a junkie," my then therapist offered. "Hairdressers are serial partyers," my social worker added. Needless to say, I allowed their reproaches to scare the dream back to where it had come. By then I had a child to rear, and working menial jobs in group homes with severely emotionally disturbed children felt far too familiar. And the long commute was eating up my small earnings. In two years' time, I found a cosmetology school. I committed myself to the grind, and then I graduated.

After beauty school, where I learned to work with the myriad of textures found in the Black community, and a succession of apprenticeships where I learned to work with a variety of other hair textures (Asian, European, Native American, and more), I dedicated myself to apprenticing for two years at the swankiest, most high-end salon in town. There the stylists donned designer clothes priced well above the average rent in the Oakland Hills, ate out several times a week, and traveled home in the evenings in taxicabs. I waited for buses that barely showed up and was habitually late picking up my son from after-school care.

Working at Savage Hair Salon would mean that I'd *made* it. All I wanted back then was to be a hip mom: with the right hair, the right clothes, and stilettos, oh my! I was willing to do anything in order to become what they stood for: #CoolAF

The first time my boss stuck his tongue in my ear in front of the *entire* salon, I laughed off the embarrassment of it, as in *that did not just happen.* My sudden feeling of humiliation made no room for believing that it *had* actually happened. Although I was surrounded by a salon full of stylists and patrons, no one acted as if they'd witnessed anything out of the ordinary. No one flinched. No one came to my defense. It was as though, in a single moment, a tsunami-size wave of disbelief had washed over the salon, leaving each person waiting for the next to act on what everyone had seen yet no one saw. The gaslighting was f**king epic. As a result, I too was unable at the time to take action on my boss's behavior. I became terrified instead. Up until that moment I'd felt as though I'd made a home at Savage, plus a few friends, which for me was no small feat. I was unwilling to lose what I'd worked hard to secure for myself and my child.

The hiring manger told me that I should *feel lucky* being the first African American woman offered employment there. Instinctively, I felt that speaking up would be seen only as the word of a lowly assistant against that of a worldly and super successful white professional male business owner. Think *The Devil Wears Prada* in the hairdressing world, featuring Harvey

Weinstein as Miranda Priestly. Although I was no stranger to having to fight the good fight on behalf of gaining equitable opportunities for myself, I just didn't want to be forced to be *that* girl to fight that war so soon after leaving foster care and losing that battle.

And then there was that time the boss told me to go to his favorite hotel, book a room, and wait for him. He made further commentary on what he planned to do to me. However, I refused to dignify his crudeness with a theatrical outburst, which would only have broadened his audience. Instead, I pulled my butt muscle so tight I could suffocate a tick, a trick I learned from a friend about staying cool under pressure. Let's talk about cowgirling TF up! All right then! Any thought of a tear getting shed was choked off in its infancy. I'm nearly certain my face belied my efforts to appear impassive. How many of you have been there and done that? How many times over?

"Don't be *so* sensitive," my boss told me, elbow-tapping his sentiments onto my arm as I stood beside him, breath held, terror blasting its way from a bygone time of horrific child abuse. At that moment my boss became my mother's live-in boyfriend, Mr. Benny. Both felt inescapable. Unsafe. While what I am describing is absolutely not acceptable, once the trigger of my own shame got pulled, trauma had free rein over me. It's as though the past was hijacking the present. What once lived in the past can come alive in us, once again in the now.

It's as though the feelings, the fears, the anxiety, or whatever emotions appear grab us by the throat and render us completely unable to access any healthy adult, self-loving response. At least that is how this intrusion worked in me. Trauma does not ask permission to show up. Trauma trespasses across time barriers. That day, I abandoned myself, momentarily forgetting all that was good about me. And because of my inability to confront my boss, his behaviors increased in frequency. The more demeaning his behaviors, the more defenseless I believed myself to be. It was as though I were under a spell of complete and utter powerlessness. The more I convinced myself that nothing was happening, the worse I felt about not doing anything. I did not know that my inability to take a stand made me an unwitting accessory to my feelings of helplessness. I felt trapped in a cycle of impenetrable denial, dread, and defenselessness.

Pause to Consider

What injustices have you accepted unwittingly or otherwise? How have you swallowed your self-respect in order to bury the bitterness, a survival reaction you may have relied on in similar situations? What was the result then and now? Take your time to think about these questions. Jot them down in your journal. Mindful awareness is an enormous act of self-love and moves us toward reclaiming our rightful place in our own dignity.

From Blaming to Reclaiming

Getting out of bed each morning to drag myself to work became a taxing undertaking in the days and months following my boss's initial harassment. Every day I concocted scenarios of how to quit or sabotage my way out of that job. Self-sabotaging, as in catting out or leaving without a trace, back then was like a superpower that weirdly enough allowed me to exit awkward situations without having to engage in confrontations with the people who preferred avoiding them anyway. I'd left a swath of such situations in my wake. I knew enough, however, not to take the fall for this one. Something in me wanted to play it out. Also, simply quitting would have prevented me from collecting unemployment. While a single act of sabotage, as in blackmailing him, might have encouraged my boss to approve my unemployment claim, I would have lost self-respect. So I stayed steady. When he'd say crushing things to me, eventually I'd say something to myself to flip the script, a quick reframe. Mostly I'd tell myself *he's really talking about his mother, not you.* Believe me when I tell you that playing the dozens in group homes had prepared me well for this situation and worked magic for me. It helped me to laugh at him, even if it was just to myself. Do keep in mind that I had not yet learned the powerful nature of such attributes as kindness and compassion. "Yo' mama" jokes *were* my attributes of kindness. It was either that or a straight-up get-in-his-face-and-have-at-that-ass type of confrontation. I was more afraid of my own rage than his.

One day during a staff meeting, an opportunity presented itself. A manager asked if anyone had anything to add before the close of the meeting. She'd restated their "open-door policy" before encouraging the room of mainly women to step forward. *Speak up*, an inner voice encouraged. In front of forty people, including the front-desk staff, the laundry lady, the coat-check lady, and all the apprentices and stylists, I publicly outed my boss and all the myriad ways he'd planned to defile me. No one seemed surprised. Instead of having my concerns met with gasps of incredulity, or even compassion or empathy, I was encouraged to "brush it off," to not be another Anita Hill. The salon manager, a woman who I *so* naively imagined would be neutral, actually suggested that I was taking it "way too personally." *WTF?* I stood up and walked out. That same salon manager came after me, encouraging me to reconsider, coaching me to "not let him win." I thought about my son, his after-school basketball team and how much it meant to him. Being an only child was a particular kind of burden for him, especially given he was an extrovert with ADD. I needed to support his socialization and his therapy. I leaned into giving the situation *one more chance.*

The morning after the staff meeting, I received a phone call from one of my colleagues. Through hiccups, sobbing, and long pauses during which she struggled to find her words, she eventually confided that she and several other apprentices had lived for months on end afraid to go into work alone because of the boss's before- and after-hours harassment of them.

"When you told the truth, we had to fess up to what's been going on," the caller informed me. "We thought we were the only ones." As the designated leader, I worked with the others to come up with a plan to push through the situation until we could find other employment. From that day forward, we agreed to never enter or leave the salon without a buddy. I encouraged each woman to speak up for herself and her buddy if a public humiliation ensued. We became support resources for one another. We traded off picking one another up for work each day, often staying past quitting time to honor the principles of our solidarity.

That day, I was honored to say yes to standing with and for those women. We began taking our power back, which led to standing stronger in our own skin, in our dignity. Slowly but surely the owner backed off. I stayed employed for as long as I could until one of the senior colorists beckoned my assistance by calling me "slave girl." I. Was. Not. Having. That. Shortly thereafter, each of us, in our own time, gave our notice.

I was the first to leave. And later I was also the first to open my own hair salon, which was grounded in the principle of treating my employees with the utmost respect. My intention was for anyone who worked for me to feel empowered to step up and speak out, but more important, I made a vow to myself to never provide them with cause to have to step up and speak out. And should I have unintentionally caused any of my employees harm, I was willing to place my ego on the line and take responsibility.

Acting on my own behalf and that of others was an act of unconditional love. Allowing my feelings to rise and fall, experiencing them as they presented themselves, was all about my ability to become familiar with my personal power and my goodness, and to accept that I mattered, that I'd be able to bring myself back from my feelings. I gave myself a chance to see that my contributions made a difference and that the differences made as a result of my actions were honorable. *That I was honorable, that I too could be love in action. And so can you.*

Bootstrapping Takeaways

- Admit there is a problem when you see one.
- Speak out on your behalf and that of others.
- Find your "yes" in the face of doubt.
- Collaborate with others.
- Stop blaming someone else and do something on your own behalf.
- Stand in your truth.
- Endure under strain toward a reasonable resolution.
- Make room for a potential trauma response.
- Permit your humiliation to become your motivation.

Zoom in: Now that you've had an opportunity to read examples of the steps taken by Mandela and well, yours truly, to stand in our dignity, it's time to get to work. Return to your earlier responses. Once you've read through your notes, select the reflection that has a bit of heat for you. Spend some time musing on the details of what happened. Perhaps there were instances when you didn't speak your truth. What did you do instead? Maybe, like me, you found yourself in a position of wanting to do the right thing but due to a trauma reaction or other reasons, you were unable to act from your highest beliefs about yourself.

Let's take a closer look. Using one of the bootstrapping takeaways I identified on pages 79–80 and 86, begin a reflective conversation with yourself. For example, if you were to consider facing your fear, what would it look like to grant yourself permission to do so? What do you imagine would get in your way? Name one fear that holds you back. And as you work your way through your responses — addressing all the points that hold value for you — go slowly and act with tender regard toward yourself. And know this: by naming your feelings and then sitting with them, you become a loving witness for yourself. By acknowledging what is true for you, you hold space through mindful awareness for your innate self-worth to shine through. These tasks, although they may seem simple, are open invitations to grant yourself permission to embark on your loving journey toward unconditional self-love — the theme of this book.

Dignity Quotient (DQ)

If you've made it this far into the experience, permit me to give you a whopping *thank-you*! In my work as a teacher and coach,

I've learned the value of giving and receiving gratitude and the grace it bestows on our hearts after we've engaged in deep, soulful work. There's one more invitation I'd like to extend to you. There's no requirement to do it *immediately*; however, I am asking you to commit to coming back to it before moving on to the next chapter.

Now that you've taken some time to become more intimate with yourself, let's discover a little something about your relationship to your dignity. The Dignity Quotient is a metric devised to assist you in better understanding this relationship. As you saw in the story of my boss's boundary violations, I quickly lost sight of my capacity to stand up for myself, leaving me feeling powerless against his aggressions.

Put a check next to each statement that is true for you:

- ❐ I allowed another person to overstep my boundaries this week.
- ❐ I remained silent in regard to something that mattered to me.
- ❐ I said yes when I really should have said no.
- ❐ I give away my time to others, hoping they'll give to me.
- ❐ I treat others with more kindness than I treat myself.
- ❐ I defer to self-effacement in times of distress.
- ❐ I am — sometimes — unaware that I need my own permission.

How did you do? Whatever the outcome of this little quiz, celebrate you right where you are. Who you are today is perfect! There is nothing wrong with you. Make this learning as fun as you'd like it to be. And go ahead and commit to transforming every check mark into a powerful act of consciousness raising. By the end of the week, write yourself a permission slip that'll empower you to move from a place of dignity and worth. Perhaps you'll feel ready to say no and mean it. Give yourself permission to do something kind for yourself. I am notorious for gifting myself shoes! Lord have mercy on my inclination to pamper myself so creatively. Your sky is as limited as you allow it to be.

Lovefirmations

I am worthy of my own permission.
I permit myself to stand in my dignity.

Below you will find a meditation practice designed just for you. The intention is to gently and lovingly pour the words offered here into your heart. I can hardly think of anything more potent than slowing down and gently nurturing the soul. It works hard for us, our soul does: breathing, holding, awakening, and inspiriting us to move toward love's openness. Give yourself permission to be with yourself in a time of quietude.

Meditation on Dignity

What do you need right now? A sense of your worthiness? A spell of time to connect with what is now and has always been significant about you? A moment of grace in which to honor yourself? All these states of being originate from within you, through you, as you. They are as close to you as your very breath.

Find a place where you can easily get comfortable. Once

you've done that, take a moment and connect with your breath. Take a few deep breaths, and ever so slowly drop into the moment. Once you've settled in, think back to a time when you had an experience you are extremely proud of. Pay attention to where you were and what you were doing. Were you alone or with others? What pleasure did you revel in? Allow the situation to slowly come into view, unfolding as it will. If you land on something in particular, stay with it through three deep breaths. Notice how you're feeling. Name the feeling. Locate the feeling in your body, place your hand there, and make a mental note of the feeling.

Now turn your attention back to your special moment. Take in all that's good about it. Perhaps there's joy and excitement, laughter and celebration. Allow whatever you're experiencing to be; nothing more than your own acknowledgment and validation is being asked of you. Now take three deep breaths at your own pace. As you turn your attention to the present moment, how are you feeling? Name one to two feelings for yourself. No rushing; it's not about getting it right, because you are perfect as you are. When you find your one or two feelings, recognize where they are in your body. You may not notice the where, and that is okay. Gentleness is the key. Are you experiencing any sensations in your body right now? If so, where? Breathe your loving attention into that place. If not, stay as you are, and breathe your loving appreciation into this moment, into your entire being. Place your hand on a part of your body that you intuitively know could benefit from your touch. Breathe a Lovefirmation into this place until you feel whatever is there beginning to soften, to give way. Stay with this for as long as you desire.

Notice how all you need is your own consent to shift your

attention, to be right where you are, experiencing that which you desire. Repeat after me:

There is only one sun, one moon, and one me, and like each celestial body I too am unique in the way I serve a purpose in this vast Universe, filled to the brim with all the yeses I can possibly imagine. I am safe, I am trust-worthy. All that I am is a result of showing up right here, as I am. I am worthy of my own attentiveness and love. I am worthy of staying in connection with myself and my feelings.

Kick-Ass Strategy #4

Grow Through
What You Go Through

Think like a queen. A queen is not afraid to fail.
Failure is another stepping-stone to greatness.

— Oprah Winfrey

Don't go through life, grow through life.

— Eric Butterworth

I think Eric's phrase above is not only catchy and clever, but it also captures what I've come to understand about myself in relationship to what is good enough about me.

Growing through what you go through (like a queen) allows you to pause and consider the very choices and experiences that make you who you are. This tactic is a venture toward slowing life down and cultivating a sacred opportunity, a chance to step ever more deeply into the composition of *you*. In this way you create an opening to get up close and personal with the parts of you that may be begging for your attention, parts unintentionally disowned, ignored, or suppressed. You're also presented with the choice to act on your own behalf, to become the interventionist you so urgently need. You become the authority on and arbiter of what right action means to you, thus stepping into your own permission to heal yourself.

Remaining stuck in an emotional rut drains us of our light, our agency, our joy; it can be a nasty business. Using your life force to compulsively fuel outdated ways of thinking and of viewing yourself in turn feeds repetitive and outdated actions that will likely lead you back to where you started: feeling stuck, overwhelmed, constricted, and disconnected from your life's purpose. This is no way to live. Or worse yet, we're left doomed to repeat the patterns of our versions of hell on earth, not so unlike our ancient brother Sisyphus.

Pause to Consider

- How would it benefit you to become unstuck as a result of acknowledging and exploring the familiar ways you are with yourself?
- What's one behavior or a way of thinking that you are willing to reconsider in exchange for having more inner spaciousness?
- Who are you when you're not being your best self?

When You Go Missing

Katherine Spence, now a successful independent business-woman in the entertainment medical field, knows firsthand the value of the strategy we're exploring here. Today her life is filled with caring for cultural icons such as Dwayne "the Rock" Johnson and the likes of Chrissy Teigen, Cher, Rihanna, and a whole host of A-list celebrities that could fill the bed of her cherried-out custom-built Ford F-150. But in no way is it lost on Kat all the work it took to get to her heart's desire, which was to grow herself into a person worthy of her self-respect. Here's her story.

Born in 1964, Kat was adopted three days after birth. Although Kat grew up in what she calls a *wonderful* family with conservative values, complete with a doting mother, a dedicated father, and an adopted sister who adored her, most of her life she'd felt a deep and palpable inner loneliness. Kat was not alone in losing that vital first connection with her biological mother. That year, in the United States, 135,000 other babies were also adopted. Nor could Kat know that what she felt was a common experience among adoptees worldwide — preverbal mother loss.

By the time Kat reached young adulthood, she'd already mastered the art of filling in the piece of the puzzle that was *always missing* inside her with late nights, speedballs, and cringeworthy blackout episodes that made returning to her day job as a customer service agent at the local Vons a laughable conceit. Unable to grasp the fierceness of her addiction, eventually Kat was demoted to bagger, then parking lot attendant, until finally she was released from the company entirely.

Everyone Kat knew exhausted themselves in their failed attempts to support her in some kind of recovery and healing. The ones who loved her most, her parents, thought Kat may have suffered neurological damage during birth or even inherited some type of faulty temperament. All they knew was that one moment their beautiful lifeguard daughter with the sunny disposition was first runner-up in a beauty pageant and the next she'd been denied the right to walk across the stage for her high school graduation, kicked out of Catholic school, and dismissed from every job she'd landed.

"I arrived home after a late-night binge, and there, in the front yard, amid the garbage cans that had been pulled out for collection, were my shoes, books, and clothes, everything I owned, tied up in plastic bags. Can you believe they were stacked next to the garbage cans? Dude, my sh*t was literally out on the curb," Kat shared during our conversation. "I couldn't help myself," she stated in a voice so small her words were nearly inaudible.

Kat was already so far gone by the time her parents cast her out that their last act of publicly shaming her only drove her further from her own power and ever more deeply into the throes of her addiction. However. Something helped Kat change the trajectory of her life:

I awakened one morning, upside down, naked, and twisted up in a closet, feening for my next hit. I had no idea how I got there. There I was, ass pinched into a corner, my neck smashed into my breasts like a cracked-out humpback. It took me nearly half an hour to get to where I could just sit on the floor, and all the while I wanted more: more cocaine, more forgetting. I just wanted more of what I was feeling: more emptiness.

The question that flashed across my mind was: What are you willing to do to get more, Kat? How much more of you are you gonna give? And then a sound broke through the moment, or perhaps it was always there, it was hard to tell. It felt like the sanest stream of consciousness I'd had in, like, forever. At first it felt surreal, as if it was coming from somewhere in my body, and like the insatiable huntress that I was, I began to pat myself down trying to locate the sorrow taking over me. It took me a moment before I saw the little feet, the soles dusted with dirt. They jabbed the air fiercely, as though all they had ever known was to kick and fight with life.

I managed to pull myself up by hanging on to a dresser. Standing over the dresser drawer, I could see there was a baby lying in it, its face reddened from the screaming. I didn't know how long she'd been there, left all alone by her parents, who were somewhere in the house. In my haze I offered the infant girl my finger, and after a while I picked her up and felt the sadness and rage rock her little frame. Knowing early on I didn't want children, I was surprised at how the baby's cries opened the floodgates of my own unshed tears.

Far too messed up to do anything different, I left the baby in the living room with her parents and somehow dragged my raggedy ass back to my own parents. By then I weighed less than ninety pounds, and my mother had no idea who I was. Not allowed inside, I was given a tent, food, and essentials to rough it out in the backyard. And I did just that. I knew enough about myself to know I'd never accept my parents' paying for a treatment center. That would just affirm my shame. Instead, I made deals with them that would assure little wins. I stopped using. Just. Like. That. Cold turkey, they call it. We agreed that, after thirty days of no drugs, I could move back into my room. I'd find a trade or training program and complete it. I remembered how I had felt as a lifeguard. The CPR training was my favorite: the idea of using my breath to resuscitate someone who was having difficulty breathing on their own felt right to me. I came alive at the prospect. Also, I committed to talking with a counselor and agreed with her diagnosis of ADHD.

As an EMT, I've saved a lot of lives, babies, children, and adults. I've also lost a few. It comes with the territory. I've learned to respect and accept the limits of what I can and cannot do, and not a day goes by when I'm not grateful for that baby, her wails, her will to fight, those tiny feet striking the air, telling somebody, anybody, "I'm here. I matter, come and get me."

I later learned she was taken from her parents and placed in foster care. That baby helped me save myself. I owe her a lot. But also, as I held her that day, I had flashes of being held by my mother, the one who chose me out of love. No matter how they showed it, from gently coddling to fiercely drawing an uncrossable line, I knew my parents loved and wanted me, even though I had often challenged that love, at my own expense. Their stern consistency helped me make a difference in my personal life and in the work I do. I pray often that that little girl is also getting the love she needs.

It comes as no surprise to me, or anyone who knows me, that I've worked most of my adult life in complex, chaotic circumstances, first as an EMT, then as a psychiatric nurse in an acute mental health facility, and now as a director of a mobile medical services agency. You might say that I've replaced my need to self-destruct with its opposite, the positive desire to preserve life, not just my own but the lives of others I'm called to respond to.

Emotional Pulse Check

If this feels like the perfect place to slow down, go ahead and do so: take a breath and allow whatever is arising inside you to be as it is. No need to do anything other than sit quietly and allow whatever feelings or sensations that arise to settle in their own time. Stories such as Kat's have the power to connect us not only to her humanity but also to our own. If you find yourself identifying with Kat's journey and something in you becomes triggered, pay attention to the sensations. Commit to staying with whatever arises. Allow this to be an opportunity to be gentle with yourself.

According to author Kristin Neff, self-compassion is the kindest thing we can give ourselves whenever suffering finds us. She advises her readers to place a hand on their heart as an act of self-compassion. If you feel called to do so, place your hand on your heart and check in with yourself. I like to think of this benevolent act as taking your emotional pulse, or as a way to self-soothe. For you dog lovers out there, have you ever noticed how a dog will lick its paw when it is hurt? Apparently, dogs, like us humans, have a built-in capacity to self-soothe. Instead of placing their paws on their hearts, they just lick 'em. I can't overstate the importance of developing such soft skills as self-regulation and the ability to show warmth to yourself.

Now ask yourself, *What am I feeling?* Where in your body do your feelings originate? Place your attention right there. Is there a tinge of discomfort, a tugging? Whatever the felt sense that arises, commit to being with it for however long it takes. There is nowhere to go but right where you are, and right where you are, everything you need is at hand. Whatever feeling is the most vibrant, turn your attention to it — especially if it's a bodily sensation — and ask the feeling what it is trying to tell you. Listen. Make mental notes. Jot them down, if you like. This way of paying close attention to what your body is experiencing is a technique from philosopher Eugene T. Gendlin's groundbreaking work *Focusing*. Make a promise to come back to the moment and spend some real time together. Often our bodies have their own ways of making contact with us. I've learned to use the power of focusing as a tool to better understand whatever felt sense is making an appearance.

At any point on our journey together, I encourage you again and again and, yes, again to gift yourself with a moment to step back from reading and take note of your experience. Over time, doing so cultivates a sense of emotional sophistication you can rely on. Also, my hope is that this will assist you in sharpening your sense of listening and feeling and offer you the space to mentally record what's happening for you. This seemingly innocuous act holds a powerhouse-worthy vibe of self-love. Maybe you want to send a burst of joy not only to the child who lives within you but also to the inner child Kat eventually reconnected with, as well as the baby discussed in her story.

In my work, I've come to realize that many of us feel as though we were denied the love we wanted and truly needed. And although it's true that we can't change the past, we can honor the remembrances, the feelings, the miscreated situations that may have left us raw, exposed, and perhaps feeling far too vulnerable for our own good as they revisit us in the present moment.

Once you've taken your emotional pulse, grab your journal. Now let's slow down and be with ourselves in a more intimate way.

Pause to Consider

- In what way(s) did Kat show up that resonated with an experience you've had, positive or negative?
- How did Kat eventually pivot and improve her situation?

Bootstrapping Takeaways

- Hold space for yourself.
- Allow your heart to be broken.
- Acknowledge what you are feeling.
- Define what being grateful means to you.
- Explore what it means to grow through your circumstances.
- Create a way to pivot any situation.
- Draw a line of self-respect in the sand.

What experience might require you to engage in a bit of self-reflection so that you can grow yourself to the other side? Take a moment and sit with this question, and when you're ready, respond to it by writing in your journal.

Facing the Fear

Upon emancipation from the residential treatment center at age eighteen, I attended San Francisco State University. I loved it. However, I was far too free-spirited to be corralled into classrooms in the middle of the day, forced to pay attention as this or that professor droned on about nothing that could have satisfied my need to be free. Not to mention the fact that I'd been locked up and lorded over and had missed far too much of my adolescence in solitary confinement to believe that anyone knew more than life had already taught me. I eventually dropped out of college. I made a vow, however, to return and finish my degree when the time was right.

Even as we go through challenges, it's important to find a way to hold ourselves accountable. Twenty-five years after abandoning my initial attempt at pursuing a degree in social work I decided to return to school. I've never been a fan of leaving anything half-finished, not to mention I'm all about making good on the vows I make. It took me nearly a year and a half to complete my bachelor's in interdisciplinary studies at California Institute of Integral Studies. A month before graduation, I received notice that I'd been offered a dean's distinguished fellowship to attend grad school at the University of California, Riverside, to study creative writing and writing for the performing arts. Within two weeks of earning my degree at CIIS I moved to Riverside. I was forty-six. And although

I'd worked my butt off in therapy identifying my attachment style (insecure … duh) and understood that most of the adults in my life had been far more interested in my meeting their needs than the other way around — all of which added up to a general anxiety disorder treated by a daily dose of hydrochlorothiazide, which also managed my blood pressure — *still* … I had no freaking idea what lay ahead.

Three movers hauled box after box of my life's possessions up the steep flight of stairs leading to the second floor, to the one-bedroom apartment reserved for graduate students. This was to become my home for the next two or three years. To admit that I was terrified would be an understatement of epic proportions. Insert mouthless emoji.

The truth was that I'd never lived alone for any significant length of time. If I'm *really* going to be transparent, I'll have to admit that I'd acquired an inclination for staying in relationships way past quitting time, unconsciously using the situations for what I now understand to be the need for safety (although of course now I understand that safety, my own, begins with me). Furthermore, once I'd recognize that the relationship I was entangled in was dead in the water, I'd stay for as long as it took for me to find another someone. And I'm humbled to admit that off I'd go — unconsciously — to eventually end up pressing the repeat button.

I was stuck in a serious cycle of, *what*, exactly? I couldn't name it then. However, I've since come to learn that so much happens in the preverbal stage of our development, and as a result of having no words to articulate what's happening, the body becomes the default vault, the holder of all we've experienced. As psychiatrist Bessel van der Kolk confirms, "The body keeps score." And given the right circumstances, those earlier repressed emotions and experiences reappear. It's as if they come bearing their own olive branch, and all we need do is stop running from the pain that more often than not comes with the package. Like small, uncared for, needy children, my losses showed up over and over again, needing my love now, needing my adult self to clear the space and grant them the right to be seen and heard. It's as though a form of personal clemency was required, a holy cleansing.

The moving truck and drivers leaving was all it took for the terror, initially masking itself as a passing fear, to land and expand into a full-blown anxiety attack. I was aware of the anxiety disorder that I'd dealt with for three-plus decades, but I wasn't sure how prepared I was to take the emotional truth of it head-on. My heart rate increased. I began to tremble. I was sweating, and all this was happening at once till I became so tense, I felt immobilized. Have you ever felt terror to this degree, to where you felt paralyzed and unable to respond to your needs? If so, then you know what I'm talking about right now.

I was frozen in place, my back against the front door. It was as though I'd lost touch with time and space. And perhaps, not so unlike Kat, I was suddenly psychologically and emotionally naked, all twisted up and upside down, with my back against the door of a long-held trauma. Although I had no context for what I was feeling, somehow I knew I'd been there before. And this very knowing is what stayed me. I'd not only been there before but, I reminded myself, I had built up a tenure in that no-man's-land. This time would be, had to be, different. More than anything I wanted to know what I was going through and to assure myself that I could meet my needs. "I got you," I repeated to myself. "I got you, lil' girl. We're working toward being okay." Just meeting myself with those words provided some comfort. Clearly, my psyche had experienced something that wasn't going to go away all by itself. It needed me to be on board 100 percent.

Growing Through the Fear

That night, and every subsequent night for the next six weeks, I was unable to sleep in my bedroom. My body remained on red alert. It sensed danger. All I could do was allow whatever was happening to happen. It was clearly my turn to be the adult to meet the situation head-on and heart-on. Radical compassion was essential. So instead of forcing myself to do otherwise, I'd follow my instincts. Each night when I was ready to at least try and get some sleep, I'd gather up my blanket, pillow, and my stuffed bear, Charlie. Right at the threshold of the door I slept, Charlie in my arms. I made it through the first week without incident. I was truly amazed that nothing horrible had happened to me. Nevertheless, for a while, every day when night approached, my mind seemed hell-bent on convincing me that my death was imminent. Each day brought a different outcome. The more room I made for my fear, the better able I was to stay with it. Of course I allowed myself to grieve, to unwind from around the axle of whatever was holding my psyche hostage. Sometimes I sobbed; at other times I lay awake and spoke kindly to the aloneness and the abandonment that showed up. The more ground I was able to recover for myself, the easier the approach of nighttime became. The adult in me was learning to show up for the kid who had been left behind so long ago without instructions or a road map back home to myself. I had to learn to befriend the darkness of my aloneness. So often, through the years, when people would ask me about my upbringing, I found myself speechless. I did not have a simple answer. I wanted to be like everyone else. At the very least, having a grandparent or single mother or father who raised me, not to mention a full-on nuclear family that was halfway functional and intact, was the narrative I searched for yet could not find because it wasn't my story. The friends I had all came from fairly unbroken families, and I can only imagine how easy it must have felt for them to say, "Let it go, Genie. Just let it go." I get it, I *really* do get it, that it's not easy to be with someone whose loss is ambiguous. Now I get how uncomfortable people became when hearing my story of abject neglect, abandonment, and homelessness (in the sense of not having the family to return to celebrate a birthday or holiday, or even just to wash a load of clothes).

Sometimes the ones who were meant to love us, in my case my father and mother, were not able to. Therefore, when there are no funerals held to ritually demarcate the living from the dead, occasionally the hope of a potential reunification, no matter how slim the chance, flickers within. Those of us who are in limbo with understanding the loss of a significant relationship, whether it's with our parent(s), friends, lovers, or a family member, are left with the weight of disenfranchised grief. Meaning we don't feel entitled to our deep sense of loss because the finality of the loss does not get acknowledged or validated and therefore becomes compounded and delayed. And when, for whatever reason, no rituals, personal or public, are performed, when we do not or cannot honor the fullness of our experiences, it's not so easy to let them go. It takes awareness, these things do, and time and patience in order to uncover and encounter the unconscious motives that drive our emotions.

By week two, and after much contemplation and reflection, I had a better understanding of where I'd come from: two teen-agers who were not able to take responsibility for what they had created. Simply stated, I was the product of an unwanted pregnancy. Some parents find themselves in these situations and somehow make it work. Mine did not. The terror and anxiety about my origins had finally come home to roost. And because I committed to stay the course, before long, a sense of safety began settling in, a trust unlike anything I'd ever experienced. And when sadness showed up, which it most certainly did, or any other emotion, I held on to Charlie and spoke Love-firmations into her ear, letting her know just how brave and incredibly wanted she was. Then came the day when I was ready to sleep on the sofa. For a feeling of extra security, I installed a safety lock and a doorstop. Maybe that was two safety locks and three doorstops? Just kidding. I needed my inner child to know not only that I could meet her requests but that I was eager to do so. With each passing day, my relationship to my trust deepened.

Weeks three and four flew by. With my strengthening sense of self, I was able to shower without barricading the door; for the first time in my life, I enjoyed closing my eyes without the panic that someone was going to come from behind me. I allowed the soapsuds to rain over my lids without the fear that should an intruder arrive I'd be unprepared. I no longer moved through my home as though someone were chasing me. I was better able to move more slowly, more freely. I began to feel what it was like to actually be a self on my terms.

It was in week five that I made a pallet on the floor in the narrow passage between the living room and the bedroom. I was close enough to the door to escape if I needed to, and

within arm's reach of sequestering myself in my bedroom behind closed doors should the situation call for it. I worked to
not judge myself too harshly for my thoughts. Instead, I gave
my loving attention to whatever showed up, coaxing myself to
get through whatever was happening, minute by minute, breath
by breath, all the while holding myself, allowing my emotions
to flow. By then I was ready to sleep on something a bit cozier
than the floor. So I made my bed into a haven of comfort fit for
a queen, with European-style square pillows dressed in soft-
pink velvet coverings; other pillows of all sorts and sizes; dust
ruffles; and percale sheets and comforters and quilts to match.
I made my arriving at my bed a destination from the heart of
my deepest desire, to be held in beauty and softness, to be safe,
to live in my own skin. #OMOT.

Week six arrived. I was careful not to judge my process,
belittle my needs, or find *any* reason to accept shame for what I
was experiencing and creating for myself There was nothing at
all wrong with me. Instead of judgments, I found ways to celebrate my journey, to support the speed of progress necessary
for me. And on the first night in my bed, Charlie in the crook
of my arm, I read myself a bedtime story from *Her Stories: African American Folktales, Fairy Tales, and True Tales* by Virginia
Hamilton. I wanted to hear the stories I imagined all Black
children should hear; narratives built on the ideas of different
possibilities. I tuned in to the fear and excitement of having
made it into the bed. I'd slow down and allow my body to get
acquainted with the feel of the sheets, the pillows cradling my
neck and upper back; I held myself within myself.

And once I felt that I was truly present and in my body,
I asked the small tinge of fear if it would be all right to speak
directly to it, and it gave me permission to do so. What I came

away with is a better understanding of the things that frightened me and why. A string of memories appeared. They were the evergreen messages I'd received as an institutionalized, and pathologized, child: that I was nothing, that I was unwanted. That I was dangerous, mentally unstable, incapable of ever having any real sense of autonomy, that I was the reason no one in my family of origin ever sought me out. It had never dawned on me that in order to feel safe in my own skin I would need to dismantle the lie that I was dangerous; that I would need to embrace the fact that I was something and someone amazing as opposed to nothing; that I was capable of sound mental health; and that even if I were unstable, I could learn to become balanced. And the mere fact that I was there, in my bed, five weeks later, dealing with my inner world from a place of autonomy was absolutely brilliant. That night, and I'll never forget it, I realized how afraid I had been of my own shadow and just how deep and paralyzing those suppressed beliefs, perpetuated by systemic racism, classism, and a surplus of other isms, had become.

Eventually, I got in touch with the truth that I secretly resented the fact that I was left to care for myself. It took some time to recognize that I was moored in feeling sorry for myself and that it just wasn't working for me. I worked to expand the breadth, width, and depth of living, trusting, and being on my own. I made dates with myself for attending theater and movies and kept them. I learned to eat alone. I learned to like it. A lot. Each day I checked in with myself and listened to what my needs were. It was the first time in thirty years I hadn't been in therapy, and I appreciated the time to grow into a more intimate relationship with myself. At the time, it was as though ending my previous way of relating with my partners had become the portal to a new way of coming into relationship with myself. In fact, it was a time of personal growth that allowed me to come face-to-face with who I thought myself to be: kind, gentle, and quiet, verging on being somewhat shy. It was as though grace had nudged me and held the space for me while I lovingly, over time, reparented myself, and thus began the journey of shedding the ways of being that no longer served my highest good. In other words, my circumstances presented me with a chance to do something different, break a fixation on being helpless, avoidant, and dependent, again understanding that these were ways of being that served me as a child, kept me safe, gave me a sense of belonging. I was opening to mothering myself in ways that permitted me to grow up, hand in hand with my spirit in my own way and time. I was better able to grow through what I went through. And for this, I am immensely grateful. Learning such lessons takes time and energy. Although I had begun the journey of healing, it is fair to say that I would revisit these themes of aloneness, reparenting, disenfranchised grief, and letting go. More on that later.

Now, it's important to note that each person's life experience is unique to them. What is true for you is true only for you and your particular journey. The ability to measure just how estranged we are from our own experiences, I believe, rests in our willingness to spend some time alone, stand in the sometimes cavernous pain of our primal wounds, and commit the time and energy it takes to pay attention to our deepest selves. In my case, giving all my self away in order to belong to even the slightest crumbs meant I'd have a lengthier and more challenging recovery. Each person's homecoming will be different. The point is to stay the journey, to shed the masks and the false selves. Eventually the face you see in the mirror will be your own, as opposed to the makeshift version of yourself you've accepted due to someone else's inability to see you.

Pause to Consider

Are there places inside you that frighten you? What are you avoiding doing, being, or feeling? Which fear-provoking memories do you turn away from or tune out? My experiences have led me to believe that the more I am able to answer these questions and remain willing to step into my growth edge, the closer I can move to the essence of who I am: calm, tender, and generous. The more I understand my journey, the further I move toward self-acceptance instead of believing someone else's story about me and as a result engaging in self-abandonment.

Pause to Consider

What have you gone through? What happened to you?

- Try to recall an experience that pushed you toward your growth edge.
- How did you know that you were going through something different?
- What was your initial response?
- Who did you allow to support you?

As a trainer in the human services field, I am frequently engaged as the expert on overcoming seemingly insurmountable odds. Always, after a presentation, I am asked, "What got you through those really tough times?" And of course the answer to such questions is partially why I'm writing this book, to explore what I know to be true for me and to share those findings with you. There are and were many ways in which I was able to think my way into surviving.

But more than thinking, I had to operate from a growth mindset and put the best of those thoughts into action, fueled by an everlasting hope that things would work out for me. I knew, deep within, that I *was* the only hope I had. Remember, I am all for faithing it until I make it. As a result, the idea of hope that I aimed to live blazed one pathway after another for possibilities to present themselves. No matter how large or small the openings, I always found a way to multiply whatever came forth into something more. Faith, hope, and courage were but a few of the attributes I relied on. They are part and parcel of my natural inheritance. I am free to use them at will. And so are you.

Now ask yourself what you are willing to grow through:

- What three areas in your life are in need of growth?
- What does the term *growth edge* mean to you?
- What does a growth mindset mean to you?
- What are five positive things you have gone through?
- How did you grow through them?

Me-Time Practice

The first time I heard the phrase *me-time* I was a summer camp counselor-in-training director for the San Francisco Bay Girl Scout Council. On the first day of camp the hiring director asked, "How do you like to spend your me-time?" To say that I was panic-stricken doesn't even come close to describing the chagrin I felt. There I was, in my late twenties, and I had zero clue as to what me-time was. Not to mention how uncomfortable I felt even considering the *me* that I'd suddenly put into question. I've had nearly three decades since that time to cultivate an understanding of me-time as well as a practice of spending quality time with myself. I journal, listen to my favorite music, make my own music videos (that I secretly pray will go viral just for the thrill of it). I have it on my list of ways to spend time with myself to learn how to do TikTok. Why not?

What are some of the ways you spend time with yourself? Perhaps you're uncomfortable (as I was) with getting that close to yourself, or maybe you're unfamiliar with the concept. Or perhaps you need to be alone in order to recharge. Whatever the case may be, try to push yourself to your growth edge with the questions. Permit yourself to become ever more intimate with you. I'm excited about your curiosity!

Choose one of the Lovefirmations below, or create your own. Set a timer, perhaps for ten minutes, and allow your pen or pencil or fingers to move nonstop. If perfectionism shows up with her hands on her hips, desperate to micromanage your time, tell her to back up, however gentle or direct you choose to be. A boundary is just that, a boundary. It's where perfectionism ends and your free will begins. When the ten minutes are up, immediately stop writing, take a breath, and acknowledge your act of loving-kindness toward yourself.

Lovefirmations

I am better able to know what I am going through.
I can grow through it.
I accept myself right where I am.
I am love.
I am capable of meeting my own suffering.
I am enough on my own.
I am never truly alone.
I am okay by myself, with myself.

Kick-Ass Strategy #5

Compose a Permission Statement

*I have learned from every single character I have played.
Something emotionally, spiritually, psychologically true . . .
I could not do anything that would not enhance
humanity, especially women.*

— Cicely Tyson, *Oprah's Master Class*

How often have you turned to just about anyone who would listen in search of answers to your most deeply held questions about what to do, how to do it, who to do it with, and quite possibly what to wear while figuring it all out? Well, I officially hereby appoint you the boss bish of you. All you need is love, as in your love coming through loud and clear from your heart of hearts. The awesome strategy I provide in this chapter, the Permission Statement, offers you a chance to access your kick-assery abilities, making them front and center and personal and at your disposal.

Drafting a Permission Statement is an act of enormous generosity toward yourself. It's evidence of your willingness to get on board with who you are, and it offers you the chance to examine your values and beliefs and to own your inherent right to flex your personal power. That's right. You get to gather *all* of who you are, not just some of the more fabulous things about you, in one place and become your own mood or vibe. Isn't that what is often said about iconic personalities such as Cardi B and Nicki Minaj? Who doesn't want to be in the company of a queen, or at the least someone who owns her power in such a way that molecules change when she walks into a room?

Pause to Consider

When was the last time you brought all of who you are into a particular moment? Ruminate on that question for a minute. Consider some of your desirable and not-so-desirable attributes, and then think about a time when you may have felt completely and unconditionally seen and held in pure acceptance and with psychological safety. What was it like? What were your thoughts at the time? Who were you with? What did you take away from that experience, and how does it continue to live in you? What if you could have more voice in how you get to show up in any situation, regardless of how anyone else feels? What would it take for *you* to be a safe experience for you?

I know you may have a ton of responses to all these questions. But it's in the examining of these experiences, the mining of them for their gems of wisdom and insights, that we are led along a path of personal power and of up-leveling our excellence on our own terms. Take it from someone who had no peers or mentors to reflect my most salient assets:

- Charm
- Confidence

- Courage
- Can-do attitude

And of course, this is just to name a few. We are all such complex beings who possess countless positive and negative personality traits. In our lifetimes, we face many situations to either improve or flat-out make a mess of by succumbing to our fears or worse yet our unchecked relationship to avarice. We can face our situations with courage, strength, and grace or with the spite of a pissed-off alley cat. I'm all about transforming those not-so-desirable traits by growing them toward a higher standard of self. This isn't to say there is no place for those moments when we lose our sh*t but to suggest that there is a way back once we've let loose.

In this exercise, take your time and peruse the words and phrases listed below and on the next page. Then, when you're ready, pick from the list the twelve that best describe you. Be generous and have fun. Some of the words may not be familiar to you, while some will seem to fit you perfectly. Again, take a leap of faith and try on a different way of seeing yourself. Push toward your growth edge, whatever that might mean to you. And if you can't find the word or expression you are looking for, feel free to write down your own.

Once you have identified and circled the initial twelve words or phrases, reduce your twelve down to six.

Visionary	Invigorating	Enthusiastic
Meticulous	Motivating	Dedicated
Thoughtful	Inspiring	Uncompromising
Considerate	Skilled	Forthright
Sensible	Competent	Driven
Brilliant	Commanding	Organized
Complex	Leader	Decisive

Gentle

Dependable

Reliable

Principled

Professional

Personable

Practical

Ambitious

Spontaneous

Playful

Courteous

Positive

Respectful

Conscientious

Mindful

Tactful

Sensitive

Tolerant

Assertive

Adaptable

Resilient

Multifaceted

Flexible

Deep

Dynamic

Resourceful

Capable

Open-minded

Accepting

Judicious

Persuasive

Epic

Fantastic

Knowledgeable

Successful

Efficacious

Well-mannered

Fierce

Tight

Extra

Savage

Salty

Finessing

Woke

Fresh

Exciting

All that

Blessed

Bodacious

Badonkadonk

Bomb diggity

Choice

Def

Hellacious

Popping

Smooth

Solid

Rocking

On fleek

Legit

Like a boss

Champ

It's all good

Caring

Super

Great

Kind

Compassionate

Empathic

Loving

Trustworthy

Loyal

Supportive

Responsible

Expert

Dedicated

Honest

Innovative

Kick-ass

Imaginative

Progressive

Amazing

Intelligent

Generous

Progressive

Relentless

Champion

Advocate

Activist

Abolitionist

Shamanic

Now, take some time and consider how you wish to give yourself permission. Using the six words you chose that describe your most revered attributes, begin to craft your personal Permission Statement. Incorporate those qualities into a statement like the one below.

I am _____. Courageously I grant myself permission to _____.

In the interest of _____, my purpose is to _____. It is like me to _____. It is like me to _____.

Here is an example:

I am determined and passionate, a gifted speaker, trainer, and coach. I am world renowned and highly sought-after. Courageously I grant myself permission to move and inspirit others to be their personal best. In the interest of transformation, my purpose is to fiercely utilize my talents to support each human I am asked to hold space for. It is like me not only to know my purpose, but to be on purpose. It is like me to know that I am a child of all that is good. It is like me to know that I am a perfect emanation of Spirit.

As this example statement shows, you can go all out to find the words that will help you proclaim your statement. That's what your Permission Statement is, a proclamation of what's possible for you at any given moment. Think of it as a road map back to your center, a private sachet of divine prose that holds the secret sauce of you. When you know who you are, it's difficult to buy into anyone else's version of you. And when and if you lose your way, as we all sometimes do, feel free to refer back to this small manifesto. Have it laminated, and carry it in your wallet. That's how I roll with it!

Kick-Ass Strategy #6

Be Big (and Small)

Grateful for small things, big things, and everything in between.
— Holly Smith

Mentors of mine were under a big pressure to minimize their femininity to make it. I'm not going to do that. That takes away my power. I'm not going to compromise who I am.
— Alexandria Ocasio-Cortez

Thank you for your willingness to grab my hand and allow me to walk beside you during what I hope will be a powerful exploration. The intention behind the strategy in this chapter is to offer you as much insight and opportunity for personal growth in reading it as I have gained in writing it. In identifying *bigness* as a core blind spot and the Achilles heel not just for myself but also for anyone else who has been charged with shining the floodlights of our megawatt personalities, I have felt moved to explore this dynamic and to glean a few jewels of loving course correction. Being big has offered me a lot of learning; therefore, this strategy will be allowed to take up as much space as it requires or demands; I'm here for it. There is no need to apologize, no need to shrink: the invitation is to stand center stage in who you are and to feel it, be with it, and own it, big or small.

Identify with BIG or Small!

How many of you have been told that you show up as *too big*, or conversely, that you play *too small*? If you have not had either of these experiences, perhaps you know someone who has, or you've had your own feelings about someone taking up too much, or not enough space. Whatever the case may be, instead of reading the questions in order to answer them for yourself, consider walking in that other person's shoes.

Pause to Consider

- How did it feel to hear that you were *too big*?
- What did it mean to you to say that to someone else?
- How did it feel to be accused of playing *too small*?
- What did it mean to you to say that to someone else?
- How did hearing that you were too big affect how you understood yourself then, and how does it affect how you understand yourself now?
- How do you think your bigness or smallness has affected others?
- How has experiencing someone else's bigness or smallness affected you?

———⊗⊗⊗———

As you consider the questions, pay close attention to what's happening in your mind and body. What are you thinking? What are the sensations? What emotions are arising as a result of your responses to the questions? Go slowly. Check in with yourself. This may be the first time you've been asked to consider how others see you in such an intimate way, and it could be triggering. Or you may have lots of tenure in having to "check yourself" on someone else's terms; either way, I suggest you go gently.

If you're able to identify an emotion, go ahead and name it. Often naming something lessens its energy, giving us a chance to transform the feelings into a more manageable state of being. Given how often I've bristled from hearing about how big I am, it's in turning toward it, facing it, and naming it that I have found the most comfort, disentangling me from the *power-over* dynamic that feelings can ensnare me in.

Speaking of something having power over you, I've come to recognize that we are a culture that proudly celebrates all things big. We like our burgers big, and those interested in branding their personas, passions, and expertise via digital distribution strive for the biggest followings on social media platforms. We like big companies that provide big solutions. Some of us prefer our bangs teased so high they touch the roof of the car while we're driving around drinking 7-Eleven Big Gulps. I'm just saying. Our Afros are applauded for their height and width. It's like walking around with our own personal sun or moon on our shoulders. And when it comes to french fries — I digress, sorry, not sorry — we like ours from McDonald's, and we prefer them supersize, and lightly salted. Please. Thank you very much.

That's all fine and good for Mickey D's, but if you're anything

like me, and you've been told that you're a *big personality*, that
you're *too much*, which you translate as "I'm not wanted" and
"I'm about to be abandoned," then the next thing you know,
you're lost in a big-ass trauma response.

Have you ever stopped to wonder how you became a big
personality? And if you have been accused of disappearing
in plain sight due to your playing too small, what conditions
shaped you? Big or small, having to mold yourself around
someone else's views of you poses its own challenges to work
through. If you feel that your life has been affected by people
you believe either take up all the space or leave you to fill it,
how has that been for you? For me, it all comes down to transforming and integrating who we are on our own terms, to get
24/7 access to our unconditional love. I understood my own
bigness as:

- A control tactic to minimize my presence
- A need to be all-forgiving
- An expectation to give all of myself away
- A need to become all-understanding
- A need to assume all the responsibility
- A one-way, first-class ticket on the invisibility train
- A way to perpetually turn the other cheek until my
  neck feels as if it's a disco ball of self-abnegation

Does any of this ring a bell for you? In what ways did you
come to understand your bigness or smallness? How did this
play out in your life? How did you learn to not have any needs?
How did it come to pass that you deserve to have everyone else
meet your needs at their expense (and yours)? Take a moment,
find your journal, and write down three ways in which you

understood yourself to be either too big or too small, or how your life is affected by others who possess these traits.

Now write down how these ways of being have played out in your daily life. What has it cost you to play these roles? Write it down in your journal.

Exploitation

From as far back as I can remember, I was encouraged to be the "bigger person." Even before I fully understood what this instruction meant, I was busy fulfilling the demands of others who expected me to shoulder my weight with adult sensibilities. The quicker I was able to leave my childhood behind, the better for me. By adolescence, I was fully committed to taking the high road. I'd allow bad behavior to go unnoticed, even against my better judgment. I transformed turning the other cheek into a masterful display of exonerating anyone of any infraction. It was as if I were saying by my actions, *Who are you accusing of having needs? I'll show you how need-less I can be. Just you watch!* It was as if I were hardwired to be solely about other people and *their* needs. Off I went, denying, swallowing, diminishing, and apologizing for how I felt. I had no sense that this was all at my own expense.

No matter what, though, if my bigness, that is, my ability to be the bigger person in any and all circumstances for others, was code for belonging, getting love, being accepted, and guaranteeing that I did not piss off anyone who had the power to make or break my getting by, then I was down with that. If a sycophant is what was needed, that's exactly what I'd be. I saw my willingness to please as an easy sacrifice, considering what would happen if I held anyone accountable. Where I came from, standing up for myself was synonymous with rejection, or annihilation. In other words, holding others responsible for their behavior, especially as a young person, was considered dangerous. I had been there, done that. As far as I was concerned, as long as I had skin on my bones and a place to lay my head at night, I was willing to sacrifice myself to whoever needed me to do so. The last thing in the world I ever wanted was to be ousted, or worse, tribeless.

Perhaps you have some idea of what I'm sharing here, or maybe you have firsthand experience of it. No matter the circumstances, people from all walks of life are subjected to harsh conditions. The ways we learned to get through our childhoods become the same means — if we don't recognize and transform them — we use to navigate most of our adult relationships. How we were treated is how we will treat not only ourselves but others as well. We've all learned myriad ways of traversing our circumstances in order to get through, in order to survive. Our brilliance in persisting is what supports us, as adults, in changing those undermining ways of thinking into unconditional acts of self-love. Meeting our own needs is part and parcel of individuating from our parents and from the behaviors that no longer serve us, and stepping into maturity. I can't think of an employer, a partner, or a friend who wouldn't appreciate being in a healthy relationship with a thriving and emotionally conscientious adult.

To me, at least, bootstrapping my way to adulthood by tracking, then hacking, the shame that bound me is nothing short of Divine providence at work on my behalf. And if you've managed your own version of challenging relationship experiences, I hereby invite you to consider the efforts you've made that have contributed to your success.

When You Give Yourself Away

I was forty-something when I began the journey of breaking up with the self-deprecating behaviors that ruled my life. My excessive modesty had become the downside of always defaulting to being the bigger person, taking more than my fair share of the onus, and working overtime to make everything better for everyone else. You might have thought that age and experience would've shifted how I saw myself. But what I've come to understand about my resistance to behavioral change is that I tended to not pay attention to the red flags signaling when a belief was no longer serving me. It has taken me running smack-dab into disaster before I'd get the hint that something had to change. It has been said that we do what we do until we get tired of doing it.

Minimizing my importance, simply because I did not have the awareness, has shown up in myriad ways in all my relationships. As a result of feeling deep-seated unworthiness, I've unwittingly set myself up to be taken advantage of on countless occasions. Of course, I never saw it in the moments, days, and years that I allowed it to happen; it's only in hindsight that I've slowed down and taken the time to put together the pieces of the puzzle, allowing me to see the truth of my actions. It was in my college years that I had the most practice at losing myself to others. Back then, I gave away so much from what I believed was my being *nice*. It did not dawn on me that my behavior was potentially manipulative, as well as an exercise in sidestepping intimacy. Without having adequate relationship experience as a result of my unstable childhood, how could my tactics be anything other than what they were — *tactics*? Now I see how my interactions and ways of being in relationship were survival mechanisms rather than authentic personality traits coming from the pureness of my spirit.

I'd listen to my friends' stories and feel overwhelmingly compassionate about the difficulties they'd encountered. If I loaned my friends money, I did not hold them accountable for paying me back; when clothes were borrowed, whether asked for or literally taken out of my closet, I did not have enough personal power to ask that they be returned. I often insisted on paying for dinner on dates. Which I could not afford. If something came up missing from my apartment, for instance, a piece of jewelry, and I saw a friend wearing it, it was very hard for me to find my words and call her out on it. I didn't know what I didn't know, and that was how to say a clean *no* without it triggering a crapload of feelings about my potentially being abandoned. And as stated above, my sense of belonging was tied up with giving myself away under the pretense that I was big enough to handle the consequences.

Pause to Consider

- When have you given yourself away under the pretense that as a bigger person you could afford to lose more than someone else?
- In what ways do you imagine you've given in order to get?

I often used this way of overcompensating in order to keep the peace, no matter the cost, with my sister. She had no misgivings about pointing out how much better my life was as opposed to hers (never mind the fact that she'd been adopted into a family who adored her, while I spent much of my adolescence in and out of other people's homes). However, because

I wanted whatever scrap of love my compliance with her demands promised, no matter how ludicrous it seemed, I always acquiesced. After all, I was supposedly the pretty one, the one with amber eyes, freckles, and a bigger personality, which somehow equaled better but also "guaranteed" that the world would treat me better. Yet again, I assumed responsibility for having my genetic code express itself the way it did, differently than hers. And in the end, she never expressed that she liked, loved, or wanted much to do with me (which I now understand, given the circumstances that shaped both our upbrings). Not to come off as cavalier, but at what point do we have to save ourselves and let others decide (or not) to do the same for themselves? Eventually one has to recognize that life does not always go as planned, that there comes a time when we just have to accept the disappointment and move on. *C'est la vie!*

While most of these experiences eventually led me to over-function for anyone at every turn, I'd never considered that people were more capable of caring for themselves than I was for myself. Caring for them was all I knew, and in my own way I understood that putting other people's needs first was what it meant to get my needs met; it was the surest way to be seen for what I do as opposed to who I am. For me, being the bigger person meant ignoring my own needs in the face of someone else's desires. Looking back, my mind *still* has a hard time computing what I've given away in the name of being the bigger person, in the name of "belonging." Don't get me wrong, it felt good, for a moment, to feel needed, to have earned a reputation as someone with a *big old heart of gold*, someone who would *literally* give you the shirt off her back. It was all good until the line of people who wanted the shirt off my back was so long it wrapped around corners. It was all good until it wasn't, and I recognized I'd become a magnet for the needy. It would take me until my late forties to accept that the good I gave was in fact the good I wanted to receive as well as the good I'd always been. I believe that at one time or another, many of us humans have been unwitting victims of such thought patterns. As with any personal attributes left unexamined, our blind spots have a way of coming from out of nowhere and bringing with them the lessons that must be faced or repeated — until we grapple with them courageously and have that reckoning with ourselves.

It would take another decade for me to get in touch with and own the shame of it all: the self-abandonment that resulted in my innocently aiding and abetting against myself. Here I want to make clear the distinction between victim and victor: although it may be true that I had not a clue as to what was going on (how could I, given that I was tasked with being my own parent at such an early age?), my spirit knew and kept me steady until I developed the ability to know the difference. *No harm, no foul,* in the sense that all parties concerned were, I believe, doing the best with what we all had. If manipulation was a survival tactic you used to get your needs met and keep you safe, then that's your best until you're able to commit to doing the work to know better in order to do better. Whether playing too big or too small, if it was the best you had and the result was that you survived, then good on you; it was an act of self-preservation as a child. It was a genius survival skill that has served you well. The up-leveling skill, however, is to recognize when a belief or behavior no longer serves you and to break the fixation by grappling with what inner strengths would better serve you as an adult in manifesting your deepest desires.

Having It All?

Not soon enough, turning the other cheek simply for the sake of turning the other cheek or because I felt I had no other options would run its course. I mean no disrespect to those of you who have found comfort and solace in the Good Book and its effort to encourage us to observe proper decorum. However, for *me* my kindness was one time too many mistaken for my weakness. I was simply deferring the inevitable: a confrontation with my low expectations of myself and of other people as well. Not only does assuming the role as the bigger person set us up to be a bit grandiose, but it also robs the person who chooses to play small the opportunity to manage their own life Oh, boy, can this dynamic get out of hand if left unchecked by all parties involved.

By the time I'd begun to consider that my life was not working, I'd had quite the life of being big. In some ways, I actually felt larger than life. I had beaten the odds, and I'd worked hard to close the gap on my disadvantages. I'd worked even harder to have a piece of the American Dream, not just for myself, but most important, for my kiddo. Nothing was going to keep me from giving my then-teenage son the life I knew he deserved.

Some might have said I had it all: a life partner, Emma Mac, whom I loved. I believed she loved me in return, despite our differences. I believed too that our love was enough to smooth over any rifts or challenges. Not only was I the co-owner of a thriving salon on the top floor of the historic Shreve Building in San Francisco's Union Square, but, as mentioned earlier, I was also the first Black hair salon owner on trendy Fourth Street in Berkeley. My son, Michael, a sixteen-year-old scholar-athlete, attended a boarding school that guaranteed 98 percent college placement.

In early 2001 I'd landed my first book contract. As a result, Emma Mae and I purchased our first house together and my first home *ever*. We lived five blocks from the salon. I could have walked to work or ridden my bike. I chose to drive. I simply loved having a parking space slated for the "salon owners." We hired a personal chef who prepared meals five days a week, and our laundry was washed and folded, wrapped in craft paper, then finished with twine. I love the little details. We had a housekeeper who came once a week, as well as a gardener. And if that wasn't enough goodness, getting the first dog I'd ever had was the cherry on top.

And in 2003, all that goodness went bad. Or did it?

I was once told that famous musicians never traveled with their bandmates, and that many professional athletic teams preferred not to fly on the same plane in case the plane met with tragic circumstances. Some inferred that couples who lived together should never work together, and that it was inevitable what happened next. A few times I'd considered what another someone had said in regard to "putting all your eggs in one basket." Although I saw the logic for the athletic teams and the musicians, given the millions in revenue that could be at risk, I believed that we were the exception. I believed that together we had a better chance of beating the odds of our constant togetherness than any couple we knew. As quiet as it was kept, I knew that our secret sauce would be my ability to adapt in any situation that might come our way. After all, I was the one who'd survived the treacheries of a Dickensian childhood, dubbing me the uber-resilient one, the creative one, the one with the Midas touch. Everyone asserted that I was the bigger person(ality). Everyone took it for granted that I had and always would land on my feet. I was "street smart," they said, although I knew absolutely *nothing* about "the streets." I knew that comments like that had more to do with my skin color and others' limited perceptions and experiences of Black people than with my actual story. I've come to acknowledge that hard-won emotional intelligence, intuition, and, most important, a connection to the soul source is what held me together, and learning to follow that nearly imperceptible inner voice. Don't try and attribute my hard-won thriving to the "street"; I give no one permission to accuse me of any less than who I am.

Be Careful of What You Ask For

It was one thing to say that I wanted to write a memoir, and another to put my derriere in a chair and get it done, to the tune of a six-figure advance. I now believe that Emma Mae didn't think I'd finish it, see it through to the end. Though I agree that it sounded absolutely outlandish, even to me, that I could actually pull it off, write my story, I never heard her direct resistance to it once the process was well underway. I would have done all that I could to accommodate her, to work it out. I'd go more often to the counselor. Soon enough, however, there was no room for the changes that were occurring at lightning speed. One of us seemed to always come in too big and the other far too small.

Pause to Consider

- Have you ever experienced the dynamic described above in any of your relationships?
- How did you react or respond?

We worked steadfastly to agree to disagree. And no matter how much we tried, we were rarely, if ever, on the same dance floor moving in tandem for any sustained amount of time. Soon enough, our rhythms became disjointed until we eventually danced that dance of inharmoniousness to death. How I wish I knew then what I know now. I would have slowed everything down, posted psychic sentries at every entryway possible, physically, mentally, spiritually, and most definitely emotionally. I cannot say enough about boundaries.

To make matters more complicated — because that comes with being human — I was entombed in a Honda Odyssey minivan on a ten-city book tour with my partner when the woman I'd written the book about literally showed up out of nowhere. Seriously. Like a ghost. I was torn in two directions. The Honda Odyssey minivan idea was our last attempt for my partner and me to bridge the gigantic gulf that had widened between us. My attempts to reach her failed; her attempts met with the same fate. We just could not reach across the profound loneliness we both felt and offer ourselves and each other any lasting comfort, empathy, or compassion. And yet there was Jeanne, the once-upon-a-time almost mother I'd been estranged from for twenty-seven-plus years. Jeanne was one of my counselors at the shelter I lived in as a child, the one the police took me to. She had wanted to adopt me but was turned down by the courts. Jeanne was all I'd ever wanted. And there was my partner, a frightened woman who was dreadfully concerned that I would meet someone as a result of my new-found success and abandon everything we'd built. And there was Jeanne whose kindness was otherworldly. I felt desperate for that kind of love. I believed I needed her kind of love. And when Emma Mae and I agreed to allow Jeanne to move in with us so that she and I could get to know one another again after such a long estrangement, the proverbial sh*t not only hit the fan but flew in every direction and didn't stop until everyone and everything had become unrecognizable.

The more attention Jeanne gave me, the more she mothered me, the smaller I became, and the bigger the chasm between my partner and me grew. Jeanne had even offered to adopt me as an adult. Even while I was drowning in the reunification I'd prayed for my entire life, I continued to do all that I could to hold on to both Emma Mae and Jeanne. And because they were each caught on the brambles of their own unrecognized and therefore unmet needs, no one seemed able or willing to be the adult I needed. I researched adult adoptions, I called up friends who either had been adopted or had relinquished their child to try to understand what was happening for every-one involved, and what we might expect in allowing Jeanne to adopt me. To say that I was as lost then as I'd ever felt hardly captures the maelstrom of unprocessed grief that arrived along with Jeanne. No one was prepared. I. Was. Not. Prepared.

I allowed Emma Mae to convince me that as a result of Jeanne's reappearance, it would be in my best interests to sign over my half of our joint ventures. That was a lot of money. I was terrified of losing both Jeanne and Emma Mae. There was no such thing as in between. No safe ground. I was told that my son, who was off at college, and I would always have a home. Any-body who knew my story understood how much that first home meant to me, how I'd trusted another human being enough to go in half on a house that was worth a nice chunk of change. That I'd sunk my advance money into a future of belonging to someone and something in a forever kind of way. That was huge for a little Black girl all grown up, acting like the only adult she knew how to be.

I wanted my partner to like me, to be my friend and my family, even if the romantic relationship wasn't able to survive; the larger context of family would be our saving grace, my saving grace. I believed her when she said she had my back. I had no reason not to.

Before Emma Mae and I ever agreed to date, I had only one caveat: that my son would never be abandoned or rejected as a result of things not working out between us. It was a deal, one I'd never expected to break. It was out of a trusting desire to always have a place for my son and me that I had signed over my half of the assets, which for me was everything I owned. That was then. And instead of continually blaming, and thus shaming, myself, I eventually began the journey of reclaiming myself. The way I saw it was that I'd chosen myself. I've since learned that knowing where you end and another begins has the potential to slay drama in its infancy. And those of you who are masters at drawing that fine line in the sand between what's yours and what isn't have something magical to teach the girls and women in our world.

Having boundaries is the ability to draw that line, lovingly, of course, to demarcate your worth, your limit, your threshold for "that's enough." Boundaries have a sort of resilience built into them, an elasticity, if you will. Boundaries can support us in going between feelings of bigness and smallness, ways of being that are often called for. Yet having and exercising your limits allows you to experience these ways of being on your own terms and without giving all of yourself away — along with your assets.

Emotional Pulse Check

Let's slow this down for a moment. Pause. Take a breath. Pay close attention to what you are feeling in this moment. If this story resonates with you on a personal level, turn your awareness toward what comes up for you. Where are the feelings arising from? Are any judgments forming, and if so, what are they? I normally get sensations in both my abdomen and my throat when I'm having an emotional response to something that hits home. For many people the stomach is often emotion central for reactions.

If this is true for you too, go ahead and place your hand on your belly, right on the spot where you may feel discomfort or any kind of stirring. Can you name what is happening? Whatever it is, allow it to pass through you. Then ask yourself:

- In what circumstances has your bigness or smallness jeopardized your well-being?
- In what ways do you justify your bigness as the means to an end?
- How do you understand sabotage? How have your blind spots resulted in self-sabotage?
- How many relationships have you tried to save at your own expense as a result of a shadow belief or a blind spot?
- In what ways have you become aware of and healed your blind spots around being either big or small?

Hilarapy

Lizzie Allan is an Englishwoman who spends her days in the quaint British Columbian town of White Rock. There she lives with her partner, her stepdaughter, and their Maltese, Max. (A photo of the dog wearing a bow tie graced the cover of a community magazine. I'm just saying.) Lizzie, a certified mental health counselor, funnels her passion and her bigness into what she affectionately calls Hilarapy. And when I tell you this chick is knock-the-wind-out-of-your-gut funny, I mean just that.

I met Lizzie during a ten-week Zoom class. All twelve of us — from all over the world — were interested in studying the Christian-inspired principles of Ernest Holmes, a New Thought teacher whose spiritual discoveries have inspired metaphysical luminaries such as Iyanla Vanzant, Louise Hay, and Michael Beckwith. We were in good company. What struck me most about Lizzie was the expansiveness of her presence: along with being drop-the-mic funny, she was open, generous, and engaging. She had no fears sharing among strangers, and on our first reveal let us in on the fact that she had once, while recovering in a psychiatric ward in Thailand, become Jesus while finding her way back from a deeply transpersonal psychological journey. (It really doesn't get any bigger than that.) When I asked Lizzie what it has been like for her to manage her sense of bigness, this is what she had to share:

This memory does not sound like very much on its own, but for me it was huge. It's Christmas and I'm at my grandmother's house. My dad is one of five, so it is a huge Christmas gathering. My uncle is teaching me to juggle; I must be six or seven. I come into the kitchen, where everyone is sitting around the table, and say, "Look, look, I can juggle." Then I drop the balls and pick them back up again, saying, "No, no, it's fine. I can juggle. I can juggle." Then I drop the balls and my grandmother stands up and shouts at me, "Elizabeth, get out! Go away and come back when you can do it properly." When I left that room, I felt alone and cast out of the family. I was so ashamed my face went bright-red, and I boiled with anger, thinking, *I am never showing that woman that I can juggle again.*

I actually got to be a really good juggler. But that experience stopped me from performing for years. Up to then I was getting really good roles in school plays, but it all went downhill from there. I could not even get into the chorus of a musical when I was a teenager. And then I got a bit part as a Serbian soldier. I had two lines. My dad drove down from Oxford to see it, and I messed up my lines because I was so conscious that I had to get it right or I would be rejected. I could not even remember my two lines as a Serbian f**king soldier!

My sense of being big is tied up with perfection as well, and criticism. I am too much, and I am not good enough. I have to be perfect or I will be rejected: those were my childhood beliefs. Because I have the experience of trauma, I was a young person without an emotional language, without the ability to see beyond her own experience. Instead of being able to say, "Oh, well, my mom is not well" or "Oh, well, my mom is struggling with her own trauma," I thought, "My mom is reacting like that because of me." My mom and dad both went through enormous trauma as children. My dad was physically and sexually abused at boarding school from the age of seven. My mom had a schizophrenic, alcoholic doctor for a father, and everyone believed the doctor. Although none of that actually happened to me, I carry the anxiety and the traumatic memory passed down by my parents through their wobbly raising of me. They were both addicts when I was growing up.

If I had feelings, they would come out as anger. Then I would be told, "Lizzie, you are too much," which just confirmed what I already believed. It was so deep in me and so strong. It was all unconscious. I really believed my mom hated me, well into my adult life — I am still doing work on it. I was so awful to my mom not because I wanted to be but because I was just an out-there person.

One day, when I was twenty-three, I said, "I don't know how this is going to go, but I'm no longer going to deny what is possible for me." It was an expansive, creative feeling coursing through my body. I let go of the curse that I was mentally ill. I gave myself permission to no longer sit on my dreams and desires. I gave myself permission to show up in front of people and allow myself to not be good enough, not be perfect, and stand on the stage anyway. I was twenty-five when I got onstage again. Then at age twenty-nine, I went into recovery. I needed to be clean. I wanted more from the limitless nature of reality. I wanted to be somebody who had an impact on the young people I worked with. I wanted to be somebody about who others would say, "She makes it fun being clean and sober, that's cool." My recovery became the origin of Hilarapy, a unique blend of comedy and therapy.

Bootstrapping Takeaways

- Acknowledge how your efforts toward healing, no matter how big or small, have supported you.
- Transform blaming yourself into reclaiming yourself.
- Identify and let go of the fear(s) that bind(s) you.
- Find the support you need, and come up with an action plan.
- Discover and master ways to move between being big and small.
- Define for yourself what it means to have boundaries.

⌬

Are you ready, willing, and able to better understand who you are in terms of your emotional growth? How will you grant yourself the permission to be all of who you are, both big and small?

Build a Foundation That Supports Your Bigness

The moment when life gets messy might be just the time to spend your energies getting the chaos under control instead of denying your need to connect more deeply with yourself. Continuing a dysfunctional way of being may feel comfortable, but it would be more helpful to practice having access to your own goodness before giving it all away.

1. *Become aware of your emotional signature.* Can you give yourself personal attention on a regular basis? Do you have enough of you to meet your needs first? Is there enough of you left each day to enjoy yourself? How are you saving some of your own goodness for the future?

2. *Discover your boundaries in as many situations as possible.* Only you can determine what that means to you. It might mean saying no to everything until you feel ready to move forward with people. Think of boundaries as a codependence elimination diet.

3. *Have at least one hobby that you love.* Life can't be just about work, chores, and socializing. Find something that you've always wanted to learn or explore, and begin doing it. You might learn to appreciate what you are capable of creating, being, and having on your terms.

4. *Take care of the small things.* Walk your dog, eat, brush your teeth, keep your house tidy, always wear clean underwear, keep your kitchen and bathrooms clean, engage a therapist, 12-step groups, Hilarapy. All these little things have much more impact on your life than you realize.

As you know by now, when your life comes undone, it can be tempting to go all in on the patterns that keep you stuck. Part of their appeal is the fact that these behaviors are a distraction. You might also believe that your life will have more meaning if you can save someone other than yourself, if you can please them, if you can get validation from them by trying to be for them what you're terrified to be for yourself. However, chasing down others in order to avoid your own needs creates imbalance, which is something you already have in excess if you're unsure of how to be with who you are.

You will be happier and ultimately more successful if you can master the day-to-day issues of *your* life first. There will be plenty of time to share yourself in a healthy way with others after you've mastered unconditionally loving yourself in your way and on your terms.

Kick-Ass Strategy #7

Be the Subject Matter Expert of You

I've been tested by the fire, and the fire lost.

— Governor Ann Richards

If you are looking for ransom, I can tell you I don't have money.
But what I do have is a very particular set of skills,
skills I have acquired over a long career.
Skills that make me a nightmare for people like you.

— Bryan Mills, *Taken*

You better say it! Bryan Mills, Liam Neeson's character in the blockbuster drama *Taken*, pulls out all the stops when speaking truth to his antagonists. Anyone who doesn't know where he stands is sure to generate the opportunity for him to show them. I believe it's a good thing to know up front where you stand in a situation. Knowing what you're coming up against helps you make choices, weed out any chance of confusion, and circumnavigate potential conflicts that can quickly turn into unwarranted commotion. In the case of an action-packed film, it is precisely what the actors are aiming for, the disorder, the drama. But it ain't what we're after!

Let's put a bit of spin on the above quote, which I believe is one of the most attention-grabbing, moment-stealing, chest-bumping, stop-you-in-your-tracks, don't-let-your-mouth-write-a-check-your-ass-can't-cash monologues in contemporary cinema. The words are well chosen and exact, and also have an air of mysteriousness about them. They embody hope while at the same time giving you the sense that a can of straight-up kick-assery will be opened on anyone who chooses the wrong path. Okay, I know. I got carried away there. I couldn't help myself.

I chose this quote not only for its undisguised meaning and the skillful way the words are strung together but also because I have used it many times while onstage. Sometimes I use it as a humorous way of establishing my credibility with my audience by telling them I have a particular set of skills that includes surviving an itinerant and seriously disturbing childhood and making a conscious decision to mitigate the effects of the historical trauma that threatened to follow me into my adulthood. That I made this decision so that my life and my child's life, and the lives of anyone interested in being inspired, might be different. That I've not only made lemonade out of lemons but worked bare-handed the places that threatened to harden my heart. I grew love from a flicker to a steady flame. Where there appeared to be no way, I became a way. And these are the actions that fostered willingness into possibility, persistence into integrity and opportunity. My intention is always to invite people to face their lives with intention, to turn toward the challenges, no matter how large or small, with the courage to transform what they may see as lead into gold. These are the skills that permit me to be the one standing before them. These are the skills that I am here to teach to anyone who is interested in becoming their own resident alchemist. I use the energy to get them curious and engaged and in the moment. I have also used this quote in a few circumstances to ward off unwanted attention from stalking social media creepers. I know you all know what I mean; therefore, I resist the temptation to digress yet again.

Not only is it essential to have a *very particular set of skills*, but it's equally vital to know to what extent those skills can serve you. Knowing this supports you in several ways:

- It helps you represent yourself honestly.
- It helps you be at ease with the essence of you.
- It provides you with a chance to explore areas for potential growth.
- It minimizes the need to overpromise and underdeliver unless, of course, that's the razor's edge you prefer to teeter across, barefoot.

Knowing the scope of your skills can be a valuable tool when you need to step it up and be your own cheerleader. When I talk about being the subject matter expert of you, I am inviting you to consider the depth, breadth, and width of *all* of you. What are your unique talents, your ways of navigating beautifully through this one life you are living? What do you know to be accurate about you and, as a result, what prepares you to make your way without needing anyone else's permission to do so?

That's what a subject matter expert is: someone who owns their ability to identify their unique talents, who knows the value of what they bring to the table, who accepts that they are the go-to person when it comes to their expertise. And a subject matter expert will not compromise their integrity.

And that right there is what I believe to be true about me — although it's taken me most of my adult life to understand who I am, to know what I bring to the conversation. I am aware of my value. I've come to accept that it is okay to be an expert on me, it's okay to be responsible for my needs and wants. It's more than okay: it's a necessity for thriving. Given that this is, after all, a personal-growth manifesto, I would be remiss if I didn't continue to admit the lengths I had to go to to arrive at what I am sharing with you.

Being the Expert on Your Own Expertise

By the time I attended my first weeklong writing workshop, I'd been a writer for what felt like five minutes. I can't recall, exactly, how I learned about the yearly writing retreat held every summer, but I was grateful for the partial scholarships I received to attend. To take an entire week off to explore the art and craft of writing is no small feat for an emerging writer and especially for a writer of color. Because I don't wish to put the entire workshop on notice for the actions of a few untutored individuals, I choose to refrain from giving any identifying details about where I was. However, let me just say this: for me to be in the company of such literary stars, artists who have made considerable contributions to our country's literary, film, and theatrical canons was a huge stroke of luck.

As I said, I was a brand-new female Black author. I knew absolutely nothing about craft. Actually, I didn't know the first thing about writing, let alone that it was *considered* a craft, but I was there because I wanted to learn more about what I didn't know. And like so many literary spaces I'd come to experience over time, it was not lost on me that I was one of the only Black people out of about 125 at the workshop the entire week. Maybe you already know the toll the responsibility of representation takes on a person. And if you don't know ... keep reading.

It was around day two that I would start to understand that I didn't know what I didn't know and that sh*t was about to get *really* real. But what I did know was that there were several white women who made it their business to inform me of what they thought about me, my writing, and who I'd stolen my "unoriginal" voice from.

It was during lunchtime that I happened on a reading designed for the workshop participants. The lucky ones, the readers, would get selected through a lottery system. By then I'd read only a few times in public, but I was quite comfortable with it. Also, I'd just attended a morning workshop where the facilitator had read my work as an example of how well I'd (unknowingly) accurately incorporated a literary device known as an "objective correlative" (*say what?* thought the country girl who learned to read from the back of a cornflakes box). Only the Lord knew that I had no idea who the hell T. S. Eliot was and that I surely did not care, at that time, to know. I felt embarrassed not knowing what I didn't know, and therefore unable to add anything to the conversation. I was happy when the workshop finished and thought going to hear others read their work would lessen my own discomfort as well as take the attention off me.

On entering the building, I was handed a lottery ticket and told there might be a chance I'd get to read. Assessing the room and the thirty or so people assembled, I felt assured I'd have no such luck. I took the ticket and sat down alongside a woman I'd met earlier. We sat through three readings before I heard my number called. I was hesitant. My instincts suggested that I not read. Some of the readings before me had depicted a romantic version of bucolic life in rural New Hampshire or a grandmother who had left her favorite grand-daughter the rocking chair she'd used throughout her life to rock and to instill love, calm, and a sense of place into those she loved. And then there was that one reading about how downtown Detroit had selfishly diminished the home values of the residents of Bloomfield Hills. I waved the moderator on saying, "It's okay, I really don't have anything prepared anyway." But the attendees weren't having it. And then there I was, facing a group of people I would have to spend four more days with, after possibly getting self-conscious and tangled up in my own words.

To play it safe, I picked the piece I'd used to pitch to the acquisition editors at the various New York publishing houses I'd recently visited. My body swayed as I listened for the right moment to begin, and then I dropped in, my body listening, swaying to the feelings. The words were hot, honest. Raw. They flowed from me with ease. And before I knew it, I was done. I didn't realize there would be feedback. In my opinion, it takes a tremendous amount of compassionate intention to give feedback in a way that is beneficial for both giver and receiver. Feedback in a writers' workshop is generally geared toward offering the author constructive, insightful, and structural comments regarding the piece being workshopped. It is not supposed to place the writer herself in front of a firing squad. In my understanding, the craft of writing is just that, a set of techniques and devices intended to support the work into becoming its best form of expression. In my work with people, I work diligently to remember the history of their vulnerabilities, and I aim to deliver my responses accordingly.

There I stood, in front of the mic, waiting. I was informed by one young woman that I was a thief. A literal *word robber*. I didn't know such a thing existed. Apparently, I had intentionally stolen, verbatim, the cadence and syntax of all the best Black writers ever to exist. I learned that I had *clearly* plagiarized their voices, tones, and authority. None of the women who stood up and spewed what felt like vitriol in my face said one positive thing about my work; rather, they vehemently worked to eclipse my efforts. I was told that no one had given me permission to put all the movement and hand motions and lyrical verse into my work the way that I had. I was accused of giving a spoken-word performance. I was told, and this is the punch line, "*That* voice has already been done. You're totally impersonating Toni Morrison," she said. Someone else yelled out, "Gwendolyn Brooks and Alice Walker."

Even as I write this, I feel the power of those fellow writers' words. My rage built up as it mirrored the energy vibrating from their bodies as each woman shook her head with conviction and the self-proclaimed expertise on the subject matter of *my* experience. I was not at the time aware enough in the area of creative writing and the nuances of voice and tone, or well versed enough in the rhetorical modes of the craft, to defend myself, nor was I educated enough about the hideous nature of systemic racism and blatant prejudice that existed within that presumably safe literary experience. I wanted to intellectually punch back, to defend myself, to get bigger than the situation by dominating all of them with my own feelings of outrage at their inability to monitor what came out of their mouths. Had I met them beat for beat, I have no doubt that I would have been placed under arrest for using that particular set of skills also known as a laying on of hands. The experience felt that threatening and violent for me.

In the years after that event, and as a result of pursuing an interdisciplinary education, I became more aware that what these women were saying was that there was only one way for me to present myself as a Black writer and that there was no room for my particular way of being outside of what they felt they had the right to dictate. Chimamanda Ngozi Adichie, the venerable Nigerian novelist whose TED Talk "The Danger of a Single Story" has garnered more than 25 million views, warns us "that if we hear only a single story about another person or country, we risk a critical misunderstanding." And this is exactly what I believed to be the case regarding my situation.

This became clear to me: There was only one accepted Black woman's voice in contemporary American writing, epitomized by the work of Pulitzer Prize–winning authors Toni Morrison, Alice Walker, and Gwendolyn Brooks. Their perspectives have been distilled into the singular sanctioned voice presumed to represent the entirety of the Black woman writer's experience in America. There was no room for my interpretation of my experience as a Black woman writer. My presentation skills were out of bounds, mostly misunderstood, and therefore unsanctioned by the self-appointed story committee. There was only one way for me to be, in their eyes. In regard to them as writers, oh, sure, it was absolutely expected of these women, in their MFA programs, to identify with the likes of T. S. Eliot, or Jane Smiley, or Elizabeth Bishop, to allow the works of those culturally sanctioned and widely assigned writers to shape and inform their own point of view or approaches in syntax, voice, and style. But for me to do so from that "one" voice composed of three of America's most prolific and esteemed writers was to be assumed a "thief."

I cannot say what any one of these women intended to give with their feedback, but I know what happened for me: I felt as though I'd been a casualty of a drive-by, or a survivor of a hate bomb, and what was left of my pre-presentation self was my shadow scorched against the carpet I was pinned to. I felt robbed. But though I was tempted to retaliate, clearly the best thing for me was not to act from a place of payback. This was one of those times when kick-ass became an inside job as opposed to an outward expression. I intuitively knew it was in my best interests to turn my set of take-no-prisoners survival skills inward. It felt nearly impossible, but that's the work, isn't it, to be a big person by playing smaller than seems humanely possible in a triggering situation. When we override the fight response and instead grapple with not knowing what to do, staying with the vulnerability of each moment, we make space for meeting the situation with something other than violent words or actions.

And there was something else. Although in the heat of what happened I had no access to the information, the fact was that two weeks earlier I'd inked a two-book deal with one of the top seven publishing houses in the world. That I'd actually sold my work in progress to a wonderful editor. So while these women were, in my opinion, merciless in their comments, eventually, after my trauma response subsided, I was able to get back in my body and recognize the truth that what I had just read had been acquired by the aforementioned editor. And ironically enough, during the rounds my then agent and I had made to different publishing houses, I'd met an acquisitions editor at Little, Brown who'd compared my writing to Morrison's *The Bluest Eye*. I remember informing the editor that I hadn't yet read the novel but had planned to do so. Nevertheless, no thanks to the enormous power of the negativity bias, the pain of their remarks left me shaken to the core. I would need to grow through what I went through, and of course this would take time.

In regard to becoming the subject matter expert of ourselves, this event revealed to me that I was clearly untutored on the craft of writing. I recognized that in the face of those women, I was "guilty" of relying on my intuitive guidance and the organic process of trusting in myself, never mind that those abilities had allowed me to complete my first manuscript. I will admit that although that wasn't the first time I'd experienced something similar in spaces where I was among the few people of color, it was the one that left me doubting my skills. The result, on the outside, was the publication of my memoir, *Somebody's Someone*. However, on the inside I made a solemn vow to never again allow myself to be that vulnerable with other writers. In 2015 I graduated from the University of California, Riverside, with an MFA in creative writing and writing for the performing arts. Because my degree took sixty-four quarter units to confer, mine is considered a terminal degree, the highest ranking within my field. I've no doubt that if asked, I'd teach the hell out of a creative writing or theatrical class on craft. It would be an honor to do so for a historically underrepresented demographic, who like me could very easily find themselves confused and believing that their organically inclined approach is erroneous or unsanctioned. The more representation we have across the disciplines of the language and writing arts, the better chance we will have as a culture to truly honor diversity, inclusion, and equity and to experience the truth that our unique stories and voices matter.

The Accidental Speaker

As odd as this may sound, it is only recently that I've learned the value of the strategy I'm proposing here. No, seriously. For many, many years after that writers' retreat, I felt a sense of detachment from all things that pointed to naturally talented me. Although the writing and subsequent publication of my first book led me to a speaking career, I became self-conscious and doubtful that I had the qualifications to adequately represent myself, or even my story. Unlike the character Bryan Mills, I was unable to identify at that time what my "particular set of skills" was. It wasn't enough to just be naturally good at something. Again, I didn't know how to own that truth in order to give myself the permission to be who I was. And, just like the writing, speaking fell into my lap without media training or a speech coach. Things rapidly evolved from there.

At that time, I was a hairdresser who was well-known for cutting hair, sewing in weaves, and delivering an awe-inspiring set of highlights, finished off with a banging balayage. Writing and speaking were my side hustles. Loving the energy that existed between the audience and me, I wrote in order to speak. And in terms of the relationship I'd already cultivated regarding my comfort level with people, speaking in front of them was a natural move. However, I did not understand how to maximize my experiences into a scalable business model. In the beginning I rarely requested a speaking fee that was commensurate with my time, including the effort I put into customizing a presentation to fit my customer's needs. I'll say it again: sometimes we don't know what we don't know until we need to know. I did not know my speaking worth because it wasn't clear what it was I brought to the table that encouraged people to continually hire me. Also, because I didn't have an agent representing me, I had no clear idea of how to package myself, what was considered an acceptable pay range, what the hell a "one-pager" was, or that I actually needed one. Secretly I felt illegitimate. For the longest time, when people asked me what I did for a living, I wouldn't stand in my truth, I wouldn't admit (fully) that my belief in Spirit and how it moved and encouraged me to express the truth of who I am was how I'd achieved much of my destiny. I truly believed this; I just wasn't sure how to say so with confidence. I didn't grow up feeling seen for my gifts, supported, or encouraged to go the distance to cultivate those abilities into anything I could be proud of. I had a ton of permission in one area of my life, haircutting, and not so much in another. I imagine this is true for so many of us.

How many of you are familiar with harboring a host of insecurities about who you are? It's more common than you may think, to not believe you have a right to express yourself in whatever way feels right and true for you. I get it.

I'll never forget the day I stepped onto the stage for my first speaking event. It was for Kaiser Permanente's Women's Wellness event at the Bob Hope Theatre in Stockton, California. I was scheduled as the opening speaker, to be followed by the honorable governor of Texas, none other than Ann Richards herself. The actor Marlee Matlin was to close. In my soft-pink power suit, I took to the stage. I think I may have mentioned the fact that I was wearing a full-length Spanx to smooth the cellulite in my thighs, which of course drew a huge response from the audience of hundreds of women. Listening to Governor Richards speak, witnessing the ease with which she delivered her words, and the conviction, had a major impact on me. She held the audience in rapt attention without raising her voice and with zero antics. It was all story. Hers was a master's lesson in decorum at the lectern. Later, in a photo op, I expressed my admiration to Governor Richards, and that's when she said, "Your story is amazing. Don't ever stop sharing it." Without a doubt, her words helped me believe in the possibility of pursuing speaking as a career.

However, until I could make my way to accepting, without shame, the full truth of how I came to be who I was under the circumstances that had shaped me, I saw myself as an *accidental* speaker. That way, if I didn't measure up, I wouldn't have to take full responsibility for falling short. Oh, don't get me wrong; clearly, as I said, I felt the power of Spirit's hand guiding my affairs while addressing and inspiring the audiences I have stood before. Even with the light and love fearlessly shining through me in front of all those people, and after receiving the best compliment from a highly regarded stateswoman, I was missing the narrative, the personal relationship with myself, my own permission, that caused people to hire me again and again and yes, again. Thank you, Spirit, for all the good that has made my life bountiful.

Pause to Consider

- Are there ways in which you ignore how Spirit shows up and shines out in your life?
- In what ways do you downplay your skills or your capacity to be effective?

How does it feel to recognize what you've pointed out? Know that you are not alone. So many of us have fallen into the trap of not knowing or accepting our full worth. We allow others to talk us out of our ability to be strong, to boss it like it's nobody's business. And I get it. How do women and those of us who identify as historically underrepresented folks give ourselves the permission we so often need to be bigger than a suppressive society wants us to be? It takes courage on steroids, many times, to realize our dreams. It gets exhausting, I know, but no matter what, don't allow anything to get in your way. Ride out the uncertainties, the confusion, the rejections, the misplaced projections that there is no room at the inn for you. And when evidence presents itself that you are doing a great job, as in the case of Governor Richards offering me encouragement, take it. Work with it. Make the effort to integrate such sentiments into your perception of yourself. These things take the time they take. And often building your confidence muscle gets more taxing before you see or benefit from the improvements.

Speaking of time, let's take a breath. Exhale. Now extend an act of kindness toward yourself as you work your way through your awarenesses. How will you congratulate yourself for being generous with your time in doing these exercises? Take out a permission slip and identify five ways you can completely, indisputably, and nonnegotiably celebrate *you*.

Too Talented to Have Such Low Self-Esteem

I was in the campus screening room at the University of California, Riverside, where I attended grad school, shyly acknowledging what I'd just experienced. Seven actors had participated in a staged reading of a play I'd written that was selected for the university playwright's festival. I was beyond excited. My love for anything theatrical began in high school. *Camelot* was the first musical I experienced, and Alvin Ailey's *Firebird* got me juiced for the sight of Black folks en pointe. And although the

Ebony Fashion Fair shows were just that, fashion shows, the theatrical flair was afoot in each show, and I loved it when I was lucky enough to sit in the audience.

"What do you think?" my professor asked.

"It's okay," I answered.

"What do you mean? It was great," he said, a look of confusion on his face.

I didn't know what to say. So often I seemed to understand the emotional underpinning of plays or books, and I could explain them from that perspective, but just as often I felt strapped for the intellectual language to express my understanding of the ways in which art expressed itself. As someone whose Myers-Briggs showed up as I/ENFP (an introvert/extrovert, intuitive, feeler, and perceiver), my right brain ruled everything about my burgeoning personal aesthetic. I needed time to go inward in order to bring what I understood outward. And you can best believe that once I understood it, you would be hard put to shut me up!

Not to mention the fact that I was standing in a dream come true, a member of the audience watching a play that I wrote, something that my professor and his colleagues chose to have mounted for the entire campus to see. There were rumors that reviewers from the Kennedy Center American College Theater Festival would be in attendance. I was everywhere else but there, really hearing this professor or knowing how to answer his question. Someone, a friend, stood beside me, and my professor turned and said, "She's too talented to have such low self-esteem." That was hard to hear. I was happy that my crony seemed to let the unintended slight slide. I, on the other hand, did not. I felt the sucker punch of it in a deep way. Yet I also listened to what my professor had said, loud and clear. Perhaps the time had come for me to become curious about my relationship to my own talents. And like so many other things in my life, I of course had no idea how *good* I was at any of them. It was one thing to *feel* some way about something, and another to feel emboldened enough to find my words and say as much. Also, I had not made the connection that the same Spirit that moved me while onstage also had a hand in helping me write plays. What I wouldn't have given to have grown up with a chorus of inspirited voices *amen*ing me on to victory and telling me that I was talented in many ways.

Anyway, what my professor said wasn't news to me. Given how averse I was to name-calling and labeling due to my history, I couldn't name my inability in the moment as low self-esteem. I've never been a person to put myself down; rather, I prefer to admit that I don't know something if in fact I don't know it. It's been a weird paradox of sorts. On the one hand, I'll get inspired to create, following the intuitive impulse and doing whatever needs to get done, and on the other, when it lands positively, I go all introverted. Or perhaps the truth of the matter is that I'd somehow lacked the ability to identify with the fact that I am actually a creative person. At times I became freaked out trying desperately to put into words how images and instructions came to me in visions and dreams. As a hairdresser, I completed a twenty-four-month training program in six months. The first book I ever wrote, I sold for a hefty six figures; and then my first one-woman show had a successful six-week run that was extended and mounted in various venues across the country. These bouts of fortune weren't supposed to happen to people like me, because they are meant for those who've given blood and toiled through trials by fire, witnessed and validated by coaches, mentors, and experts, before earning entrance onto the world stage. These experiences merely scratch the surface of the incredible fortune I have had in following the instinctive impulse within. I literally had no awareness that I should feel good about myself as a result of these things. It wasn't until I had a conversation with another professor that I began to see the patterns in the way I experienced creativity. What I've come to understand is that there is such a thing as visual spatial intelligence, which means that I, like many designers and artists, poets and metaphysicians, have a keen ability to see and sense deeply within and to use what's considered the mind's eye.

I could give you countless examples of times I have driven around the country — until I knew better, of course — meeting with this consultant or that specialist and then yet another one. Yep. That was me at many points in my life, searching for the next level of my own permission I didn't even know I needed. I've spent way too much money employing other people in the service of pointing out to me what was not self-evident: that I am worthy of my talents, that my way of showing up in the world is evidence that I exist in my own goodness, and that my talents are expressed as evidence of Goodness itself expressing through me. For some time to come, I was at a loss when it came to understanding how I worked as a creative person and taking responsibility for what I'd created.

Don't Share Until You're Ready

Many people feel dissociated from their interior experience: that deep landscape of emotions, feelings, and spiritual sparks that reside within each of us. It is a dwelling of sorts, a place of true refuge if we allow ourselves the freedom to go to the deep recesses of who we are. It takes practice, a recognizing that your dreams are yours to create. It also takes a willingness to coalesce your gifts with that of the Divine inspiration available to us all.

I'm gonna go back in time a bit here. I'd signed up for a creative intensive. It was one of four electives I could choose from in the BA completion program I'd enrolled in. The workshop lasted several weeks, which meant I'd have the chance to explore my relationship to creativity in a way I hadn't before, and I'd also have the time I'd need to spend with the discoveries that arose. Little did I know that this very class would provide me with the insights I'd long desired.

With beginner's mind, I began school again. I buried my attention in each and every project I was assigned. It was a lovefest between me, myself, and I. Eventually I learned that not everyone I showed my work to was meant to see, hear, or even know about it. That some things, especially those of a creative nature, needed time to incubate, to fluctuate, to come into their full maturation. I learned the importance of protecting one's creative process until it felt right to share with people with whom trust had been established. Oh, if only I'd known about that before attending that writing workshop, LOL! I could truly have saved myself some unwarranted trouble.

How many of you have innocently had your hopes dashed or your dreams murdered right before your eyes by sharing your work too soon, or with people you believed were safe? This isn't to suggest that there is no room for constructive criticism but to indicate the value of waiting until both you and your project are ready. Once you feel certain enough of where you are with your creative endeavor, it is up to you to decide who shares values with you in regard to their craft. I call anyone I've chosen to trust my SPOT, Special Person of Trust. After a time, and while building an even deeper creative relationship,

I promote them to acting as my creative *spotter*, someone who has my back, my sides, and my projects' best interests at heart.

One day, while on my way to school, I found myself parked fifty feet from Target's parking garage. In my car I sat, poised for the right-hand turn that would put me on time to pick up my final project but late for my class. Tears streaming down my cheeks, I sat. Idling. The impact of my intensive professor's words were finally having their moment. I've always had a penchant for responding late to comments, feelings, good experiences. I am certain it's a delayed processing mechanism left over from the successions of trauma responses I've experienced. It takes me a while to get on board, and once I do I go all in.

You're an artist. These were the words Alec, my professor, had spoken to me. Three little words. So simple. But I felt that Alec, someone I'd trusted, had lied to me. He'd only wanted to shut me up, throw me a bone, confuse me.

I couldn't accept that this whole time I'd been an artist and that no one had ever said as much, had noticed my skills or encouraged me to go all the way with them or had me tested to see if I possessed a high degree of visual intelligence. Perhaps they had? Lord knows I felt as if I'd lived about a hundred lives by this time. Perhaps it was *I* who wasn't prepared to see myself as I was. What I knew to be true was that my sister was the natural-born artist. She'd won all the school contests when we were young; we attended the same school three grades apart. Her paintings were displayed in galleries and local museums. If I let my sister tell it, which I did on countless occasions, I was the one whose father could actually be identified. How dare I have *her* share of artistic talent as well? Although we'd been estranged for nearly four decades, it was at that moment when I felt the weight of how much I'd downplayed anything that pointed to my having any differences or capacities that might give me an advantage over someone. It felt dangerous, somehow. Especially if it meant it might hurt them or that they wouldn't like me. Oh, my Lord, the ways I'd learned to erase myself in the face of the threat of not belonging. I'd learned it was easier, and perhaps safer, to deny my God-given goodness than own my blessings and risk further rejection.

Eventually I got it together and pulled away from that curb where I sat bawling like a baby. I made it to class. Although I was late for the start of that day's agenda, I had caught up to a clearer understanding of my relationship to the art of creating art. Granted, for years I, like many people, had walked around with all those repressed myths about who I was: flat-out bad, a nuisance, a bull in a china cabinet, crazy, and therefore un-lovable.

As you may have gathered by now, it is by grace that I've kept pushing it, coming through, and showing up for myself as an artist. It has taken the time it's taken, and the more I stayed with the creative impulses that showed up as opportunities to discover who I am, the more open I became to what was true and possible for me. And so a thought arrived one day: per-haps my *gift*, or talent, was the art of perseverance itself, and if I could stay with it, develop a relationship with it, then perhaps in time I'd have a better understanding of who I am and of the distances I am capable of traversing as I become the expert on the subject matter of being just plain old me.

Who Do I Need to Become?

It's been nine years since I sat in that creative intensive class along with eleven other souls searching to discover what it meant to engage with the creative force, to trust in our instincts enough to call ourselves *artists*. That we have a right to belong to that which is ours, that which defines what it means to be us, to be human, to be individuals in our own right.

Since choosing to step into what seems to have always been true for me, that I am an artist, I have exponentially increased the work I do in the world, and in right relationship to it. Recently, I signed up for a visioning class. I wanted to have a clearer idea of the scope of the project that would become the book you are now holding. I had written memoirs, but this was to be a different kind of book. During the meditation that is part of the visioning work I'd committed to doing, there are five questions, one of which asks what I must embrace in order for my vision to be realized. That is how the strategy for this chapter came into being. During the time I was quietly connecting to my inner world, I realized that I'd needed to embrace the truth that I am the subject matter expert of what *already* is and of what can become possible.

In my heart the words blossomed, and I felt in alignment with Spirit, with what has always been true for me. There is nothing you or I need to sacrifice for this awareness. All you need to do is recognize the particular set of skills that make you uniquely you and then own them, live them. I am a speaker, an author, a teacher, a coach, and on a good day, a singer.

Who are you?

Those age-old questions of why people have hired me or why I didn't feel I had permission to accept my talents have less power over me now. Sure, from time to time I hit a hiccup and need a moment to get back on track. But this is what I now know is true for me, and I intend to avow it here for all to see: *I am the subject matter expert of perseverance!* I bring that quality of being to everything I do. And so it is!

Pause to Consider

- What type of learner are you? How have you come to understand yourself in relationship to how you learn?
- Does the feeling of detachment and confusion I described resonate with you? If so, in what way?
- Have you ever been in a situation where you were unaware that you were going to receive feedback from strangers regarding something you felt vulnerable about?
- How do you manage feedback?
- What do you need in order to make the receiving and implementing of feedback a success for you?
- What is the scope of your particular skills or talents?
- In what ways are you the SME (small and medium-size enterprise, in case you didn't know) of you, yourself, and you?
- How do you compromise your integrity in relationship to your skills?
- What do you know to be true about you?
- What is it like you to do?

Lovefirmations

I am my best supporter.
I am an artist.
I am creative.
I am Spirit embodied.
I am worthy of the skin I was born in.
I root for myself in all situations.
I offer myself praise and deserve the compliments I give myself.

*I use my successful experiences to remind myself of my
    abilities and to motivate me.*
I am knowledgeable.
I am someone I can go to.
I trust me.
I celebrate the positive changes I make.

Mirror Work

Taking a moment to search inside yourself is a quick practice
I like to call mirror work. This simple self-care practice offers
you an opportunity, like so many of the exercises in this love
manifesto, to connect with yourself and to practice relying on
your own insights.

1.   How do I know when I need a pep talk?
2.   What is one inspiring thing I could say to myself each
     morning?
3.   Why is it important to express kindness toward myself?

Bootstrapping Takeaways

* Discover how your skills best serve you.
* Understand the scope of your skills.
* Protect your creative endeavors.
* Accept that you are an artist, a creative.
* Remain willing to step into your vulnerability around
  your skills and talents.
* Cultivate your spotters!

Spend some time with each of these takeaways, exploring
what each of them means to you. A good way to approach them

is to turn each statement into a question. For instance, starting with the first takeaway you might say, "How have my skills best served me?" and so on. The words *how, why,* and *what* are strong clarifiers and can lead you deeper into the praxis of personal inquiry. As always, have fun discovering the best of you!

Kick-Ass Strategy #8

Receive for Yourself as You Believe in Yourself

*When I dare to be powerful, to use my strength
in the service of my vision, then it becomes
less and less important whether I am afraid.*

— Audre Lorde, *Sister Outsider*

And whatever things you ask in prayer, believing, you will receive.

— Matthew 21:22, New King James Version

It was day one of the Presidential Physical Fitness Award tests, and I was going to beat every girl in my PE class to the top of that rope. I had to. There was no other option. This was all I had. Most of the white kids at my school appeared to have everything they could ever hope for; me, I had my ability to see things in my dreams. And what I knew is that I wasn't leaving school that day without that much-coveted blue patch with the eagle in the center with its wings spread and the six stars crowning the number 1. For all I knew, it was the *actual* president's insignia. I imagined that if I won someone might inform the president, and perhaps Mr. Nixon would consider meeting me. But first things first. I needed to kick some middle school…

Phwwwwwhht! The shrill from my PE teacher's whistle exploded in my ear, and off I went. One hand over the other, I crawled up that climbing rope. *You're doing good,* I remember thinking while scooting upward with the speed and precision of sheer determination. I would out-climb both the girl to my left and the one gaining speed on my right. It was though I'd held my breath and decided not to let it go until I tapped the top of the metal rung that held the rope to the gymnasium's ceiling. I'd previewed all of it the night before, in a dream, from the bottom of that rope to the top. Therefore, I believed I would win. To tell the truth, I climbed that rope alleging to myself that I already *had* won.

I would prove to my gym teacher that I was the fastest and most fit of all the girls in my school; in fact, I'd show everyone I was as tough as any boy. The guys I lived with in Austin, before that fateful day when I ran away, forced me to literally box my way to a chance to hang with them, play their games, in order to prove I wasn't just a girl. In my mind, I was a bona fide tomboy, all muscle and effort. This was my chance to put truth on its feet and go into action. Even when I was forced to wear ankle socks with lace, and, God forbid, a dress, I remained loyal to sitting with my legs wide open. This was something *real* girls did not do. But the guys, they dismissed my unladylikeness as nothing more than my being a "wildcat thang," as they used to tease.

And with that wildcat thang, relying mostly on my upper-arm strength, I tapped that top rung and heard the shrill of the final whistle.

That one act of winning my much-coveted badge gave birth to something I could count on, no matter if I won or lost (although I definitely preferred to win), and that was believing in myself enough not to give up on myself. Most of the time, I entered contests or competitions at a seeming disadvantage. At least these were the conditions I'd come to understand as time went on. When people asked where I trained, or how long I'd apprenticed, they'd express concern that I might not be up to the task when I explained that I had a *feeling* that I could do it or that I had seen myself do it in a vision.

Hearing once that I would "be the first to place in any category by virtue of a feeling" did not deter me, however, from staying true to what I believed, what I'd seen. From time to time it may have made it a bit harder to hold on to my truth, but what mattered most is that I tried and succeeded on my terms. Many times, it felt as if my efforts were only valid as long as I'd spent countless hours or days learning the thing in plain sight — where my actions were observable by anyone who could attest to the facts. I couldn't trust people to support me in the ways that mattered to me, as in seeing the whole nature of my person. So I was offered chance after chance to work harder at learning trust in myself. I couldn't give up. My hope for you is that you never give up either.

Dree-ee-ee-eam, Dream, Dream, Dream

By the time I was fired from the job I took as a result of not knowing how to manifest the job I *really* wanted, I'd figured out everything I needed to know about pursuing my heart's desire: becoming the hairstylist I always felt I was. I was thirty-one, my son was six, and I was exhausted from desperately working toward the domesticated life of being a mom and a wife, which felt more like a continuous disaster in the making. C'mon, who was I fooling? I was the girl who'd failed thirty foster home placements and ended up in residential treatment. Girls like me were allergic to people and the closeness that domestication promised. The upside was that although I was failing at the *wifey* role, I was a good-enough mother. And while it's been said that self-report is the least reliable kind of report, in the case of my mom-ing skills, I beg to differ. Go ahead, ask my son, if you don't believe me. I was and still am a Boss Mom! Because I want to set a good example for my son by expressing my most authentic self, I hereby admit I was an accident waiting to happen at that job I was thankfully relieved from.

The job was at a group home, and I did want to make a difference in those children's lives. I meant well. But I got it; I was still too close to my own experience to remain objective. So, yes, it was I who took the kiddos out to Baskin-Robbins for sundaes. And yes, it was half an hour past their bedtimes. My treat, of course. I wanted them (I put the onus on Little Red) to have the experience of having an ice cream simply because they wanted it. That just has to happen sometimes in these institutions. You feel me? I know. I digress. Let's get back on track with what I was born to do.

Okay, so it's the first day of beauty school. *Yass!* If you're a hairstylist, colorist, or barber and you're reading this, can I get you to pump both hands in the air?! It was such an exciting experience. How my then husband and I arrived at an agreement for me to attend beauty school remains a mystery. Nevertheless, I owe this dream come true to that guy. On the first day of beauty school classes, we had a visitor from the Redken products company. The salesperson was selling tickets to something called the Cosmoprof Beauty Show, which was scheduled four months out. Being the curious person I am, I asked what a beauty show was. I learned that it's an event that hairdressers, makeup artists, and nail artists at every level attend and learn tricks of the trade, buy products, network, and drink overly foaming beer out of plastic cups. In the middle of the day. Along with those same round tortilla chips drenched in five pumps of melted cheese spread, topped with a gazillion jalapeño peppers, that you can also find at baseball games. So delicious. It's all legendary. It's like the Mardi Gras for hairstylists, with lots of parties and shows and fun to be had by all.

The product rep also explained the competition aspect of hair shows, the various rounds that one must win in order to advance to the next, and then to the finals. I asked if brand-new students could enter and was told that all I needed was three hundred hours in order to qualify. She asked if any of us were interested, and of course my hand was the one reaching for that ceiling. That's when our cosmetology teacher chimed in that the school prefers to reserve such experiences for their seniors. And there they were, an interracial boy couple. Both cuter than all the women in the room put together. I could tell by the way they cooed and blushed and batted their mascaraed eyelashes that they were clearly the teacher's pets. For the moment, I dropped the matter.

Until later that night, when I had one of my dreams. That's where I saw it. The hairstyle. In 3D. On my way home I'd picked up one of those hair magazines from Walgreens. There was a photo of a Vidal Sassoon hairstyle that was mesmerizing and all the rage. And that is the look I'd taken into my dreams in order to figure out how to cut it. Not only did I see the entire cut from a 360-degree perspective, but I also noted the texture of the hair, the silkiness, the sheen. The color. As you know by now, this is my learning language. It was as though I were watching a movie, step-by-step, as though I already knew how to accomplish what I intended to do. I'm not kidding. In my sleep I worked through each stage, as the sales rep had discussed earlier that day. The dress my model would wear was black. A sheer strip running diagonally through the dress's midsection not only added dimension but also complemented my model's curves. These elements accentuated the asymmetrical shape of the cut. The sheer panel on the dress would move in one direction while the line of the cut moved in the other.

I awoke the next morning and called Nichelle, who I referred to as my sister. She and I met while we were in foster care and claimed one another as family. I asked if she'd be my model and agreed to split the winnings. I just felt it in my bones that we could win. Which we did. All three qualifying rounds. And the finals as well. I offered the ribbons and the smaller trophy to the school to place on display. They refused the offer. The leadership didn't seem particularly happy that the boy couple had not won. Nor were the boys. Fortunately, my understanding of office politics was nil to none. I may have had an affinity for winning on my terms, but that didn't necessarily make me popular. I *had* to go for what I knew was right for me, my heart, my spirit. And let's just say, my teacher found it difficult to support my independent spirit. Nevertheless, I could not allow that to stop me from following my instincts and moving from my integrity.

The straw that broke the camel's proverbial back for me was during the second preparation round. Wanting to be inclusive and hoping to create an opening for my teacher and me to work together, I asked her about applying color to relaxed hair. She replied, "You won the first round without asking me anything; I'm sure you'll figure it all out." In all honesty, my intention was not to become an outsider. I was following my spirit, believing as I saw things unfold. And of course, *now* I get it. Being a team player didn't come naturally to me, and how could it? I raised myself, for all intents and purposes. My strength was never in relying on others to balance the load. So axioms like "Take one for the team" or "There is no *I* in team" were lost on me in my early career experiences. During the two decades plus since I was in beauty school, I've learned the value of working independently as well as with others. I learned to flex my expectations against those of others, and I aim to create win-win situations.

And it has taken me most of my adult life to learn that I'm not now, nor have I ever been, someone to play solely by the rules, whatever that means. Perhaps I have a sort of social dyslexia when it comes to understanding or accepting that there is only one right way to do things. Does this resonate with you? I've become well aware that going with what we believe or know to be true for us doesn't mean our truth will always sit well with others. Difference can often mean being targeted. This in turn can deter you from going for what you want for fear of standing out. So instead, you wait for someone to give you permission to be great. Well, what if that permission never comes? Then what? What happens to your chance to be all that you can be? Remember the words of Rabbi Hillel, "If I am not for myself, who will be for me?"

Sometimes it has to be like that; we have to be for ourselves. And we need to learn to discern when those times are, something I've chosen to explore on my own journey. Let's keep it real. Fifty-three percent of Americans are not aware of the pay gap between Black and white women. And as an educated and underpaid Black woman — a member of the most underrepresented demographic in the country, who will lose an average of a million dollars to white men over the course of my career as a result of race and gender — I have seized opportunities to reinvent rules in order to get things done, pay my bills, realize my dreams. Ninety-nine percent of the doors I've walked through I've chosen to carve out of a closed-off wall in order to get a seat at the table. And given the information I just laid down for you, dear reader, I must inform you that there have been times when I've had to build my own table out of necessity. I know that I am not alone in this. And for the record, simply because I think that this is the moment to highlight these findings: Black women are just as ambitious as white men — and just as likely as white men (41 percent) and more likely than white women (29 percent) to say we want to become top executives. But even in the same job, Black women are paid less.

We are all socialized beings. We are led to believe, in one way or another, that we can't, shouldn't, or dare not go faster, or that we dare not present as too different from the people around us. This thinking is pervasive in family systems, schools, and workplace environments. When we strive for our own sense of greatness, the chance of being singled out, ridiculed, not accepted, denied promotions, discouraged, undervalued, and the monster of them all, feeling shunned, can feel like a price we can't afford. This can result in our dumbing ourselves down in order to fit in. We lower our standards, we hide our talents so far down we forget they are there. Believe me when I say I've done my share of that. But know this: sometimes we must take the risk of being the outsider by being who we are in our own way and on our own terms, regardless of the outcome. How else will we know what we are made of if we don't test the limits of our abilities? How else do we become the innovators and disrupters who transform the status quo and set a new ideal of inclusion and equity?

What I've learned from Mordechai, my fabulous therapist-teacher-spiritual-spotter, is this: if I want to heal from the fixations that defined my childhood and from the limitations imposed on my present, I must do so by first recovering from the introjections I experienced while growing up. Introjections are the opposite of projections. Introjections are when we take on other people's beliefs, feelings, and attitudes and make them our own, most often in an attempt to belong. Here is a list of some introjections that may sound familiar:

Men don't cry.
Black women deserve less pay simply because of their race and gender.
Women are not strong.
Girls are not supposed to be smarter than boys.
It's a man's world.
There is not enough to go around.
Women deserve less pay than men.
White people are paid more than other people because they're smarter.
There is only one story to define anyone who isn't a part of the majority.
No one wants to read Black stories.
Be quiet before I give you something to cry about.
No one wants to hear what you have to say.
You are too much.
You are a loser.
You're never going to get it.

Your kind should go back to where you belong.
You are the reason there are no jobs for people like us.
You're disgusting.
You're hopeless.
You are such a piece of sh*t.
You'll never make that happen.
Dream on.
There can only be one Oprah. Why bother trying.
Nobody wants to hear from a know-it-all.
As if you could ever make that happen.
Women ask to be harassed.
If only you hadn't _____, it wouldn't have happened.
No one will ever believe you.
It's better to fit in than to stand up and be alone.

Pause to Consider

- Do any of the above introjections resonate with you, and if so, in what way?
- What are some of the introjections you've heard that have made you question yourself?
- Have you ever changed your dream(s) because you fear believing in yourself?
- Take a moment to check in with yourself. What are some of the thoughts moving through your mind?

I Just Had to Have That Part

Let's turn our attention now to a young woman who is most impressive when it comes to believing in what's best for her.

Meet Angela Fairley, actor, activist, and manager at a start-up company. I first met Angela while perusing her *selects*: live auditions taped for a casting director, who then sends to the director, and from there an actor either gets selected for a call-back audition or cast in a role. It was an amazing opportunity to have a voice in choosing the actor to play the role of my younger self in a film depicting a slice of my life.

It is an industry fact that "life rights" holders are rarely allowed, or more truthfully said, *wanted* on set during the making of the film about their lives. And I completely understand the logic behind it. So my being in Winnipeg for the sixteen-day shoot of the film *I Am Somebody's Child: The Regina Louise Story* was already beyond belief. And then to have the chance to volunteer as a consultant was an unexpected perk of being there. The entire train ride from San Francisco Bay to Seattle and then on to Vancouver to catch the train to Manitoba, all I could think about is the actor who had stolen the hearts of both the casting director and the director with one simple act: when in the presence of Ginnifer Goodwin, her supporting actor, she tapped into the truth of her own foster care experience and allowed the emotion to come through in an authentically touching and overwhelming way. The result was the believability of her emotional truth. She really got me and my experience. Not only did Angela permit herself to *go there*, but in doing so, she invited us to trust in her capacity to take us along with her and bring us back. That is how the power of believing can present itself, whether in acting or in real life.

The day came when I would meet Angela in person. What stood out for me about her was what I observed while on location with her. She was impeccably organized, always on time, and arrived on set raring to go, no matter how late she'd worked the day before or how long she'd be expected to go each day. I wanted to know why landing this role meant so much to her. This is what she told me:

I have always wanted to be an actor. It's always been in my soul. There were a couple of really defining moments that I hold on to when I think about what helped me decide to make acting a real possibility. A lot of them were in my last four years in Florida. In high school, drama was more important than my classes. It was just acting, acting, and more acting and anything that involved the drama department. I began to realize when one of my friends said, "We never see you anymore" how much I'd given my life over to drama. I pushed everything aside to give it more of my attention. There was another moment when I realized my thing was going to be drama. My school had something called the International System Society. If your school participated, then it could get inducted into the society. When you are in the society, you can compete and go to the district showcases and perform your pieces, from a solo monologue to your entire school putting on one act.

It was in my junior year, and I got to go as an observer. At the end of the festival there was a showcase. The best performances of the festival were picked to perform at the end, and I saw a performer who later became my friend. He chose contrasting monologues that were specific in timing, as in back-to-back, and they had to land exactly. His performance was amazing. Everyone was awed.

I remember watching him do his thing and thinking, "Wow. I want to do that. I want to be there." And then the following year, my senior year, I entered to do a monologue because I was so inspired by what my friend had accomplished. That year I was the person who won the best in show for my monologue. I got to perform on the stage exactly where I had seen my friend the year before.

I remember the moment when I found out I had won best in the show. It was the biggest and happiest moment of my life. I had worked so long on those pieces; I gave so much to it. I did not think I would win, so I just felt really good about what I accomplished. They had this little scholarship opportunity that I could apply for and perform another monologue. I applied for it and won. They gave it to only one person in the entire district, and they gave it to me.

At that time, I was always watching Will Smith interviews, and in one he said that "there are people who are more talented" than him, but he had such a strong work ethic that he could surpass them. When I won the monologue competition and the scholarship, it really showed me how that was true. There were people in my troupes who were naturally more talented than me, but I was the one working so hard for so many hours. Winning justified the necessity of all my routines and all I had been learning. It gave me a lot of hope. As I think about where I have been and where I am now, in Los Angeles after driving across the country to relocate, it feels really overwhelming. And then to learn that I would get to be part of making a movie that I needed to see while growing up, part of telling a true story, was a dream come true. What I loved the most about acting was telling real stories, stories that would show all those little girls about hope, and possibility, about where they could actually get themselves to.

To find out that I was going to be in *I Am Somebody's Child* was unreal, and also not surprising. It made sense, because it is what I had always wanted. It was a defining moment in respect to everything I have ever done, everything I have ever fought for. I was told, "You know, you shouldn't go to LA" and "It is not going to happen for you" and "It just doesn't happen for normal people; this is not realistic." I gave myself the chance to do it anyway.

Bootstrapping Takeaways

- Follow your dreams anyway.
- Learn from those who inspire you.
- Dream! Periodt!
- Align with your deepest intentions.
- Challenge the beliefs that threaten to limit you.
- Stay true to your own course.
- Get inspired, and stay there.
- See in yourself what you believe in yourself, even if no one else does.

Pause to Consider

Take a few of the bootstrapping takeaways and engage with each in a conversation with yourself. Be curious about what it means to you. How might any one of the takeaways help you go for what you know to be true about you? Spend some time writing, expressing, and exploring. Remember to be gentle with yourself. There's no need to become critical or judgmental. This is simply an opportunity to be with yourself and allow whatever shows up to be exactly what it is: a chance to become better acquainted and perhaps more intimate with yourself and your dreams.

Kick-Ass Strategy #9

Allow Your Spirit to Triumph

*You can start with nothing, and out of nothing, out of no way,
a way will be made.*

— Michael Bernard Beckwith

*There is a law of faith and belief which is just as definite
as any other law in nature. This law utilizes the Creative
Principle of Life in such a way that all lesser uses
of It become submerged. This is the triumph of Spirit.*

— Ernest Holmes, *This Thing Called You*

We've all been there. We've all had our share of challenging circumstances, debilitating conditions, hurdles to overcome. We've experienced setbacks that, depending on our frame of reference, have been opportunities to set us up to come back. We've encountered limiting and fixed mindsets and petty contrivances and have been the instigators of a host of experiences far too numerous to list here. This is my offering, to acknowledge the magnitude of our spirits' journeys in the quest to have our human experiences. All this is to say that within us lies an immutable and universal truth: every day that we breathe ourselves awake, sit upright (or lounge); every day that we dare to love, laugh, live from our courage and our faith; every day that we face our loss, our emptiness, our aloneness, our feelings of being betrayed, of feeling shamed, lost, unimportant, disremembered, unaccounted for; every day that we embrace our joy, our freedom, our belongingness, our inclusiveness, our values and virtues, our integrity; every day that we are able to overcome any lesser beliefs about ourselves, as in, "I can't" or "I am not" or "I haven't a way forward," our spirit has indeed triumphed.

It goes without saying that what I inscribe onto this page is purely my own understanding of the nature of Spirit. I recognize that mine is but one way to interpret life, and my hope is to contribute to the myriad of ideas that already exist concerning what governs our lives. I leave the specific naming of it to you because I believe it is our work to do. It's your God-given, inalienable right to have a say in what is true about you and your relationship to spirituality, or whatever you want to call it. Through the ages we have grappled with our thoughts of what it means to live as both human and spirit. My invitation is for you to do the same, if you don't already. If you'd prefer to gracefully decline, no worries. It's more important to me that you live your life as best you can from the sovereignty of your truth rather than feeling coerced or bullied or, worst of all, shamed into doing what your soul doesn't feel called to do.

What does Spirit mean to you? As we move through this strategy, keep an open mind. I'm aware of the nerves that can be struck when it comes to such heated topics as race, religion, and politics, when it comes to our personal beliefs made in the quietude of our own lives challenged, made public. As a once-upon-a-time hairstylist, one of the golden rules is to *never* discuss those aforementioned topics. I believe my success as a business owner in the myriad of spaces I navigate owes partly to my devout adherence to this rule.

It is here on these pages, with my own permission at the helm, that I've dared to wrestle with the genesis of my beliefs. Someone once said, "I write to see what I think," and it is in the "spirit" of these words that I encourage you to write your self into a better understanding of what it means to allow your spirit to triumph. Whether you identify it as God, Allah, Elohim, Creator, My Lord, the Universe, Spirit, Mother Earth, or whatever, I believe that there is something greater than all of us humans combined, and we are but a reflection of that Presence.

Reaching Back

Although I've intimated already what life was like for me as a child, I would be remiss if I didn't reach back one more time into that horn of plentiful craziness, if only to highlight what I now consider some of the most salient and powerful occurrences of my life. Many of which, I might add, inspired me to become the woman, friend, teacher, advocate, artist, coach, writer, and human being that I currently am.

I've come to appreciate the value of examining my lived experiences. And as such, I recognize how important it is to look back and pay homage to the children we once were. They are our real sheroes and heroes, the gifted ones who braved the days of childhood with hope, enthusiasm, love, and kindness. Unconditional forgiveness. Children know unconditional love like nobody else. I don't know about you, but my younger self paved a path of success for me. There's no real way that I would've learned the value of belonging to myself had it not been for that resourceful girl of my past. *I love you, Red.*

In regard to that whole scary childhood chock-full of Dickensian characters, I promise not to go on and on and carelessly, vicariously traumatize you. But I do want to share the incidents that allowed my spirit to take the helm of my life's journey. Now that we're all on the same page, let's go!

John 3:16

"You gonna be a nothing...you the reason nobody wants you!" Boom! And just like that the bombs are dropped. Lethal. Although I am a firm believer that those who do not possess a clear understanding of their own pain are more likely to unconsciously project it onto others, this does not mean you must grant someone permission to be cruel to you. The perpetrator may or may not recognize that a statement like the one opening this paragraph has the potential to decimate connection and safety. When fear and shame is all we know, we may not comprehend — in the moment, or ever — that dropping such a bomb has the power to scorch someone's sense of identity right out of its becoming. Forget about trust. Forget about personal regard. The stakes are especially high if the one hurling the invectives is our caretaker or loved one.

This may not come as a surprise, but if you've had a safe enough childhood, it might be disconcerting to know that children actually hear messages like this on the regular. Every. Day. Perhaps you've been spoken to harshly, whether as a child or an adult. Our bosses, lovers, friends, frenemies, relatives, and strangers have said horrific things that have knocked us for six.

And you, my dear reader, may've unintentionally hurled a few unkind words toward another without fully calculating how they would land with that person and that the unintended consequences may be that of hurt, suffering. Guess what? It's okay to allow what's true for you to arise, and to feel and express your feelings, whether you're the receiver or the perpetuator. And, no, your experiences need not be as dire as mine or anyone else's to be valid for you. I only ask that you get honest with yourself and your feelings and attempt to be with what is, eventually forgiving yourself for doing the best with what you had at the time.

Each of our stories is relevant. They are our experiential signatures, our representatives of our pasts. We all have a right to belong to our stories, for better or worse. And the choice is always ours as to whose narrative we will follow. If we choose to give what's true for us away in exchange for some other thing, it's imperative to know what's at stake, and at what cost you're willing to lose yourself to another's agenda. The more you're willing to hold on to what matters to you — dreams, hopes, desires, good vibes, and feelings that are, again, signature to you — the better able you will be to hold fast to your faith and beliefs. To have access to what is true for you is your personal power. It is from this storehouse of fortified will that you will find your inner capacity to flip the script on what no longer serves you. The outdated beliefs, gone! The feelings of being less than, gone! The need to play games in order to feel in control, gone! The truth that there is something greater than what can be seen with the naked eye, something that awaits your permission to let it work on your behalf: permission granted! For me, my *greater-than-me* moment, my go-to for before, during, and after I've entered the ring of fire has been

John 3:16: "For God so loved the world that He gave His only begotten Son, that whoever believes in Him should not perish but have everlasting life." For reasons that remain somewhat mysterious to me, that passage holds a truth both magical and real. *Bible!*

And the Soul Felt Its Worth

Growing up in South Austin had begun to feel so dangerous, I knew that if I were going to make it to that far-off place of untold freedoms that all little Black girls dream of called *grown-ass*, I'd have to learn to untether myself from my situation, my people (for better or worse), my favorite neighbors, Sunday school, digging for gold in my backyard, collecting soda bottles in a pillowcase and redeeming them at the corner 7-Eleven in exchange for Little Debbie cakes. One of the advantages of my childhood hyperawareness was my ability to pay close attention to what was being said and *how* it was said. Facial expressions conveyed crucial information; frowns, glares, half smiles, pinched brows, side-eyes, sly eyes, and rolling eyes all had their own meanings, depending on the situation. I became adept at recognizing other people's energy: someone happy to see me coming usually had a wide smile, which invited my smile, both smiles relaxing into comforting exchanges that slowly melted into common connection. Headshaking, arms akimbo, tongue thrust into the side of a cheek, clear signals that patience was nowhere to be found. A clenched-jawed "yes" indicated agreement was given but wasn't clean or sincere, and if it also had the power to somehow suck all the air out of the room, a storm to be reckoned with was sure to follow.

At school and church I was reminded, frequently, that I was

pretty and smart and would one day grow up to be someone special, even "remarkable." On the other hand, at home, the moment I walked through the door, the tension was nearly too thick to breathe, let alone navigate. At home I felt invisible until the next time I was used to busk for shoes and food. It was moving between those two environments, church and school, that made it abundantly clear that I was more dissimilar to the people I lived with than akin.

As an adult, over the years, many of the people I've worked with have told me how they too have felt like imposters in their own homes. Many reported it was as if they'd been plopped down into the wrong family. They had wondered whether or not there were adoption stories they had yet to be told because it was clear to their hearts they did not belong to their families of origin. In my case, it was true. I did not belong to the people I originally lived with. This became a fact I was unable to ignore because of the way I was treated, and it was something I was not willing to accept. And although I'd failed to reconnect with my biological mother, I would later go on to become a foster child and eventually be adopted as an adult.

Pause to Consider

- Have you ever felt as if you didn't belong to your family of origin?
- What about your colleagues or friends? Have you ever felt like an outsider among some of your supposedly "deepest" connections?
- Have you felt alienated or disconnected from yourself?

Once I decided I'd had enough of the excessive and painful alienation I felt whenever I was home, my mind was made up. Believe me when I say I did not overthink this. I was full of bounce-back and empathy and was ever willing to accept responsibility for my actions. And because I was desperate to be loyal to someone and also to feel the lightness of joy that I was sometimes able to touch on, I gave myself a directive: the next time my abusers struck (literally) would be their last, as I wrote about earlier in the book. I did not mince my words or allow fear to have a moment of my time. I now recognize that I made my first covenant with my higher self, or spirit, when I was eleven. Even then I knew with uncompromising certainty that no one was going to just magically appear and stop the abuse and save me.

And I knew with the same certainty: I was all I had. I gave myself permission to *come through for myself.* That day I stepped into something different. It wasn't just a vow I'd made, or a pact, as I'd called it back then. That day, as I look back on it, was the day my sweet girl, Little Red, stepped into that power of faith and belief that rendered all the lesser beliefs — of not being wanted, good enough, worthy enough, or loved — insignificant. That day, my inner child became aware of her truth, that God did so love her that he'd given his only son for her survival, that she would be safe to step out on pure faith. Her belief in God's word made it possible for His promise to deliver in the moment. I am reminded of my favorite line from "O Holy Night," which also happens to be my favorite Christmas carol, "and the soul felt its worth." That right there is what happened the day I decided to believe in the power of Love's word. That day, Spirit moved in me, through me, as me. That day, my soul felt its worth and as a result inspirited me to take leave of my abusers. That decision more than likely saved my life.

Pause to Consider

- What does it mean to be for yourself?
- How has your spirit been on your side?
- What does "the soul felt its worth" mean to you?
- Have there been times when you haven't been for yourself?
- In those times when you weren't down for you, who or what were you turning your attention to?
- What have you felt called to turn away from in your best interests?

Take a moment to consider the questions I've posed. Perhaps you are experiencing questions of your own. Pay close attention to whatever is happening for you in the moment. Turn your attention to the places that might frighten you, especially if you have a herstory of a particularly complex upbringing (violence, abuse, neglect, shame).

Triumph of the Spirit

Let's fast-forward a bit into my adult story. During the time when I lost what most might consider everything as a result of my breakup with Emma Mae, I lived in Marina del Rey for several years with a friend before moving back to the Bay Area and starting my undergraduate completion work, which of course paved the path for grad school, when I'd turn right back around and move to Riverside (it's humbling to see how foster care lived in me as an adult, the moving here and there). I resided two blocks from the beach, and I walked a big part of the Strand every day. It was on one of those walks that the Universe gifted me something in the most unexpected way. I'd heard a lot about the Agape Spiritual Center and its extraordinary orator, Michael Beckwith. I'd listened to him in the film *The Secret* and made a vow to visit the center first chance I had. By then I was emotionally, physically, psychically, and spiritually spent. Literally tapped out.

It was on one of my walks when I found myself leaning against a concrete post looking up at the belly of an airplane flying overhead, wondering where the passengers were going. As I turned to head home, I saw a postcard-size advertisement for an event at Agape Center on the walkway. "Cute meets" can happen in many contexts, I suppose.

Off I went to a Wednesday service, and then both Sunday services, until attending Agape Spiritual Center became my new norm. I was not one to attend any particular services with devout regularity. I am absolutely cult averse, and anything that feels too mired in religiosity always gives me cause to check in with my common sense in terms of what's being asked of me in order to "belong." But with Agape, I wasn't having to question any red flags because there were none. The way Michael Beckwith spoke touched me in such a way that I returned again and again, eventually becoming a member. Often, he had conversations with guest speakers like Alanis Morissette and was featured alongside other luminaries considered at the top of their game: Marianne Williamson, Wayne Dyer, Gregg Braden, and Caroline Myss, all people whose books I've read and whose workshops I'd participated in.

It was no easy thing to lose all the personas that made up my identity — salon owner, hairstylist, cultural organizer, first Black business owner on an exclusive street in a much-coveted area, someone able to afford my child's boarding school, and a partner — not to mention my extended family, my love life,

my sex life, my home, my assets, the insurance waiver protecting my hands, which I needed to maintain my business, and,
most important, my self-respect. This of course all goes back to
dignity. And that is exactly what I chose to fight for, to reclaim,
my right to recover from a soul-crushing experience. One of
the most challenging realities when taking on the responsibility of raising yourself is that there is no one to fall back on, as
I've mentioned before and cannot seem to stress enough. And
when I say no one, I don't mean that as a metaphor or as an
exaggeration. I'm not rounding the corners of truth in order
to enhance your reading pleasure. When I say that I, like so
many who have been emancipated from the foster-care industrial complex, had no one to lean on, I mean it. There. Was. No.
One. However, as Spirit would have it, I now see that was the
perfect place for me to be. The simple fact that I was able to say
there was no one set the stage for the work I needed to do to
become the someone I needed to be for myself and the work I
would soon enough pursue.

Each day on awakening, I read books that over time began
to remind me of who I was. I attended the Agape Center as
much as possible, and I drank from the chalice of a truth that
began to revive my body, mind, and spirit. I learned to pray by
using spiritual mind treatments. With a spiritual mind treatment, also known as affirmative prayer or scientific prayer,
we arrive at the realization that there is one infinite, universal Presence in the Universe that permeates everything; and
that because this Presence is everywhere, It is within us as well.
Every day that I affirmed my right to be alive, to be a child of
all that is Good and worthy, I'd gain a bit more hope. I listened
to music. The kind that revives the soul when nothing else will
do and a certain kind of resuscitation is needed. I listened to

Yolanda Adams, Sounds of Blackness, Kirk Franklin, the Clark Sisters, Esther Nichols, and Tori Kelly. I read books by Iyanla Vanzant and other New Thought writings.

I encouraged myself to move within the emptiness until it began to fill with what was real and true about me, until once again I was able to feel my own life force moving through me, in me, and as me, until once more my soul felt its worth. It's so easy to get caught up in the game of life, in believing that all its accumulated accoutrements define the entirety of who we are. When I lost it all, $1.8 million worth of assets (at that time), it felt as though the world had swallowed me whole. But the truth is, having to lose that other world, that outer layer, the one composed mostly of material assets, is what I believe placed me in the best possible position to find my one true life, that which never depreciates but only appreciates with my recognition and honoring.

And not so unlike what Jesus's resurrection stands for, new and everlasting life in the Spirit, I too believed my spirit back to the truth of who I am. In other words, I chose to give my essence a chance to triumph by believing it would, to believe that Spirit is the source of everlasting life. Thank you, Rev. Dr. Michael Beckwith, for speaking from the truth of your highest good, which invited me to rediscover my own.

As an adult, when referring to the number of the material successes I've experienced, I've had people chalk it up to the "triumph of the spirit." I've never quite understood what that was until one night in my Spiritual Roots class when I was presented with a question based on a quote pulled from Ralph Waldo Emerson's essay "Spiritual Laws." The assignment was to fill out a questionnaire pertaining to the domains of my life: family, work, spouse/partner, friends, and community.

The main question was, *What do you uniquely bring to life?* I answered, *I bring the power of persevering faith to life.* At first what I had written felt somehow flat, as if I was performing the question instead of answering it from a place of wholeness; it felt intellectually rather than emotionally true. But as I continued to answer the remaining questions, I began to see a pattern of how I show up, a blueprint of sorts.

I not only saw but felt the truth of who I am: this spirit who has believed in the power of perseverance, someone who as a child learned to trust her intuition when there was not a soul to be found for her to place her trust in, a spirit who has spent her entire life working overtime to have a human experience on her own terms: beyond skin color, race, socioeconomics, opinions, prognostications of her certain failure, beyond her learned self-abandonment and self-destructive behaviors. Phew, after forty-plus years of searching, I believe I have gained an understanding of what my spirit has been up to my entire life. It has been holding me in faith, allowing all lesser beliefs to give way to triumph and joy. *My life is a unique expression of Spirit.* And so it is!

Bootstrapping Takeaways

- Have faith on your terms.
- Expand your power of belief.
- Study your understanding of what it means to be spiritual.
- Be for yourself.
- Trust your spirit to triumph.
- Believe in yourself.
- Develop your intuition.

We Are the Miracle

From the moment when I began writing my first book, about growing up in foster care, and the follow-up book (my graduate thesis) detailing my adult adoption by the beloved counselor I met while living in a children's shelter, I knew that a film version *had* to happen. I felt this truth deeply. I was disappointed at not having stories like mine represented in mainstream media and uninterested in waiting for someone else to come along and legitimize not only my experience but that of the disproportionate numbers of Black children marooned in the foster-care industrial complex.

No one, and I mean no one, was running to the screen with the story of a Black orphaned girl embarking on a (s)hero's journey and coming into her lived experiences on her own terms. That is, until I decided to follow my instincts, which pointed to the fact that the only way to change the system was to confront it with a narrative counter to the current one of limited to zero visibility for the demographic I spent most of my adult life advocating for and representing. I pursued the optioning of the film of the first book, and the story of my reunification with my counselor and her subsequent adoption of me. And later, and in the course of losing everything, completing the two degrees, building a speaking/coaching business, and training and certifying to become a Hoffman Process teacher, I managed to hold fast to the deep desire to bring my story to the small screen, also known as television. In 2018 I sold the life rights and the film went into production. More details to come in a later strategy.

My hope was that if I could get this film made, people from all walks of life and faiths would have a chance to experience the power of love and how Spirit triumphs in the lives of those who dare to believe. As faith would have it, late one night I clicked my way upon a series that premiered on OWN called *Greenleaf*, produced by Oprah Winfrey. Only a few moments in, and I knew I'd found the perfect actor to play the Gwen Ford character in the Lifetime biopic about my life. For those of you who have seen *I Am Somebody's Child: The Regina Louise Story*, you know exactly who Gwen Ford is. (And if you haven't seen it, she was a social worker at the children's shelter where I stayed for some time as a child.) Gwen is no joke. She's not having any of it. In order to play Gwen Ford, one needed to understand the importance of respecting and holding on to not just a sense of Blackness but also a commitment to fight for what it means to be all in with being Black.

The fact that Kim Hawthorne's television character in *Greenleaf* embodied the nuanced qualities of a woman from thirty years ago was nothing short of a miracle, and there just aren't enough awards to bestow upon her talents. All I can say is that Spirit's fingerprints were all over what happened next. I bolted upright in bed, pressed the rewind button, and began my character study of Mrs. Kerissa Greenleaf. Have you ever had a feeling that arrived in full technicolor and like a peacock spread itself wide all up in your gut? That's what this was. I *knew* that our film needed the depth of Kim Hawthorne's acting skills in order for us to have the perfect trifecta: the protagonist, the dynamic character, and the antagonist! Just from watching Kim on screen I could detect her genius ability not only to play the antagonist but to become the essence of that character.

I was like, "Wait a friggin' minute. That, that, is Gwen Ford." I jumped out of that bed as if ready to go fisticuffs with somebody. "Gwen, what the hell? How'd you get into my television screen and all up in my bedroom as if we were ever friends?" Oh, I was on a roll. "Gwen, how did you find me?" *There is no one else to play that role*, my spirit said.

The next morning, I texted Howard, the film's executive producer: *Kim Hawthorne. Greenleaf. Must have her. No one else. She is actually Gwen Ford.*

I was not surprised when later I heard that Kim had snagged the role. Several times while on set I had to leave because the similarity between the two women was more than I could handle. The voice, the tone, the straight-up-with-no-chaser sensibilities. The gives-no-f**ks attitude. The short-cropped 'fro. It was too much for me, and yet perfect for the film. Following Kim on Instagram gave me more insight into her true character, the fierce Black woman and actor who lives her day-to-day values as a Christian woman walking her talk. I caught up with her just a few days after the season finale of *Greenleaf*. I wanted to know what was true for her regarding her life and her relationship to God.

I get up some days, and the first thing I ask God is, "How would you use me today?" Because there is no point in my even existing if I am not going to be an instrument. Yesterday my friend said to me, "Kim, your heart is pure, you do for people, and God is always going to honor that."

I knew I wanted to act when I was eight years old. I was at school, in the second grade, and a performance troupe came to the school. As I sat in the auditorium watching those people perform, something in me said, *This is what I want to do*. There was never any doubt or second-guessing. I was laser-focused from the age of eight.

Later I went to college on a partial scholarship to study classical music because my most natural talent was singing. But what I really wanted was to act. My mother was strategic. She said, "You know you can sing. Get the scholarship for singing, then once you are in there, you can move over to acting." So that is what I did, and I became an actor.

And every time the acting life became tough and I wanted to quit, I would think of Oprah and say to myself, Oprah has gone through so much, a lot of what I have gone through too, and she's never stopped. So if Oprah can do it, so can you. This is where God entered the picture. We had just completed our first season of *Greenleaf* and were having dinner together. Oprah was there, and as we were wrapping up she said, "I'd like for you all to go around the table and share what you've gotten out of the first season. How has *Greenleaf* changed your life?" When they got to me, I said, "*Greenleaf* has given me a testimony." "What do you mean?" Oprah asked. I said, "It is a very lonely life to be an artist sometimes — and we have our moments when we just want to give up. But there is always something that makes us keep going. For me to be able to sit here at this table thirty years into a dream come true and to be able to look at the person who got me through all those times I wanted to quit but didn't, it's just a miracle. And to be able to tell you to your face that you are the reason I am on your show, well, *Greenleaf* has given me a testimony."

Oprah broke down and started crying. We were all crying. I said, "To be here, to be able to say that to your face, Miss Winfrey, ain't nothing but God." My being able to tell Oprah, "Thank you for being who you are so I could be on your show" is a miracle. People think miracles have to be like, your blindness is healed or something. But miracles happen all the time. I have on my Instagram page, this came to me in Spirit, "Stop asking God for a miracle. We are a miracle. What more proof do you need than us existing here like this? We are the miracle."

If you were to take a moment and consider the beliefs held and the actions taken by both Angela and Kim in their journeys toward the fulfillment of their dreams, you might quickly

recognize how each harnessed the qualities of what they believed to be true about themselves and the world. Each had an
experience of observing her own future in the presence of other
actors living their truths. Each allowed her spirit to guide her, to
listen as the still, small voice inside said, "I want to do that."

We've all heard the axiom "Spirit moves in mysterious ways,"
and this truth is borne out by the fact that both Kim and Angela
were afforded the opportunities to live their dreams. For Angela,
it was to play the girl she needed to see as a young Black girl
growing up in a multiethnic experience, lacking role models to
encourage her yet heeding the inner call not to give up. And Kim
had the chance to say thank you to the one person who encouraged her to keep going when giving up was but a yes away.

Bootstrapping Takeaways

- Listen to your spirit.
- Tune in to how your spirit communicates with you.
- Consider how you might pay the best of your hopes
  forward.
- Cultivate a relationship with your faith.
- Take a risk, a leap of faith.
- Believe in yourself.
- Don't give up.
- Have a contingency plan that supports you in not giv-
  ing up.

Mirror Work

Grab whatever writing tools you prefer, and spend some quality time with your spiritual self. After reading about what Spirit

and God meant for me and for Kim, how do you feel inside? How do you interact with your soul? What language feels true for you? How might you express having a relationship with God? Go easy, go tenderly, paying attention to what you're feeling in the moment. Be sure to give yourself whatever you need: compassion, generosity. What tools can you reach for from your unconditional-love toolbox? How will you use the tool to pour kindness into yourself?

Be certain to: Close your writing down with a moment of silence. Be sure to thank yourself for the time you've spent loving yourself.

Kick-Ass Strategy #10

Engage in an Exercise in Courage

You wanna fly,
you've got to give up the shit that weighs you down.
— Toni Morrison, *Song of Solomon*

You've done a great job so far, exploring one strategy after the other, burrowing in, remaining willing to wrestle with your perceptions, to look a little closer. I hope you've enjoyed engaging in the exercises, feeling better acquainted with yourself. If this form of self-exploration is a new endeavor, good for you; it is no small feat to learn to accept oneself unconditionally. And if you are a personal-growth veteran, may this foray into the mysteries of you be a loving reminder of the glorious pearls of wisdom held in the repositories of your inner world.

Now I'd like you to bring it down a notch or two by becoming aware of your breath. That's it, place your attention on your breathing, and allow it to support you in dropping down into your body. Just the suggestion of trusting the breath to settle us has a way of preparing the body to shift gears, to slow down. Become more present. I too have dropped down and into my body. I am with you. You are with me. Although we are in separate spaces, we are meeting right here, on the page, at this moment. Together, let's take a deep breath, then exhale. Take another deep breath, and as you exhale, settle down even more in your chair, on the floor, or wherever you feel most comfortable. Namaste.

Let Yourself Be Seen

One of the bravest acts I believe any of us humans can engage in is to permit another person to see us. No masks, no defending, no need to judge, no need to hide. When we can meet ourselves in our full humanity, our guards fall to the wayside, and there we find ourselves in the face of real intimacy. This act of letting ourselves be seen isn't cursory or hurried. It isn't just an occurrence during which nothing much happens between the seer and the seen. Instead, what exists is an opportunity for self-revelation. What is it to behold our own assets through another's eyes, through their natural ability to hold compassionate space?

Consenting to have another create a container for us, in which we feel safe letting them glimpse our nuances, feel the heat of the fears that keep us awake at night, sense the weight of our secret desires awaiting to blossom from our heart, is indeed a sacred act. Not only is it courageous to trust another with our confidences, but doing so points to our willingness to believe in ourselves, our true selves, that deep essence that rests beyond our surface. What does it mean for you to be seen?

In being with other humans as either teacher or coach, I am consistently asked to participate in ways both sacred and intimate. It's taken years to learn how to accept the responsibility of holding space for another. There is an art to treading ever so tenderly through the experiences and beliefs, the joys and mysteries, and the hurts of others' lives. There is very little I would exchange for the work I've committed my life to.

In being seen for who we are, sans the masks we hide behind, lies an opportunity for appreciation, acknowledgment, validation. In being seen, the disremembered parts of us become accounted for, the unaccounted-for become beneficiaries of the reckoning we are brave enough to undertake. In a culture obsessed with labels and socially constructed identifiers such as race, class, socioeconomic status, gender, and religious affiliation, it is no wonder we so often turn away from our own audacity that might otherwise be the key we need to open the door of our own healing.

Safekeeping

Over time, I have learned the value in seeing myself and in allowing others to see me as well. Some people find value in their invisibility, since it can serve as a false harbor of safety. I'm no one to pass judgment on anyone's choice. Oh, sure, I've felt like a complete fraud at times. Because you see, in my world, I was encouraged to believe that I was never going to be Black enough, American enough, or just *enough* to measure up. And in case that didn't feel low enough, I've had moments when I've been encouraged to consider that perhaps I wasn't worthy enough to grab hold of the little bit of bootstrap I'd learned to raise myself up by. And just for the record: I want you all to know that I have had enough! How about you?

To be seen is to become acquainted with what lies within you, then to welcome those with whom you feel safest to join in on the magnificence of your being. One of the most exciting invitations I've ever received to meet myself beyond what I knew to be true about me happened while I was attending graduate school. Although I was nearly twenty-five years older than the majority of the students, I rarely shied away from opportunities. Therefore, when industry professionals from production companies such as Warner Bros., Sony Pictures Entertainment, and Disney came to interview for internships, I was beyond excited to apply. To be on the safe side — if there is such a thing in the entertainment business — I all but interrogated the panel on ageism, gender biases, and whether or not equal opportunity was real or nothing more than company jargon. After the guffaws, I was encouraged to apply and assured that age and gender would not play a role in the application process.

I asked my screenwriting professor for a professional recommendation. His curriculum vitae boasted Harvard and Oxford, and he'd worked within the industry penning films for the likes of Steven Seagal. Say no more. It was a fun distraction to crush on Seagal vicariously through Robin. The day I received the recommendation letter was the day I fell in love with the possibility of myself as different from the narrative I'd loosely held about feeling like the oldest graduate student ever to walk the face of the planet. When I opened Robin's email and read the letter he'd written, I could hardly believe my eyes.

Sure, I'd had quite a bit of success before graduate school, you all know that by now, but nothing quite prepared me for Robin's experience of me. When I got to the end of his letter, I sat and cried like a baby. Yep, just like I had that day in front of Target. I was overwhelmed with the joy of hearing from someone who had seen the way I worked from the inside out. He spoke with conviction. He showed me things I didn't know about myself but that I was clearly ready and able to accept. At the time I kept my distance from men, except my son. Though I did have a couple of friends who were male identified and mostly "friends of Dorothy" with whom I felt safe. I saw Robin as a "man's man" kind of man, a martial arts, ass-kicking, mince-no-words fellow who protected the people he loved, women in particular. Yet I was so affected by the recommendation letter that I called a friend and read it to her over the phone. She also wept. Later, she and I both held a printed copy of the letter to our hearts. My friend carried my letter close to her body for the rest of the week. I carried mine around for the remainder of the quarter. Between Alec and Robin, I was beginning to gain traction in granting myself permission to accept that I am an artist.

And although it came to pass that the age difference between me and the twenty-year-old guy who'd be bossing me around during that internship wasn't going to fly (everyone was concerned with that except me), I walked through all six interviews with my head up. Someone had seen me and my talents, believed in me when I least expected it. The result is that I chose to once more release the lesser ways in which I saw myself. The fact that I was willing to let go and level up opened doors of opportunity I hadn't yet considered — a deeper level of self-acceptance. Though I may have been too old for Warner Bros., I realized that my depth of experience would serve me in coaching and supporting others to rise up to meet the best their lives had to offer.

Find Your Problem and Solve It!

Let's say you believed you had a take-to-market product, one that you, along with your two sisters, had quit your day jobs to create. You'd tested the product's viability among friends and test subjects until eventually you were ready to make a prototype and seek funding in order to scale said product into an actual business. And then comes an opportunity that is every entrepreneur's dream come true: the invitation to appear on *Shark Tank*. And there you are offered $30 million by Mark Cuban himself to flat-out buy your company. What would you do? Would you have the confidence to say yes, or would you boss all the way up and have the radical, off-the-chain, bootstrapping, kick-ass courage-on-steroids chops to say no? Unapologetically. Well, that's exactly what sisters Dawoon, Arum, and Soo Kang did. They kindly refused the offer and continued on their own to develop their product, Coffee Meets Bagel, a social networking and dating service based in San Francisco. I had the opportunity to interview Dawoon, and this is what she had to say:

Being an entrepreneur was always on my mind because my parents are entrepreneurs, especially my dad. He started his business out of high school with his brother. The three of us, my sisters and I, saw how he gave his all to his scrap-metal business. Anyone could sense how proud my father was, and how in love he was with his business. I think that always inspired us. At some point later on in our lives we thought, "Maybe we can do something that we feel really passionate about." That thought was in the back of our minds for a long time, though we had kind of put it aside to go the more traditional route.

All three of us attended good colleges and went on to get jobs at big companies. I got an MBA and just plugged along. After a couple of years of working, we decided it was a good time to do what we had talked about when we were younger. We wanted to create something to be as proud of as our dad was of his work.

In 2012 we started looking for an idea to work on. We gave

ourselves a year to figure it out, and then we started talking regularly about the different industries we could potentially get into. There were a lot! We wanted to ensure that our product would make a difference in people's lives. The subject of dating kept coming up. We were all in our late twenties and were dating, and our friends were dating, and we were all having difficulty with the offerings.

We became interested in the market dynamics, the sizing of the industries, and the competitive landscape of the dating world. We noticed that a lot of women felt very unsafe about using dating services and were frustrated at the lack of quality candidates they encountered and sick of wasting time meeting the wrong people. And as women ourselves we had a specific set of ideas of who we wanted to meet, and it was really difficult sorting through all of the random people we found on all the dating sites. We got tired of wasting our time on that, so we just gave up. And that's when we decided to create a brand that focused on quality and safety.

Today we have a few million users globally. It is amazing. It is such a gratifying feeling to know that we are impacting the lives of millions of singles. I feel a lot of responsibility for our daters, who trusted us with their time and their money to find them a partner they can create a beautiful relationship with. If I were talking to a group of women entrepreneurs, I would encourage them to believe in the possibility of going for it. What immediately comes to my mind is: find your problem. Your problem, not somebody else's, not what the world says is a problem. Recycling scrap metal was my dad's unique problem. I know there is a possibility for solving problems that no one else can see. If you can imagine a different possibility, then you are probably being called to solve the problem.

It goes without saying that to be seen fully on one's own terms is about as courageous an act as we can take in the process of upping the ante of our dreams. To keep following the yes that radiates within, that uncertain uncertainty that pushes us so far over what we thought was our growth edge, until we redefine the very notion of possibility.

Bootstrapping Takeaways

- Commit to self-exploration.
- Drop into your body and become present.
- Remove the mask(s).
- Trust yourself enough to let yourself be seen.
- Even if it feels scary, do it.
- Find your problem and solve it.
- Say no when you want to.
- Allow someone to see you.

All in One Place

One night at the California Institute of Integral Studies, the school where I would receive my undergraduate degree in 2012, I had the opportunity to interview the poet Brynn Saito, a writer in residence at that time. I asked Brynn what she loved most about the school, and her answer has stayed with me ever since. "When I walked through the door at CIIS, I felt as if *all of me* was welcome. Therefore, I knew it was the place for me." In my opinion, one of the critical components of being seen, and experiencing a place as a space to show up in, is psychological safety.

The more we open ourselves up in safe experiences, the more muscles we build for ensuring our psychological safety. We learn to have a keener sense of when, where, and how it is appropriate for us to bring all of who we are to the table. And then there are those times when we must use discernment to know how much of ourselves to expose and also whether doing so is even necessary in the situation.

Pause to Consider

- When was the first time you felt that all of you was welcome someplace? When was the last?
- What would it take for you to feel safe enough to allow someone to see you?
- What does discernment mean to you?
- How will you strengthen your psychological safety muscle?
- What would the person who knows you best say about you?
- Who do you trust to write you a letter of recommendation?

At some point, when you are feeling comfortable and willing to do so, identify someone you trust to write a recommendation letter on your behalf, for no other reason than to see, perhaps, how someone else sees you. You might have a bit of fun and have the letter writer speak to an endeavor you want to pursue in the future, as in a dream you've been wanting to work toward but could use a bit of encouragement. Or you can identify a few qualities you'd like to explore, like confidence, tenacity, and curiosity, and you can ask for the letter writer to speak to the areas you are already skilled in or new qualities you'd like to foster. Make sure they address and send the letter to you. Email works just as well.

Once you receive the letter, approach reading it with a sense of curiosity. Allow yourself to be pleasantly surprised by what is written. Hold space, no matter if the contents blow your mind or leave you scratching your head as to who the letter is referring to. If it suits you, carry the letter around with you for as long as you wish.

Later on, a week or so down the road, highlight some of the qualities you agree with, and try them on. Take a few minutes, an hour, half a day, and embody the qualities so that you feel their power. And when you've had your fill of whirling in the goodness of you, take your letter and dress it up in the frame of your choice. Then hang it someplace where you'll be heartened to glance at your likeness in prose form.

In one way or another, over the years since receiving the letter Robin wrote and reliving his words, "Regina is the one you want . . . ," I've worked to move into the truth of what Robin saw in me. Again and again, I've referred back to it as a reminder of how much more of myself I get to grow into. Accepting new and different ways in which to see and experience oneself takes time, I remind myself, all in due time.

Emptying the Garbage

In order to move past challenges and outmoded ways of thinking, we need to identify the old and work to transform it into something new. We need to move past our hurts, whether they take the form of a perceived flaw or a painful loss, in order to get to the connections we seek. It is helpful to examine our thoughts about these issues so that we can mediate the feelings and move toward change. If, for example, I need to do the work of forgiving myself or someone else, I stop where I am, take a breath, and reflect on how I might have showed up in the situation. Once I recognize my part, I take what's mine, and with the rest I do what I call "emptying the garbage." Sometimes emptying the garbage may take the shape of my deciding to call someone up and take responsibility for my part in the disagreement or offense, regardless of whether or not they do the same. I'll ask myself simply if needing to be right is the outcome I'm looking for, or if aiming for connection is a better way to go. If I am invested in the integrity of the relationship, I am likely to take right action toward addressing my part of the situation. I just don't see the value in walking around with a mess of unexamined feelings simply because I'm unwilling to see someone else's humanity and to afford them the space to make a mistake.

The exercise offered below is meant to support you in checking out the stories we tell ourselves about how we should feel. I've always been a proponent of cognitive behavior therapy (CBT) modalities, and this process is based on CBT.

In the worksheet below, you are asked to take a look at a particular vulnerability that might be up for you. With an open heart and a curious mind, become willing to name your experience, the way it shows up, your automatic thoughts, and then your "talk back" response. The "Different approach" section offers you another way to frame your experiences, one that may better promote positive regard for you and others. With this practice, it is not about what another person does or doesn't do, about whether or not they take responsibility for the harm they caused, intentionally or otherwise. I have learned to rarely, if ever, wait for someone to take responsibility for how *I* should or shouldn't feel. At one point or another, regarding every person I've mentioned in this book, whenever any type of suffering has occurred, I have taken 100 percent responsibility for my part in it. And while I cannot say the same for others, frankly, it is none of my business how each person chooses to process their experiences with me. What I know to be true is that the more I can forgive myself, the less I need to hold others in contempt for how I feel. When I move from resentment to forgiveness, I release myself from the need to be anyone's victim, including my own.

Create a worksheet like the one below to support yourself in exploring your inner world. What I love about the idea of emptying the garbage is that it provides us with an opportunity to find the best practices for transforming what hurts us into something that benefits us. Let go of the toxicity that binds you! Empty the garbage holding you to a narrative that no longer serves you. Step into courage on your own terms. In joy!

CBT Worksheet

Cause of vulnerability	How it shows up	Automatic thoughts	Talk back!	Different approach
Adoption	Sad around kids and families	My mother didn't want me.	I don't know why my mother didn't keep me. I'm assuming the worst.	Try not to make up sad stories with no basis in reality. Assume the best.
Adoption	Uncomfortable at baby showers	It is unfair that I didn't have a normal life.	My life was pretty satisfying. I want the best for my friend.	Life is not fair, and "normal" is not reality. I may be a lot better off.

Kick-Ass Strategy #11

Be with the Wild,
Wild Mess of You

People call me Stagecoach Mary. I am bold.
I smoke a big black cigar. I drink whiskey. I carry a pistol.
I love adventure. I am independent. Nobody tells me what to do.
Nobody tells me where to go. You got a problem with that?

— Mary Fields, aka Stagecoach Mary

OMG. If I didn't know any better, and were it not for the fact that my biological mother and Stagecoach Mary are 180 years apart in age, I would swear to the ethers that they are the same person. Talk about keeping it real. Talk about pluck. I digress. I've come to consider that life is more complex and nuanced than I could ever hope to portray with words such as *miraculous, spectacular, sacred, almighty, brilliant,* and *beautiful,* a mystery that at times feels like an awe-inspiring cosmic road trip that leaves us at a loss for words that fully capture just how majestic it *really* is, and: life is also messy. I'm talking hot-mess messy, and for those of you who prefer your messiness in high style, let's just call it *haute mess.* I'm suggesting that at times life can be neck-twirling, deep-sighing, deer-in-the-headlights, to-the-curb, I-ain't-got-time-for-this-mess messy.

I know you know what I'm talking about. We're human. We've all been there, entangled in our messes, in one way or another. And when it comes to doing that thing we do when we try to convince ourselves how *that person*, how *anybody*, as long as it isn't us, is the one responsible for how we feel, we further strand ourselves in the messes we make. In many cases we unintentionally project the qualities we aren't able or willing to accept about ourselves onto others. And remember a few strategies ago, when I introduced Mordechai and what he said about introjections? Well, acting in a particular way to satisfy someone else's expectations of us as a means of getting our needs met as adults can surely put us front and center in a big ol' mess.

And as we come up against the fear, or the words that reveal our deepest shame(s), it's as if we're suddenly juggling volcanic rocks and want nothing to do with them, and rightly so. But instead of slowing down long enough to examine the *what* of the matter, we react. And in protest against owning what's ours and ours alone, we abandon ourselves by projecting our unexamined experiences onto anyone close enough for our mess to stick to. It's like taking what terrifies us about ourselves, loading it into a slingshot, pulling back hard, and letting it rip. And rip it does, right down the middle of our intimacy. Then, boo-yah! What we say we value most, our connection to self and the ones who matter to us, bears the brunt of our hurt, our pain. I'm sure you've heard the adage "Hurting people hurt people."

I've heard it said that love is the mortar holding relationships together. I say that messiness is what holds our drama together, and in ways that incite detachment, loneliness, self-misunderstanding, and self-abandonment. It is true that "it's in relationships where we get wounded," and the upshot is also true, that "it's in relationships where we are healed"; these wise words are compliments of my first therapist, Lainey. This chapter's strategy is all about recognizing that there are other options besides persevering in our suffering. Being in a loving relationship can support us in transforming our hurts and pains, as opposed to living in the toxic wasteland of our wounds and blaming our loved ones for our own unwillingness to become vulnerable to our deepest unmet needs.

How to Be with Your Wild, Wild Mess

As a young person, I loved Westerns, *The Wild Wild West* in particular. The wildness of it is what turned me on, the freedom the cowboys had, how the bandits roamed the frontier free as a pack of prairie dogs until somebody would sic the town's sheriff on them and everybody galvanized their resources toward some sort of reckoning. Even the townspeople did their part to get out of the way and not interfere with the inevitable and ultimate showdown between the law and the lawless. No matter how chaotic, outlandish, or off the range the events were, the posse of good always triumphed, always transformed a piece of that wilderness frontier into a habitable place of restored order. In some ways I felt as though the characters reflected aspects of my inner wildness. Sometimes I was a wildling, unable to manage my reactions, and as a result I'd cause unnecessary consequences to rain down on me. For instance, I'd run away so frequently as a young person that eventually my wildness transformed me into an outlaw. I'd find scrappy ways to stay out of the reach of the law, hiding in hollowed-out tree trunks

and abandoned aqueducts and living off food from neighbor-
hood garbage cans. And when I'd get caught, I'd get locked up
and my freedom was taken from me.

It wasn't until I was an adult, in my late thirties to early forties, that I decided it was time to confront the mess I'd made of
my life, to hand over the outlaw that ruled my life to the frontier sheriff (my therapist). I was tired of coldcocking people,
the ones I wished could love me, for leaving me, as well as the
ones who tried to love me and begged to stay.

I did not want to continue hurting myself and others simply because I could get away with saying that "I didn't know
any better." I believed that I could learn healthier ways to engage with myself and others. I struggled with the idea that simply because I'd been mistreated, I somehow had permission to
do the same to another. I did not believe that even though life
had felt like a never-ending hazing experience from hell, that
just because I'd survived, I'd earned the privilege to bypass such
virtues as forgiveness and kindness and act out the same tragic
behaviors on the unsuspecting humans who just happened to
cross my path.

To allow myself to get off the hook by dodging, shirking,
or flat-out refusing to assume responsibility for my actions felt
not only unconscionable but also far too reminiscent of my
childhood. After all, out of the ten possible answers to determine what my adverse childhood experiences, or ACE, score
was, with 10 being the highest, I'd scored a 9. My prognosis of
having anything that resembled a *normal* life was bleaker than
bleak. This was my opportunity to flip the script, to disrupt
my legacy of generational trauma. If I couldn't entirely erase
trauma's fingerprint from my ancestral line, at the very least I'd
wash my own hands of paying such violence forward against

myself, my child(ren), my children's children, and those I'd be fortunate enough to build a sense of lasting love with. I've wanted, no, I've needed, to learn to have life on my own terms. Living as anyone's statistic seemed a soul-crushing, culturally ascribed inheritance I just wasn't interested in.

Managing your messiness can offer you alternatives to the one-way, dead-end ride of toxic exchanges had at the expense of yourself and others. The more you can respond to your own suffering instead of defaulting to your wounds, the more prepared you are to transform the situation. Isn't it a relief to know that there is a way through to the other side of our messiness? To know that there's hope and not only that, but that each of us can afford ourselves the luxury of *being* a hope?

Being a Hope

To *be a hope* is to commit to offering yourself, and then others, a chance to change and grow; you become your own version of optimism and courage, you become the DJ, the spinmaster, the one who spits beats of audacity, fortitude, and pluck. To be a hope is to stay open to connecting with what is fundamentally true about ourselves and others, that we are all worthy in our own right as human beings, that we are all *enough*. To be a hope is to not wait for someone to save you but instead to commit to living in such a way that others become inspired to save themselves. In this way being a hope becomes a legacy in and of itself. To be a hope is to rise confidently, again and again, and hack uncertainty with your powerful Lovefirmations. Let's say these together: *I am enough. I am worthy. I am a hope.* At the end of the day, aren't we all, in some way, continually moving toward the next level of our own civility, our own divinity?

Think about the possibility not only of having your needs show up in your relationship to help you get your healing on, but also of getting to be a mirror of hope for another. And please note that even if you are willing to take what shows up in your relationships and awaken to those places within you that need your unconditional love in order to heal, that does not mean it will be true for anyone else you may engage with. Each of us, as volitional beings, gets to determine the when, where, and how of coming to terms with our personal growth. Just because the timing works for you in a particular relationship, and your level of consciousness is rising, that does not always mean that your friends, family members, or partners are willing and able to meet you where you are. What matters most, once you are willing to meet yourself where you are, is that you not abandon yourself in the face of someone else's self-abandonment. Often, especially for those of us who seem to have been endowed with codependency superpowers, it's the very act of choosing yourself in the face of whatever has been your personal kryptonite that allows you to stick to your guns — like Stagecoach Mary.

Grappling

Transforming your mess into assets that will benefit you begins with a commitment to grapple with your messiness. This means you get to arrive, hands bare, heart open, and mind prepared to wrestle intimately with the qualities that no longer serve you. We've all heard the saying, "The definition of insanity is doing the same thing over and over again and expecting different results." If you meditate in lotus position with the intention of levitating six inches from the cushion within a year's time, and after a year the only thing that has raised is your blood pressure as well as your suspicion about your own mental well-being, perhaps it is time to reconsider the means you are using to meet your end goal.

Life supports us all via the law of reciprocity. We plant a seed in the earth, and the earth, given the proper conditions, gifts us with a healthy, living plant. Grappling works similarly: we take what no longer works, as in our faulty beliefs, unexamined feelings, and the lies we tell ourselves and others, and we commit to transforming their energy into a power source that fuels our agency, our permission to accept and love ourselves unconditionally.

You grapple the moment you decide to challenge your behaviors. Running from our feelings is what keeps us from our softness and provokes the inner voices telling us that we are no match for ourselves or that life owes us something and that it should be easier. I sat down with my colleague and friend Drew Horning, who is a Hoffman teacher and holds a master's in clinical social work. He also has written a book titled *Grappling: White Men's Journey from Fragile to Agile*. Drew stated that "this running or turning away from feelings and other emotions that frighten us is especially prevalent among white men. When a feeling arises, or we get the slightest indicator we are close to something that might move us, we say, 'I am out. I am done,' and we are gone." He went on to explain, "We jet because we believe we cannot handle the feeling. Half of our problems as humans, and again I'm specifically referring to men (as a therapist, teacher, and athlete, I work with a lot of men), is not the feeling itself. It is the fear of the feeling actually arriving. So we respond to our lives with, 'Oh, I might feel sad. Okay, I'm out.' Or, 'Oh, I might feel vulnerable. Okay, I'm out.'

Even the idea of the feeling coming is enough to have us alter our behavior and bolt the intrapersonal confrontation."

The counter is to grapple, to engage in a close struggle without weapons. So you replace abandoning yourself with the fundamental belief of *I am going to go toward it.* "Oh, something's uncomfortable? I am in. Oh, I am a little triggered? I am in. Oh, I am starting to armor up? I am in. Oh, I am starting to get edgy and angry because that is the one feeling I know? I'm in." Choose to become curious about what is happening in the moment. Move toward your feelings rather than away from them. Engage in the struggle. Wrestle with it, asking yourself:

- What is happening?
- What am I feeling?
- What am I thinking?
- How do I gain a degree of personal ground?

Grappling is what you bring to your relationship to sexism, to white privilege, and so on; it's something you do in respect to your own tender self. You grapple when asking the question, "What the f**k is making me feel so scared inside?" You take the thing you have armored up against and expose it, using the same power you used to armor yourself to grow into and love yourself. Instead of hiding or toughening up, we bring awareness to our internal world. Rather than dismissing things and putting them back into a paradigm that is getting smaller and smaller as the world changes, we grapple, we engage.

- Ask, "What is this?"
- Get curious.
- Allow yourself to open.

Next, ask deeper questions:

- Why do I feel this way?
- Why do I react this way?
- What is happening inside me?

Spend some time with questions like these. Journal whatever comes up for you, and consider this as a place to lean in to the learnings your inquiry may provide.

Cleaning Up My Mess

As a lifelong learner, I've always valued the results of personal-growth work. Sometimes I imagine I was born with a pickax in my hand, poised and ready to mine for what was to become, well, mine. From long-term one-on-one therapeutic relationships teaching me the importance of attunement and of not turning away from eye contact, to weekend gatherings where I learned the fundamentals of meditation practice and how to be in community with both men and women, the benefits have been tremendous. Not only have I come away from such experiences with more access to my inner world and a fleshed-out understanding of how I tick, but I've enjoyed the process of falling in love with what's true about me: that I am perfect just as I am. Life's a journey; we all know this in our own ways. And when we step fully into the work our hearts suggest we do, inch by inch, breath by breath we decide to make the amends needed to clean up the messes we've made, however unintended they may have been.

In 2015, while in graduate school, I arrived home to the Bay Area for spring break. I'd decided to attend a workshop, the mother lode of all personal-growth experiences: the Hoffman

Process. Their website clearly states that interested students consider the weeklong process when they're "serious about change." I thought myself the poster child for such a challenge: I was serious about finally shedding the limiting beliefs, traumas, and narratives that unconsciously I let define me. After receiving an incredibly generous scholarship, along with the monetary gifts I requested for my birthday, after devising a payment plan arrangement and accepting a dear friend's offer to make up the difference, I was in. It was the ultimate fifty-something birthday present.

Shortly after I arrived, one of the teachers called me by my childhood name, and before my logical mind had a chance to locate me in space and time, I was off and running. In place, that is. The mere sound of my name, used out of context, flipped my amygdala, and my fight-or-flight response kicked in. I'd never shared my nickname with anyone. *Ever.* I was ready to go all Jill Scott, like the singer by the same name, take off my jewelry, and get me some Vaseline, or baby oil or whatever it was going to take to put the person calling me by my nickname in her place. Needless to say, I calmed down, moved through my triggered state, and made a silent vow to commit to grappling my way through the seven days. Halfway in I felt caught between running down the road toward home and feeling certain that I was born to facilitate the work I was immersed in. I made another silent vow to stay the course, as well as to return one day as a teacher. The grief I'd held my entire life came out over those seven days. All the profound despair that had hidden behind designer shoes and jewels and gauche affectations began to creep out from behind the curtain where they'd sought the safety of the false self. I'd been taught to fear my inner world, taught that I was absolutely too much and that everything about me was more than anyone was willing to take on, so why should *I* take it on? I was encouraged to deny it, bury it, sex it, eat it, drink it, shop it, kill it — and me — off. Decades of living the emptiness of those false selves had taken their toll. But one thing I know for certain: they did not take my soul. I've always sensed that as long as my spirit is intact, anything is possible. I decided to grapple with the most common thread in my life: no one stayed. It was my responsibility to continue to understand the depth of this fact, to do this work to learn to stay for myself.

As if with a pile of clothes thrown into a mess on the floor, I worked piece by piece with the deeper things that terrified me and in so doing started to organize all the disorderliness I'd been living with in relationship to my mother and father and surrogates. I worked on deepening awareness of my circumstances, which led to a truer sense of forgiveness of myself and then of those who unwittingly had caused me harm. I made yet another vow, this time to give my wild, wild mess some semblance of order that I could live with more peacefully. Instead of feeling as if I were sleepwalking through my life as a grown-ass trauma victim, I stomped, cried, cursed, spit, hit, ripped, and confessed myself awake in a different kind of way, a way that supported me in moving through grief, anger, rage, and helplessness. I claimed my life as though I were rich in the type of assets that mattered most: the truth of who I *really* was and how that lived in me, through me, as me. I walked away from the Hoffman workshop more fortified and integrated. I'd created inner space by way of the peace I claimed for myself.

Manage Your Assets

When I speak of assets, what I am referring to are the highly valued qualities of being that you were born with. They live right there inside you, and over the course of your life you have had to rely on them to navigate your personal, professional, and communal relationships. The ways in which you've learned to move through your life are as particular to you as the markings on a butterfly's wings. You are uniquely you, and your assets distinguish you from others, just as your fingerprints are different from anyone else's. Here are some examples of the kind of assets I'm talking about:

- The ability to attune to your own emotions and the emotions of others
- The willingness to grapple
- The ability to be considerate toward yourself first and then others
- The ability to self-regulate and self-soothe
- The willingness to forgive
- The recognition of your own unconditional love
- The willingness to become self-aware
- The willingness to accept responsibility for your pain and loneliness

What are your assets? What do you bring to the table to sort out your messiness?

Choosing from the assets offered above, or using one you've identified on your own, write a letter to one of your assets. Ask it to share with you what it would like you to know in order to better understand it. The more understanding you have, the easier it is to advocate on your own behalf and to Boss-Hogg your messiness.

If nurtured adequately, your self-acceptance, your belief in yourself and in your talents and abilities, can activate the inherent power of your self-love. These qualities can support you in becoming emotionally successful in so many areas in your life. Financial assets allow you the mobility to explore a mixture of interests and goals such as education, recreation, travel, and creative exploration, and to have some version of the American Dream on your terms — housing, a car, the ability to use public transportation or eat at your favorite restaurants, whatever it looks like to you. Who doesn't want to live a more balanced life, to feel the benefits of peace and joy as a result of having a sense of law and order for themselves? How often do we give the managing of our emotional assets over to someone else? For those of us who identify as codependent, consider how this way of being shows up in your life and under what circumstances. What's the payoff for you to engage in such behaviors?

Bootstrapping Takeaways

- Recognize when you are projecting your unmet needs and desires onto others.
- Trust your relationships as a space to heal and thrive.
- Take responsibility for your pain and suffering.
- Become willing to grapple
- Clean up your mess.
- Commit to personal growth.

How will you begin the process of managing yourself in relationship to others? In relationship to yourself? What does it mean to take responsibility for yourself? Take some time and sit with whatever arises for you. Be mindful of how you feel, without judgment or any harshness. Return to your unconditional-love toolbox, choose a self-supportive practice, and have at it. Much love, and good luck!

Kick-Ass Strategy #12

Get off Your Back and Get on Your Side

A setback ain't nothing but a setup to come back.
— Bev Smith, 2003 BEA Warner Luncheon

I learned a long time ago the wisest thing I can do is be on my side.
— Maya Angelou

What does it look like, you may wonder, to *get off your back and on your side*? And in case you are wondering if this a sexual innuendo, the answer is no! It isn't that, or anything close to it. Some of you literal folks may suddenly feel like, *Wait, what? How in the heck can I be on my own back while I'm standing, sitting, or lying here reading? Like, that would take a Cirque du Soleil acrobatic move to make that happen.* LOL! But let's not waste another minute of time wondering. Here we go!

In 2020 day two of the shelter-in-place order found me leaning against the kitchen sink, staring out the window, favorite mug at the ready. The teapot finally whistled. I went to pour the boiling water into the cup and somehow misjudged the distance. Hot water splattered this way and that, barely missing my hand, and I dropped the cup. "How could you be so stu—" I stopped myself before that old introjection had a chance to cast its shady power over me.

No doubt, had I said the word *stupid*, I would've sent my sense of self running for cover; I might've spent the morning going down a shame spiral that would stop at nothing to convince me that I was dumb, absent-minded, careless, irresponsible. Not good enough. I took a breath, placed the teapot back into its cradle, and turned toward what I was feeling. The mere energy of the thought felt as if it had scorched my body. It was electrifying. I breathed into the sting; it was only fair to give whatever was happening inside me the time it needed to resolve itself.

Some of you may consider what almost spilled from my mouth a familiar occurrence straight out of your own life. Although I caught myself, it was not before the energy of my intent was released, triggering a fight-or-flight response. You know how we tell people, "Get off my back"? Well, it's amazing to me how I learned to get on my *own* back and insult myself for the smallest things, the tiniest mistakes. You may think my small act of insolence is no big deal. I would agree that stopping yourself from launching a self-attack is not a big thing, if it were a once-in-a-lifetime occurrence. But we all know that it isn't even close to the truth of how often we go in on ourselves in the most demeaning ways; we criticize, rip ourselves apart, treating ourselves the way we were treated as children, teens, and so on. I've seen people punch, kick, and harm themselves for mistakes best met with unconditional self-love.

It is a big deal, the fact that often we don't stop ourselves from reinforcing the belief that we've failed when we've simply made an innocent mistake or when we've done our best. But what if we did stop, as we would with a friend or loved one? What if we committed to bringing a nonjudgmental ear to our hurts, our simple mistakes? What might it be like to open our hearts to ourselves, eager to understand our hurting parts? It's so easy to hop aboard the bully train; it feels as if it's second nature for so many of us to hijack our own vulnerability. Have you ever been guilty of demeaning yourself by saying things such as these?:

You're so stupid.
Gosh, can't you do anything, right?
How could you be so __ _____ ?

If so, time to get off your back and throw a little love at yourself instead!

Love as a Gateway to You

Just so you know, I stopped typing and raised my hand as high as humanly possible. *Hells to the YAAAAAS!* I, Regina Louise, admit that I am guilty as charged and am happy to hold myself accountable. I say I'm happy because the consequences of that particular day were an anomaly in my world, an unusual occurrence, a glitch in my operating system, reminding me not only of the way I'd once treated myself but also of my own humanness. Catching myself in the act of *almost* berating my essence created an opportunity for me to segue into awareness, which slowed down the anger directed at my near mistake and gave way to my having a choice.

Choice, then, provided the optimal conditions for a better

response. I say this because although the choice is always ours, this doesn't mean that in the heat of the moment we remember. This innocuous mistake allowed me to access internal resources such as sympathy, empathy, and ultimately, self-compassion. These are the boundless qualities that set me up to receive an enormous dollop of my own unconditional love, making room for self-regulation to transpire. This is also what I believe is possible for you.

Like, whoa. That was a mouthful without a chaser, right? It can be like that sometimes. It's as though when the truth of something wants to show up and show out, there ain't no stopping it! Let's keep going.

The beautiful thing about becoming aware in that moment is that I didn't rely on old ways of being. Instead of having the familiar experience of feeling wholly estranged from myself, or worse yet, humiliated, I was able to slow everything down and move toward what I know to be true about me: that there is room to make a mistake, there is room for my kind of imperfection. I believe this is true for you as well. This knowing created a clearing for me to develop presence, to get suited up to meet my authentic needs. What I appreciate most about this incident is how I felt as though I'd caught my precious child in my arms as the danger had come barreling out of nowhere, and protected her from harm. It can be a challenge to bear witness to how self-harming behaviors live in me. Let's sit with that for a moment. Take it in. What often seems harmless may, in fact, hold the key to a more profound truth about you.

Sure, burning myself with the boiling water would not have felt great, had I succeeded, whether or not I reprimanded myself. And I imagine I might've learned the "hard way," as they say, the lesson of paying closer attention the next time.

Hard lessons have the power to help us course-correct for the next time. Hard lessons, at least the way I was taught, also held the power to shame my sense of worth right out of me — if I let them.

Pause to Consider

Were you taught, through shame, to behave the "right" way? Have you heard such messages as these?:

> *You are a terrible person.*
> *Only someone as _____ as you would have*
> *   made that mistake.*

Over time, reinforcing shame-based responses as a way to teach ourselves a lesson becomes an internalized pickax that slowly breaks apart our self-worth until we buy into the belief that there *is* something fundamentally wrong with us.

Instantaneous reactions are learned behaviors. As you can see from my example, they arrive involuntarily and remain at the ready to serve you. There is value in saying *Stop!* to someone, including yourself, when unintended harm is a potential outcome. You know as well as I that most times it's not only *what* is said but also *how* it is said that has an effect on us, whether it's said by us or by another. And isn't it a relief to know that anything learned can be unlearned or improved?

Back to the kitchen sink. Quickly, I checked in with my inner child. I asked a simple question: *Hey there, how are you?* I took the time to listen for an answer. Wanting to reestablish trust with myself, I knew an apology was in order: *I'm so sorry,*

I said. *You didn't deserve that.* I connected with the fear that showed up. *I didn't mean to frighten you. I was knocked off base for an instant.* The truth of my words resonated with me. I felt a small shift in my heart, indicating I was well on my way to making up with myself. *You mean the world to me,* I said softly.

In want of my own touch, I hooked my thumbs together, swiveled my hands into a human-hand butterfly, and laid my palms across my chest. I tapped the Lovefirmation *I love you* until the adrenaline completely decelerated and my heartbeat calmed. I recognized the ease with which I could lose my cool and say something I'd regret. I did not make arrogant promises of *never* doing that again; instead, I recommitted to the practice of moving toward myself with generosity and tender, loving care. I did so with the same unconditional way of being I'd offer my loved ones and anyone else in my life. And to you too.

Agents of Possibility

Now that I had reconnected with my feelings, the next step was to become curious. Why had I been so lightning-fast in admonishing myself for something so simple? Where had my patience gone? It wasn't as though it were the end of a chaotic day and I was riding on the fumes of *let's get this mess over and done.* I'd been awake for less than an hour and was delighted not to have to travel to work. I was excited to be home. It wasn't like me to react so quickly with the intent to cause harm to myself.

As a veteran at ducking and diving past the slings and arrows of name-calling, I knew well the zing of its aftermath. Sometime during my twenties, I'd made a vow to protect the innocence in my heart by refraining from calling myself names, being a nag, putting myself down, riding my ass, or diminishing my best efforts in any sort of way. In other words, I learned the value of getting off my back. And getting on my side is the practice I've cultivated as a result.

Believe me, I understand that what I am posing here points to a certain kind of self-mastery, but isn't that what life is all about, conquering the small things so that they don't become hidden resentments with the power to topple relationships and peace of mind? Wouldn't you prefer to move from your own truth, your own authenticity, to being a walking, talking toxic hot mess? Been there. Done that, till I didn't want to do it anymore.

Ultimately, the outcome of so many years of practice has made me especially sensitive to bullying. I did not want to be a bully, given that I was reared by so many, privately in my own home and systematically, nor was I interested in being on the receiving end of that type of venomous controlling. The child in me was not down for any of that. My practice of catching myself paid off that day, as it had many times before. Not only did this increase self-understanding, but it allowed me to give myself what I needed most: my own love. Practice makes, well, not a continuous outpouring of perfection, but it does make room for whatever we focus on to manifest into its fullest possibility.

In an earlier chapter I promised to speak a bit more about Little Red and the importance of having a relationship with your inner child. I never realized I had a childhood name until I engaged in personal-growth work. My biological mother, Mattie, called me Red when I was a little bitty thing the few times I was able to spend time with her. After a full day in the sun, my skin glowed like a new copper penny. The sun bleached my baby hairs and framed my face in red, hence the name. I remember the thrill of hearing my mama call my name from time to time. And then she disappeared. So whenever other folks used it, I hated it. It was safer for me to distance myself from that name; it made it easier to forget the good things about my mother so as not to pine for her. That is until I flipped the script as an adult and saw the value in forgiving myself and releasing the victimization that had become the stand-in for my real life. Working through the loss, and grief, through all the different stages I've discussed with you, and all that goes with holding on to such emotions revitalized the spirit of Red. It also helped me to see the good in the young mother doing the best she could with what she had, and Lord knows that poor baby didn't have much being a baby, having a baby without anyone guiding or protecting her. Keep those legs closed, ladies, until you're absolutely ready. Believe me, abstinence works!

Now I am head over heels for Little Red. I call her my inner mini-me. She's my Day One, my ride-along, my ace-boom-cool. I love how folks are all crazy about Blue Ivy, Beyoncé's daughter, and the relationship the two of them have cultivated. Modeling positive experiences and imitable character traits for Black girls remains underrepresented in the mediated spaces we occupy, yet it is remarkable to witness the strides we have made as Black people to have our truths more honestly depicted. Now we have kick-ass role models such as Marsai Martin, Storm Reid, the McClain sisters, Zendaya, and the up-and-coming Angela Fairley, and we need more young women like them to remind us of what it means to be young and gifted while also being #BlackityBlack. I think it's a fabulous necessity for us as humans — Black women, and people of color especially — to view ourselves as positive agents of possibility for other girls and women who are hustling, side-gigging, finessing, schooling, single-parenting, mom-ing, and wifey-ing their way to leading their best lives. The positive encouragement and admiration we so generously project onto celebrities and icons are full of healing energy and loaded with positivity. We can also learn to transform this practice of cultural adulation into a more balanced blend of self-acceptance and unconditional love and pour it into ourselves as well as into our families and communities. We are the ones to pay goodness and love forward unto us.

Fire in the Window

The day I almost scalded myself, as I thought about what had led up to the situation that morning, I realized it was only day two of a global trauma in the making. Thus, it was the first time someone — the governor of California — had asked me to practice the value of good citizenry by "flattening the curve" by not patronizing my local coffee shop. Observing the mandate meant I'd need to sacrifice a daily ritual that I loved more than almost anything: a Philz Coffee served as *Tesora-Ethiopian-Creamy-Light sweet.* That was a deliciousness I frankly didn't want to give up; however, I was on board with the mandate.

In my effort to make coffee at home, I became distracted, and you know the rest of the story. There was a fringe benefit in slowing down that day as well. Not only was I able to get in touch with what was going on in that instant, but more important, self-attunement led me to something I'd buried some forty-five years earlier. My making reparations with Little Red by getting off my back and on my side allowed a memory to show up. I can't recall my exact age, but I remember wanting to eat dinner. The food had sat till cold, and I wanted to have my food warmed. Everyone in my household was either busy or not around. "Do it yourself," my sister yelled from a half-asleep stupor. Although terrified at the prospect, given that I'd never lit a match before, I found a newspaper, lit the end, and turned on the gas to the eye of the burner. Rapidly, the fire overtook the paper, and all I could think to do next was turn off the gas. The flames were out of control. I threw the burning paper into the kitchen sink. Isn't it funny how memory works? I find it fascinating how objects (the kitchen sink and window) can become a metaphor for life and opportunities to heal. The curtains above the kitchen sink were plastic. They caught fire and melted against the wooden window frame.

I ran.

Thank goodness an adult smelled smoke, saw flames, and went into action. I didn't go near that sink for the remainder of the two years I lived in that house. It took decades for me to strike a match with any confidence.

When it arrived, that day some forty years later, I held the memory of that event lightly, without judgment of myself or my caretaker's reactions. It wasn't easy. I wanted to run, as I had before. I tried to justify the things that were said, the blows against my skin, the humiliation, the days I went without food as punishment. Instead, I seized the moment to acknowledge that the harsh words spoken were a reflexive reaction to the mistake I'd made. I saw the intention behind what occurred differently: had an adult not seen that fire and responded as she had, lives may have been lost. There was no comfort given me at that time, and in the face of that memory, I gave Little Red the comfort she had needed then, never mind the fact that it was so many decades later. It landed where she needed it most, in her heart. I forgave myself for that situation where I had no business assuming the role of an adult. I forgave my caretaker, and all the others I had unconsciously held blame against as well.

Establish Your Emotional Baseline

It's so exciting to know we get to do this if we choose: reframe circumstances from the past in the present. We can bring a new sense of meaning to those old feelings, should they arrive hoping for healing. You get to do that, to be the one you not only want but need. It takes more than a notion to stop a truck that's losing its brakes. That's what those runaway gravel ramps are for, to slow the truck's roll. Making a vow to become mindful of how you treat yourself is sort of like setting up your own runaway ramp: in the face of a triggering situation, you can veer off to the practice of becoming aware in the moment and asking, What do I need most right now? How do I give it to myself? *Get off your back and get on your side* is an absolute must-have in your unconditional-love tool kit.

Here is an unconditional self-love practice I use to get me back to center and to reconnect with my emotional baseline. Because I do not have allergies to essential oils, I use them in this practice. If you do have allergies, you can do this exercise without the oil or find a scent that works best for you. I currently use the Saje brand; I appreciate the themes they use for their essential oil palettes. (Check the resources section on my website, www.iamreginaloulse.com, for more suggestions.) Using Saje's scent Fortify, I dab a small amount into the "love charm," or the dip in my upper lip. Sitting in a relaxed position on a chair or on the floor, I inhale deeply until I experience a sense of calm. I repeat five minutes of Lovefirmations as I continue to breathe in and exhale. Five minutes is usually enough time.

Once I am calm, I trust that my baseline has been established. I take time to make notes about the experiences in my journal under the heading "Baseline," so I can refer to it when an experience calls for a bit of extra support. For example I might write, "lavender + calm + Lovefirmation. I am my own love charm." I mostly write it down for safekeeping in case I want to share it with a friend or client. Because I am also someone who does not enjoy being hijacked by my past, I retreat to my baseline frequently. You can also add music to the process of building your baseline, if that works for you. You can find more thorough descriptions of these practices on my website, www.iamreginalouise.com.

The LOVE of Compassion

Here is another relatively quick practice that I have found helpful in establishing an emotional baseline in a compassionate and loving way; it's what I call the LOVE of compassion. I *love* that this is something I can use in the moment of facing strong feelings and emotions. This sweet practice supports me in staying with the intensity of the moment and in quickly becoming aware of the present moment. You can find a comfortable space and simply go into this practice. The *L* in *love* invites us to *land* in our bodies, to locate ourselves in the moment. It offers us an opportunity to lean into our distress or anything that may require a bit of extra attention. The *L* is a chance for us to learn more about ourselves. The *O* offers us a chance to *observe* what is going on once we've landed. The more we sit in observation of what is happening for us, of how we feel, we will begin to open to our own experience, our own ability to move toward self-regulation. The *V* is an invitation into *vulnerability*.

The more we can face our vulnerability and not disintegrate in the face of challenges, the more muscle we build for staying with ourselves in a tender and receiving way. And finally, the *E* is where we touch into our own *empathy*. We come down into the foxhole of our own experience and become a friend to ourselves. We encourage ourselves in this place; we offer tenderness and become our own best friend. All these ways of being with yourself are examples of mindfulness, the gateway to your unconditional and loving self-compassion.

Bootstrapping Takeaways

- Slow down.
- Connect with your inner child/spirit/tenderness.
- Stop at nothing to get on your side.
- Become the one you want and need.
- Pour your unconditional love into you the same way you would into a loved one or friend.
- Cultivate self-forgiveness.
- Establish your emotional baseline.
- Cultivate patience with yourself.
- Commit to sitting in the LOVE of compassion.

Screech!

It's October 2019, and I'm on the run. I'm navigating hairpin turns and switchbacks through Penn Station, laden with shopping bags and two suitcases, when I catch a glimpse of a beautiful sistah (with a pierced nose) on the cover of *Mindful* magazine, and she ain't Oprah Winfrey. *Screech!* I slow down, turn around, and grab a copy to read on the train on my overnight trip from New York City to Chicago.

This wouldn't be the last time I'd get up close and personal with Jenée Johnson, a program innovation leader and a racial healing and emotional intelligence educator. I sensed that our connecting was divinely ordained. I wanted to meet her in person. The day I arrived home from that trip, one of our mutual friends on Facebook had connected Jenée and me while I'd been on the road. Because I tend to use Instagram more often while traveling than Facebook, I'd missed the chance to make her acquaintance earlier.

We exchanged pleasantries over chat, Jenée and I, and it wasn't until the next day that I realized that she was *the* Jenée, the woman I'd spent three days on the train ride home reading about. What was going to be had been set into motion. I love how the Universe works its magic. This woman has made an unprecedented effort to bring mindfulness into public health practices and programs through the Trauma-Informed Systems of Care Initiative in San Francisco. Her goal is to improve the organization's ability to manage change, stay resilient, inspire growth, and become a mindful culture that leads and serves with compassion.

I was thrilled to sit down with this amazing being and hear all about what goes on in her head and heart. Jenée is at the top of her game. When I was considering who to interview regarding this strategy, Jenée's face kept jumping out at me from the cover of the magazine. Black women on the cover of anything is an irregularity worthy of sincere celebration and respect because we know the kick-ass energy it took to get there.

By the time Jenée agreed to the interview, she had only two weeks earlier been peer-nominated as one of *Mindful* magazine's 12 Powerful Women of the Mindfulness Movement: 2020. The timing was perfect. How fortunate we both were!

Life Is a Gift

After connecting with Jenée, I knew that I had to get her take on the ways she poured goodness into herself the same way she would with a loved one, and I wanted to know how she inspired others to do the same:

Number one, life is a gift. And number two, you belong to yourself first. The human brain has what is called a natural negativity bias. I have heard it said that we cling to negatives like Velcro, and that positives roll off us as if we're made of Teflon. What it takes to address that, I think, is understanding that part of the negativity bias is also a very loud inner critic. And what it also takes to awaken and become aware is to believe "I belong to myself first. I am the linchpin in every relationship and situation that I experience. I am the constant in every one of those."

While I worked in maternal health, I realized that the thing missing from the work I did with mothers was mindfulness, the ability to be aware of self in mind, body, and surroundings. It takes inner courage, strength, and resilience to stay mindful, with a sense of calm, nonreactivity, and nonjudgment, and to be able to take decisive action in a wholesome direction because you have a sense of yourself. This is a practice of learning to love yourself, to center yourself, to say, "I belong to myself first." And like any other practice, you need to keep strengthening that muscle, if you will. Self-care must be a devotion, not a rehabilitation. When I am tending to my heart and what I feel, I am listening mindfully. Mindfulness is about being aware and present in mind and body. My body talks to me. If someone says something to me, and I find myself reacting, my body says, "Ah, there was a zing. What was that?" I get to investigate that. It is a practice of quieting myself and listening to my body.

Once of the first times I remember connecting inside myself was when I was a child. My mother would style both my hair and my sisters'. After each styling she would tell us to wrap our hair up at night so that the style would keep while we slept. I was never able to find my scarves. I'd get so flummoxed, and I'd run around searching for them, until one day I ran into the closet, dropped to my knees, and prayed to God over and over to help me find my scarves. Once I slowed down and calmed myself, I found them. I started to learn to trust this process of connecting to myself, belonging to myself.

Zoom in: There is a power that is uniquely yours when you understand the value of *getting off your back and getting on your side.* Or as in Jenée's example, on your knees in prayerful contemplation. You disengage with hackneyed behaviors that no longer serve you. Out with the nagging, the bullying, and the harsh handling of your emotional tenderness. In the practice of taking responsibility for your inner world, there lies an invitation to become your champion, your cheerleader. You evolve into someone who knows you better than anyone and is willing to be there for you in ways that no one else ever could. *Ever!*

Sure, it's human to believe we have at least one friend or family member who believes in us enough to drop everything at a moment's notice and shore us up in the face of uncertainty. Imagine, though, calling on your own naturally compassionate attention when you need it most. Staying connected to your own unconditional love is like carrying a first aid self-love kit, preparing you for the unexpected and empowering you to rely on yourself in any situation, no matter how unprecedented the circumstances.

Pause to Consider

Taking a moment to slow down and collect your thoughts, in your own time, go back through the strategy. Find something that resonates with your life experiences. Commit to exploring the relationship between what you've lived and the meaning you've given it. I implore you to be gentle with yourself. Go slowly. Below are some inquiries to help deepen your understanding, whet your curiosity.

- What are some of the interventions you found useful in this strategy?
- Name a time when you were harsh with yourself. How did you move through it?
- What does "get off your back and get on your side" mean to you?
- In what way(s) do you imagine this strategy can aid you in leveling up your connection with your inner self?
- What's your relationship like with your inner child / younger self?

Below you will find a list of Lovefirmations. Choose a few that resonate with you, or write your own. Perhaps you could even write an expressive letter to yourself using the Lovefirmation that speaks to you. Take some quiet time and repeat your Lovefirmation as a mantra. Set a timer for five minutes and build incrementally until you are satisfied with the space you've cultivated within.

Lovefirmations

I am me, and I am proud!
I am worthy of my own attention, and it is like me to know this is true.

I am for me, and so I am able to be there for others in a healthy way.

My life is a mirror of what I believe, what I trust is manifest in the way I live, and I live my life now!

All the love the world has to offer is mine; I am loving, I am capable, I am free.

Mindfulness is mine now; I can hold myself without judgment; I am acceptable as I am.

I am no one's victim; victory is mine on my terms; I am victorious.

I am fully capable of meeting my own needs; my needs are mine to care for.

I am patient with myself; I have the right to express love and kindness to the youngest part of me.

My heart is a clearing for my healing; I am ready when I am willing.

I have the authority to do for myself whatever needs doing.

Inside me exists a self who knows my name, my ways, and my moods and accepts me as I am.

I move through the world according to my emotional signature.

All I need to do to stay straight is to remain mindful of my own heart, to trust my own love, and to know I am my own friend first.

I can't fail me; I am all of me; I love what is, what was, and all that will ever be of me.

There is no shame in my game of loving, wanting, and befriending me.

There lives a mini-me inside me who knows how to love and be the best me.

Kick-Ass Strategy #13

Get to Know Your Inner Child

All of us have two distinct aspects of our personality:
The Adult and the Child.
When these two parts are connected and working together,
there is a sense of wholeness within. When these two parts are
disconnected ... because of being wounded, dysfunctional,
or undeveloped, there is a sense of conflict, emptiness,
and aloneness within.

— Margaret Paul and Erika Chopich, *Healing Your Aloneness*

One of the pioneers of inner child work just so happens to be a human I have profound respect for, the august Margaret Paul. Margaret's offering to the world on getting to know your inner child is best represented in her seminal classic, cowritten by Erika J. Chopich, *Healing Your Aloneness: Finding Love and Wholeness Through Your Inner Child*. Margaret is the beautiful human who was generous enough to write the foreword of this book. I have enjoyed her in-person workshops and would recommend them to anyone interested in exploring the specific nature of their inner child.

While working with Margaret — who, by the way, is not only so gorgeous she makes eighty-something look like the new fifties, but she is extremely lighthearted and playful — one of the most striking insights I had was this: the degree to which I can say yes to myself or to another person, while maintaining my boundaries, is evidence of how in sync I am with my inner child, Little Red. For many people, no matter their station in life, candlestick maker or cultural icon, it's not easy to pay it forward, to give to someone a listening ear, a helping hand, or a break that could make the difference for them. Nor, for many, is being playful and engaging in joy and laughter a natural by-product of having access to the inner child. So let's tackle the ability to give first. As humans, we seem inclined to hold on to what we value, share it with only a select few, and most important, preserve what is ours for family members, close friends, and so on.

Some may have the mindset that what they have is all they will ever get, and in the need to self-preserve and stave off the impending doom of scarcity, keep their bits and pieces close to the vest. Then there are those who give what they can but with conditions attached, unconscious motives driving their actions. And there are those who give it all away without any consideration for themselves because the giving away itself is their yes! And last are those who have more than they'll ever need in a lifetime and for whatever reason consider giving too challenging and therefore can't, won't, don't give to themselves or to anyone else. And sure, a gazillion variables inform our decisions about whether, and how much, to give.

What I've noticed about myself is that however connected

I am to my inner child has everything to do with *who* I permit myself to say yes to and how and why I do it. When I'm connected to my inner child, I have readier access to my truer self, with a greater ability to be in touch with my own kindness, generosity, lightheartedness, and innocence. I know that there is not only enough to go around but that I am enough on my own terms. When both your loving adult and your inner child are online and working in tandem for the good of all, it's much easier to know the way to your truth, or your *yes.* Children are innately openhearted, kind, and generous — generally speaking. We've all heard about the so-called bad seeds, and that's not what I'm going to unpack here. I'm talking about how most of us are able to connect with our inner child and rely on this aspect to connect us to our goodness, honesty, and ability to share, from the heart of our own innocence.

When I say yes, to my own or someone else's request, it's usually a no-brainer, as they say. It takes nothing away from me to lend an unconditional loving hand to myself or to someone else. I admit that, for a while there, when I gave to others it was from an extremely unconscious place, as you all know by now. I was led to believe that everything I received, even the most basic of human needs, was transactional. I didn't know until I was in my early forties that the "mere fact" that I'd been born entitled me to such human experiences as love, kindness, consideration, and appreciation. I give thanks to Camille Thomasson for some of that understanding. She is the screenwriter who penned my story; otherwise I'm not sure I would have known at the time the simple truth that I need not do anything to pump up my worth but can instead relish the mere fact of my existence and let that be enough. I tell you, hearing that definitely helped me put down the heavy load of working overtime in the hard department of excelling at everything I did in order to be liked.

Pause to Consider

Check in with yourself and answer the following questions:

- Who do you know your inner child to be?
- When you were a child how did you feel about being young?
- What were some of the challenges and difficulties?
- What were some of the most memorable times of your childhood?
- Was there ever a moment in your childhood that shamed you into a thousand pieces? What happened?
- How did you heal from the event?
- How are you still holding on to what happened?
- And last, how generous are you with yourself? How likely are you to support someone else?

Take some time to respond to these questions. On my website (www.iamreginalouise.com), in the resources section, you may submit your responses as possible Facebook Live or podcast topics, if you wish. I'd be delighted to further explore this subject, and many more. If you head on over to my website, you will find a letter that I've written to my inner child. I've had it for years and have edited it a hundred times. I am sharing it with you in case it helps you become more familiar with your own inner child. Sometimes I print the letter out on beautiful paper and read it to calm my inner child, to let her know that I, her loving adult, am right where she needs me to be, that I am there for her on her terms. I remind her that I am the *best* mama she has ever had and that I'm grateful she allows it to be so.

After you've read the letter I've written, take some time and begin the process of getting acquainted with your inner child. Depending on your inner child's nature, temperament, and ability to trust the imagination, they may need a bit of coaxing. They might be doubtful, afraid, preferring to hide, and judgmental. Take your time to win your inner child over. If you run into any resistance, don't hesitate to reach out. I'm happy to set up a playdate for us! And just for the record, play is an important way to be light with ourselves and our inner child. Now, I know that being playful isn't necessarily for everyone. So I've taken that into consideration and created a few word games for you and your inner child to help you practice having a bit of fun me-time.

Naming Your Inner Child

One last thing before we get to play. Many people did not grow up with a nickname or a term of endearment used especially for them. If that is true for you, perhaps it made you feel left out or not as special. I get it. It took me years to recognize that Red, as my mother called me, was an actual nickname. To make matters a bit more complicated, I took the name Vivii as my name of endearment before I remembered being called Red. Although Red has a special place in my heart and will forever be attached to the spots of goodness I experienced and therefore remember about my biological mother, Vivii is all mine. Had I named myself as a child, I no doubt would have picked Viviana. There's so much life in the name. When I teach college students, they call me Vivii. Friends close enough to know call me Vivii. I love me some Vivii. She is all things Vivi-licious and patient; she's playful as all get-out yet strong as an ox. Vivii is all things Taurean, all things fiercely strong, and doggedly determined. As if I needed to spell that out for any of you. LOL! On the Enneagram, another personality assessment tool, Vivii is a Four with a Five wing, which means she has Bohemian tendencies. Uh-duhh, as if I needed an assessment to affirm that. I am a straight-up poster child for all things Free People and Magnolia Pearl, finished off with fabulous de-signer shoes. Of course. As for the Four, I'll take it, as did Billie Holiday, Amy Winehouse, and Jackie Kennedy Onassis. Fours are also known as the "tragic romantics." Ahem, while that may have been true in my childhood when Red was going through her days of trials and tribulations, now Red has grown up into Vivii, and when a Four is in its healthiest place, it moves to the Enneagram One, which is all about growth and leadership and changing the world. Here is what the Enneagram web-site has to say about a Four who operates at One: "Profoundly creative, expressing the personal and the universal, possibly in a work of art. Inspired, self-renewing, and regenerating: able to transform all their experiences into something valu-able: self-creative." Mic drop. If you'd like to know more about your particular type, just for the fun of it head on over to the resources on my website (www.iamreginalouise.com), where you'll find links to some fun places to travel to.

Play Break: Let the Games Begin!

Do you love to play? Are you more likely to associate play with the sinking of the *Titanic* and would rather go down with the ship than stand empty-handed in the void, trusting whatever happens in the moment with sheer abandon? I get it. Play does not always feel safe, or fun, or easy, no matter what the research on the subject may indicate. For some of us, play is associated with horribly shaming experiences, and for others play feels downright terrifying. I can talk till the cow jumps over the moon, and if play is not your thing there is probably not much I can say to support you in that shift if you do not feel you are ready, willing, or able. But what I can say for start ers to that smallest part of you who continues to carry that pain is: *I am sorry*. Often acknowledgment is the place to begin before we can move on. Working toward owning and healing the pain and suffering of that child inside us who carries the consequences of their loss around with them is the next step in reimaging our relationship to playing.

Giving yourself permission to play can be a courageous act, even if playing comes easily to you, but if you are reluctant to play, it's especially so. You get to do the games I offer below in the comfort of your own space. Maybe you're like me; I've always shied away from crossword puzzles, but I've also wanted to approach them as a place of fun and adventure. You'll find answer keys at the end of the chapter, and you can use them to support yourself or to check your progress. In whatever way you decide to engage with these games, allow yourself to have a little fun if you can. If I haven't said it already, I'll say it now: have lots of fun!

WORD SEARCH

```
I  C  M  U  H  P  N  M  D  E  M  S  L  X  I
P  H  I  N  E  E  A  I  D  N  T  E  I  Y  Y
O  O  N  C  A  R  R  N  E  G  R  L  G  O  Q
S  S  T  O  R  M  R  N  T  A  A  F  H  U  U
S  E  U  N  T  I  A  E  E  G  N  T  T  S  A
I  B  I  D  R  S  T  R  R  I  S  R  P  P  L
B  O  T  I  E  S  I  C  M  N  F  U  L  O  I
I  O  I  T  C  I  V  H  I  G  O  S  A  N  T
L  T  O  I  O  O  E  I  N  K  R  T  Y  T  I
I  S  N  O  G  N  C  L  E  I  M  P  F  A  E
T  T  F  N  Y  U  D  D  A  A  K  U  N  S  S
Y  R  H  A  I  S  P  I  R  I  T  J  L  E  L
X  A  S  L  Z  X  R  E  A  L  I  Z  E  I  O
A  P  P  R  E  C  I  A  T  I  V  E  V  T  V
S  T  R  A  T  E  G  I  E  S  E  H  Y  Y  E
```

Transformative	Appreciative	Unconditional	Spontaneity
Determined	Strategies	Permission	Qualities
Possibility	Inner child	Recognize	Intuition
Bootstrap	Engaging	Self-trust	Playful
Narrative	Realize	Spirit	Light
Chose	Heart	Love	You

WORD MATCH

SUBJECT MATTER	BOUNDARIES
X MARKS	BISH
BOOT	TRIUMPHS
MAINTAIN	STRATEGY
PERMISSION	GRANTED
UNCONDITIONAL	THE SPOT
BOSS	SELF-LOVE
HOT	MESS
KICK-ASS	EXPERT
SPIRIT	STRAPPING

WORD SCRAMBLE

CSEJTUB ATMTRE PEXETR   _____

ESTNIOAOFRVILM   _____

DREMA   _____

MI LPIOSEBS   _____

ANEEGG   _____

DIWL SMSE   _____

TIIGDNY   _____

ENRIN ICDHL   _____

RDEA ADREER   _____

YJEONUR   _____

SFLE   _____

TEVRREPONSIA   _____

VRAEEPESENCR   _____

GEESNROU   _____

ALYP   _____

IIXNATFO   _____

TITVNAMIOO   _____

SVRIUEEN   _____

SIPIRT   _____

SNAWEARES   _____

Pause to Consider

- If you've done so, what was it like for you to read my letter to my inner child?
- What might be the value in connecting with your inner child?
- What time are you willing to set aside this week to become better acquainted with your inner child?
- How would your inner child like to play?

ANSWER KEYS

Word Search

Word Match

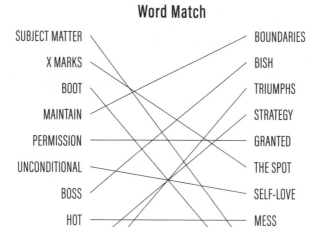

SUBJECT MATTER	BOUNDARIES
X MARKS	BISH
BOOT	TRIUMPHS
MAINTAIN	STRATEGY
PERMISSION	GRANTED
UNCONDITIONAL	THE SPOT
BOSS	SELF-LOVE
HOT	MESS
KICK-ASS	EXPERT
SPIRIT	STRAPPING

Word Scramble

CSEJTUB ATMTRE PEXETR	SUBJECT MATTER EXPERT
ESTNIOAOFRVILM	LOVEFIRMATIONS
DREMA	DREAM
MI LPIOSEBS	I'M POSSIBLE
ANEEGG	ENGAGE
DIWL SMSE	WILD MESS
TIIGDNY	DIGNITY
ENRIN ICDHL	INNER CHILD
RDEA ADREER	DEAR READER
YJEONUR	JOURNEY
SFLE	SELF
TEVRREPONSIA	PRESERVATION
VRAEEPESENCR	PERSEVERANCE
GEESNROU	GENEROUS
ALYP	PLAY
IIXNATFO	FIXATION
TITVNAMIOO	MOTIVATION
SVRIUEEN	UNIVERSE
SIPIRT	SPIRIT
SNAWEARES	AWARENESS

Kick-Ass Strategy #14

Dream the "I'm Possible" Dream

Every great dream begins with a dreamer. Always remember,
you have within you the strength, the patience, and the passion
to reach for the stars to change the world.

— Harriet Tubman

What is the first dream you remember having for your future self? How old were you? Where were you? For many of us, traveling back in time and reconnecting with the innocence that motors our dreams can provide us with a reboot of hope, joy, and possibility. If someone were to ask you, "How many dreams have you brought to fruition in your lifetime?" what would your answer be? To dream is human, and if you live in the United States or have spent any length of time there, then you are familiar with the lure of pursuing the ultimate dream, one that I believe is entirely possible to realize with a bit of old-school finessing and some kick-ass commitment: *your* version of the American Dream.

Dreams come to us in myriad ways. They arrive as thoughts

or aspirations, as visions; they pique our interests by hinting at an ambition or a goal. Dreams can begin as fantasies or daydreams in which images entice us to go ever deeper into the invisible realms of our subconscious. In our dreams lies a frontier yet to be explored. What an opportunity then, do our dreams hold for us, to get to know ourselves better, to break through limitations and fears in exchange for a sense of freedom to live our one life from our own unique sovereignty.

Our dreams can inspire us to work toward a future replete with the joys and satisfactions we imagine for ourselves. We are the instigators of our dreams, the kick-starters; we are the ones who dare to imagine our most potent possibilities and all the things we desire — each to our own aesthetics.

How do we take an image, one that appears in our mind's eye or in a dream, as a gut feeling and stay with it, nurture it, and ultimately level it up to become our version of the American Dream? By now we all know that a dream without a road map, an intention, or a way forward is nothing more than that, a dream, with no get-up-and-go.

Perhaps you've seen an automobile without any wheels sitting in someone's yard, up on cinder blocks. Let's imagine you jump into the driver's seat and adjust your side and rear-view mirrors. Yeah, now you're going somewhere (oxymoron intended). With your foot on the accelerator nearly pushing through the floor, off you go like a bat out of hell — in your mind. Although you're buckled into your fantasy of leaving town and taking the world by storm, and although daydreaming can be the beginning of all things desired, without wheels you are headed nowhere, and fast.

Well, let me not belabor the point. Without wheels or an engine, no matter how hard you try, your car, like your dreams, will remain up on cinder blocks. Your dreams rely on your momentum to move them forward. Much like that John Deere twin gas hydrostatic lawn mower, once turned on, your efforts can cut through the dense lawn of your imagination lickety-split, launching your ideas toward manifestation. (Thank you for allowing me to indulge in the lawn mower metaphor. I sometimes have fantasies about being a sexy farmer lady. I digress.)

Giving Your Dream a Set of Wheels

As mentioned above, dreams come to us in a host of different ways. Let's take a look more specifically at how we can turn our ambitions on and begin the process of bringing them to fulfillment. We'll begin by exploring what I call the skeleton, or the bones, of your dream. There are four ways in which I have incubated the visions, inklings, and ideas I've received into manifestations of things I've dreamed of:

- Visualize until you materialize.
- Engage in expressive writing.
- Build a rendering of your desired outcome.
- Take the dream to bed.

Visualize until You Materialize

Visualization is a powerful tool used throughout history to manifest one's desires by way of visual imaginings. From advertising to Olympic athletic training, some form of visual imagery is used, along with our willingness to plant in our minds the seedlings of our heart's desires. Visualization is an innate and natural psychic phenomenon. All you need to do is find a comfortable seat, settle down, and turn your attention to what you desire. Since you've gotten this far in the book, you already know what I am intimating.

You can use visualizations to inspire your desires into action. Visualizations act as motion pictures do, moving at whatever pace you — the producer, actor, and director — decide. They can be as long or as short as you want. I often write my visualizations out in script form. I enjoy including dazzling destinations and swanky venues. I encourage you to create your own visual journeys. And as you do, permit yourself to go as far from or as close to home as you desire.

I am a true believer in including as many senses as possible in my visualizations — taste, touch, smell, hearing, and sight, and all the bodily sensations that arise as a result of engaging these five intelligences or wisdoms, as I sometimes refer to these senses. Of course you are free to discover the approach that works best for you in producing results; however, for me, employing as many of my senses as I can helps make my visualizations come to life within me, and therefore I get to experience the embodiment of my dreams, as though they are happening in the moment. I love it!

Once I am present to my own awareness, I allow the images to show up. I slow down and pay close attention to whatever appears. This may take some time. Be gentle with yourself. No bullying or coercing the muses. Trust that everything will arrive in its own time and by its own means. I feel my way into my visualization as though it were happening in the now. I tune in to any sound that wants to enhance the experience, as well as any sensation. An aroma often heightens the visualization, expanding my awareness and focusing my attention. As for taste, I always imbibe something in my visualization, whether it's a piece of citrus to activate my saliva glands, making the imagery that much more immediate and real, or a full-on twenty-course meal fit for a queen. I ensure that taste is present in almost all my visualizations.

I have no qualms whatsoever about seeing myself driving down the road, blasting Megan Thee Stallion in my Tesla SE while chowing down on a half-pint of Magnolia Bakery's banana pudding.

Engage in Expressive Writing

As someone for whom writing is the medium of choice for expressing myself, I am the first person to suggest the pen, pencil, or whatever writing utensil you prefer as a front-line approach in support of your dreams. Perhaps you are already fully vested in keeping dream journals or even voice memos to archive your desires. Pat Schneider, the author of *Writing Alone and with Others*, says that speaking is a form of writing on the wind. So whether you write it out longhand or speak it out loud, the intention is to keep the ideas flowing, word by word, until you have given form to the images that refuse to let go until they are given a place to rest on paper or in a digital file.

As Bessel van der Kolk, author of *The Body Keeps the Score*, knows, the body has a way of remembering what it has gone through. Expressive writing can be used to write through traumatic experiences that may block your ability to feel safe enough to connect to the inner realm. Using expressive writing as a way through traumatic events and making meaning of them can free up previously held energies and create new neurological pathways toward healing. So writing not only provides a way to connect with your dreams, but it also can help to transform any impediments to your dreaming experiences.

Whether you record your imaginings upon waking or dictate your musings as you move throughout your day, remaining loyal to your heart's desires is essential in moving toward being a kick-ass bootstrapper. My experience is that the more faith I have in myself, the more likely I am to remain on the road to my destiny. Agency is a perishable commodity if we choose not to use it. However, when we become decisive and committed to manifesting our destinies, we open the doors to our heart's highest possibilities.

Build a Rendering of Your Desired Outcome

One of the first things I like to do when starting a creative project, for instance, a new writing project, is to build a representation of what I imagine the result will be. I first experienced what's called a rendering when the stage version of my play *Somebody's Someone* was mounted at the Sacramento Theatre Company for a six-week run. Just before the play was mounted, the stage designers presented me with a three-dimensional view of the stage and the play's various sets. As you might imagine, every aspect of that experience burst with electrified sensations, and I learned so much from it.

For the book you are holding in your hands, I began by writing down its title one year before creating the rendering. For the rendering itself I started by writing a chapter; then I drew up the proposal, the marketing plans, and so much more. Next, I assembled it all and presented the package to my prospective editor for consideration. Had I not taken the time (just over a year) to make these painstaking efforts, I can guarantee you this: you would not be reading this book that's abounding with kick-ass strategies.

Once the book was secured with the editor, I then created the second iteration of a rendering. Because my aesthetic preferences tend toward what one might consider girly-meets-frilly and all things shabby chic, which a touch of Bohemian flair, I began creating the cover of the book with images that satisfied my need for beauty, and then I laid the title on the outside and the "guts" on the inside. I divided each chapter into sections with tabs handwritten in calligraphy. Had I an inkwell and a feather, no doubt I would have found a way to include them in my creative expression. Go all out, I say, all out for what you want.

Each week that I added a chapter to the rendered version provided satisfaction and encouragement. Not only that, but the thing itself became a real representation of the future, hope in action. The more writings I added, the more evidence I had of the project coming to life. These kinds of actions reinforce intentionality, build integrity, and present your project as eye candy to your creative muse. They demonstrate your seriousness about the matter at hand, your commitment. Making a rendering of your creative endeavor is the difference between allowing it to sit idle in your mind like that car hiked up on blocks and giving it wheels and an engine so that it pulses forward to its highly desired end.

There's #OLT I'd like to say before we move on to the anecdotes: "Do. Or do not. There is no try," as Yoda so succinctly put it. I love this little bit of wisdom. I take these eight words seriously. And this may have everything to do with being a woman of hyphenated American status. I've never felt as though I've had the leisure to go at something and not succeed. I hit everything hard and running. Rarely is there ever room for grass to grow beneath my feet. So off you go getting it done, and while you're at it, be sure to go HAM — hard as a mother-f**ker! That's not Yoda's wisdom, by the way. It's compliments of both Jay-Z and Kanye West. Wisdom. Let's make it all about that bootstrapping, baby!

Take the Dream to Bed: Dream the "I'm Possible" Dream, Part 1

Now we're getting down to where we go all Teddy Pendergrass and *turn off the lights*, yeah, that's right, you hear me, and *light a candle*. Don't be shy but do come a little closer. Psych. I'm only messing with you. Yet what I'm going to suggest isn't too far off from that sultry invitation to get downright cozy with your heart's desires. I recommend that you cuddle up with your wants, engage with them, stroke your wishes, I mean stoke them, and take them into the deepest recesses of your heart while you sleep.

I am suggesting this mainly because, as you have probably surmised by now, so much of my artistic success has come about as a result of dreams. I mean, ideas about some of my deepest desires *literally* come to me while I'm asleep. And they don't just come to me; they stand akimbo at center stage, in my sleep, like a sassy little Miss Thing determined to have her say. On awakening I am moved to remember them wholly, writing them down image for image, and whatever feelings were provoked by the dream stay with me for days on end. I am a firm believer in incubating ideas during my sleeping hours. My method is simple (to me, at least): I start by taking whatever is on my mind, usually some project that has grabbed hold of me and will not let me go until I find a way to bring it to life, to bed. I welcome images into my mind without judgment, think on them, and as I'm about to fall asleep, I'll ask a question, depending on how long I've worked on the idea:

1. What more does Spirit want me to know about this project?
2. What next step should I take to move this forward?
3. How will I know this is the right action to take?

Since I was a child, this method of communication between myself and my spirit has worked for me, and in many cases has served in manifesting the answers, or at least the next step, I'm hoping for. In some cases, it has saved my life. We'll save all those lifesaving bits for another time; however, connecting with the invisible world of one's dreamscape is something I highly recommend. It's simple, really. I think of it as a complimentary gift that comes with the package of who I am, a birthright of sorts.

Have you ever used dream incubation as a way to see your goals more clearly, to step into them, and to envision the next move you might make? I have so many examples to choose from, I tell you, a lifetime's worth. However, I'll choose the one that's jumping up and down in my awareness, waving its arms overhead and chanting *pick me, pick me!*

One night before bed I'd asked, *What next step, no matter how outrageous, must I take to get the biopic of my life green-lighted?* Off to sweet slumber I went. The next morning, what I took away from the dream I had was an old-fashioned pink princess telephone. It was on a pedestal as if waiting for me to pick it up. As I recalled, Barbie had one, as did Cindy Brady, and I'd always wanted one. Without too much thought about *why*, I reached out to my friend Yvonne, who had been one of the original producers to pitch *Somebody's Someone*, the film version based on my first memoir by the same name. It had been nearly thirteen years since our initial meeting, and I'd picked her out of thirty-seven other Los Angeles producers because she had been so successful with bringing the Rosa Parks story, starring Angela Bassett, to the screen. Let me just say: how I managed to set up a pitch fest back then, hosted at the W Hotel Westwood, with thirty-seven of LA's top independent female producers, is a strategy all its own. You might have to book a private session for that one! LOL!

I'd called Yvonne and insisted that the time was right to re-pitch to the executive at Lifetime Television for Women to reconsider making our story. I had no real evidence that this was so, except that late one night I'd found my way to the network and saw that they had successfully produced three films about Black women's lives, the latest being the Aaliyah biopic, *The Princess of R&B*. Although many people had tried their best to point out to me that although I am a member of the Black Girl Magic Club and had survived some crazy shizit, this did not necessarily place me in the ranks among the Rosa Parkses, Whitney Houstons, and Toni Braxtons of the world, all of whom are pop-culture icons and have Lifetime movies archiving their legendary status. I *of course* begged to differ and continued my pursuit of making possibly the first film to document a Black girl's heroic journey through the foster-care industrial complex, a system hell-bent on her physical, psychological, and emotional erasure.

Few people are aware of the conditions in which Black girls caught in foster care adrift are forced to exist, the psychotropic drugs they are forced to take, the bouts of being isolated in solitary confinement. Talk about adultification: so many young people emancipate into a world they are just not prepared for. This demographic, not so unlike the ex-slave characters in the novel *Beloved*, occupy the ranks of what Toni Morrison calls "the disremembered and unaccounted for." As far as I was concerned, my story of the impoverished Black girl who fought her way from the bottom of a cement floor in a windowless room all the way to understanding middle-class sentence structure hadn't been told, at least not from the perspective of a true-life Black girl. Thank you, Sapphire, for writing *Precious*, and for blazing a path for the stories that we should never turn a blind eye to, no matter how difficult they may be to watch.

So there I was, hot-pink cell phone in hand, frenetically, passionately pleading my case to Yvonne until she finally said, "Okay, I'll reach out to Howard" — he held the moneybags — "and see what he says." I hung up, conducted a half-hour internet search on Howard, and called him. Myself. I do not have a lot of patience once Spirit tells me what to do. I don't know about anybody else, but once I get my marching orders, 'erbody else better get on board or get out of the way! The only thing I love possibly as much as the children in my life and Spirit is pulling on my boots, jumping feetfirst into the trenches, and getting things done! You know what I mean? I never forget, not for one second, that I am a Black woman.

Howard's assistant assured me he would *return* my call at his earliest convenience. That's how you know you're playing with the big dogs; the office assistance and personal assistants speak quickly with a "I don't give two f**ks" attitude and cut you off in the middle of your inquiry with: "I'll have him return your call." *That's all?* Click. You don't have to be so rude, B-with-an-itch (this, of course, was *way* before I discovered Lovefirmations. I'm just saying).

Two months went by, and still I heard nothing. What did I expect? It had been more than a decade since our first attempt to get the film made had resulted in reverting the life options back to me after six years of stopping and starting. At one point in its tenure as a script that might see the light of day, the film was selected by Courteney Cox to direct. We were but a signature away from packing bags, boarding planes, trains, and all other forms of travel that would take us to Canada and get the film made, when we were halted. It was a treacherous affair; shooting schedules were canceled, locations scouted went unused, and the temperature in my heart of hearts went cold, fast.

My learning curve became steeper with each disappointment. I had to learn quickly how fickle the film industry could be and what it took to bounce back. For me, it was a matter of permission to sink my incisors into the belief that this movie would get made. And that was that. Though it was intimated that the film was well on its way to becoming "one of those projects that's really good but probably won't make the cut." If I could wait out a writers' strike in order to reup the option, sit through a network executive restructuring, perform the staged version of my story at a six-week room with two shows on both Saturday and Sunday with one day off in between, perform the stage version at conferences all over the country, and finally at a mausoleum surrounded by the dead...I already had the evidence of the story's potential power as a film. My story centered on unconditional love, a love that moved beyond color and misgivings over whether one's skin color predisposes him or her to be unworthy of love's imprinting. I was willing to wait a lifetime for Lifetime, if need be.

I've never considered myself a *well-behaved* woman. However, I've always had a deep desire to go down in herstory with a bang, or at the very least a bump. Having run out of patience waiting for a return to my call from my hoped-for movie-daddy,

I reached out to another producer who I'd had the pleasure of meeting via another producer who was determined to turn my little story into an independent feature. (That dream too was kicked to the curb when that *other* producer's show, *Anne with an E*, got picked up for development.) I won't dare bog down your spirits with the scores of possible leads I'd pursued before making my next call, to A.

Yes, my dear friend A! I called and asked if she had a contact at Lifetime network, and she said she did, and the rest of the story is about how, nearly thirteen years later, my story once again had a seat at the development table. Now, I want you all to know that there is so much more to this particular story. One thing led to another, as is often the case with these things, and on May 2, 2018, Howard — yes, the OG himself — and I met at the Lifetime corporate offices and then had our first meeting with the executive signed to the development of what started out as *Somebody's Someone* but became *I Am Somebody's Child: The Regina Louise Story.*

Remain Vigilant toward Persistence

Zoom in: It was one thing to get a life rights option signed, sealed, and delivered and another to make sure that agreements between all parties were documented contractually. Up to this point I'd done everything on my own, contacted producers, media outlets, and black box theaters; written press releases; held meetings with Hollywood executives; staged meetings in romantic and fantastic places, and so on. I've always considered myself kind, and as such I know myself, under pressure, to give a lot of stuff away in order to appear "agreeable" and "easy to work with." I've had much success getting deals teed up without an agent, manager, or someone looking after my best interests. That is until I reached out to Lawyers for the Arts and retained my current attorney. I've learned the hard way that it's a challenge to be an artist and accountant, a manager and a client all the while remaining vigilant toward my dreams. However, I say to you all: be persistent. And also, maybe most important, know when it is time to level up and hire someone whose job it is to protect your intellectual properties and your best interests.

Do you feel reticent to engage with an agent or manager? Are you that person who runs to the copyright office to protect your creative work because you fear that someone will abscond with your masterpiece? I hear you. And although I am fortunate to have secured my first book deal with my then agent, I have been known to advocate on my own behalf, many times to the tune of success. However, there have been those few instances when I took my eye off the ball and lost.

Good representation takes effort, but the mission of finding the right someone for your endeavors is worth the time, money, and effort put into it. Protecting your hard work is also an act of loving yourself, not to mention a way to make sure you have someone who will go to the mattresses for you. That way you get to keep creating without having to worry about whether your efforts are being protected. Our dreams need tending to, and they also deserve our protection.

Dream the "I'm Possible" Dream, Part 2

If you haven't heard the American composer Paul Schwartz's version of "Amazing Grace," as sung by Lisbeth Scott, on his album *States of Grace*, I suggest you head on over to your favorite digital streaming service and get it in. Ms. Scott takes us to church. I'm talking 'bout the kind of church where your knees drop you down to the floor, where your mouth hangs open in search of words, where your heart is flung open in veneration, and you suddenly understand what it means to "put your hands down," in the true sense of the word, since there is no need to defend yourself against anything. And if you're lucky, you get to weep from a deep place within until the experience has run its course and you're more than happy to have had it: you're grateful. At least that's what happened to me on my first encounter with the genius also known as Lisbeth Scott. Her songs and vocals have been featured in hundreds of Hollywood blockbusters, many of them Oscar and Grammy winners or nominees. As a composer she has scored for both television and film. Her iconic contributions include songs for *Avatar*, *The Chronicles of Narnia*, *The Passion of the Christ*, *Concussion*, *True Blood*, and *American Son*.

I played that CD for the first time on a morning, nineteen years ago while standing in my brand-new salon on opening day. Lisbeth's voice moored me right where I stood. Sobbing. I understood the power of grace and its ability to humble a soul, in this case via a recording first thing on a Tuesday morning. I vowed to find a way to say thank you to Lisbeth. This desire was no doubt inspired by the audacity to believe that such a thing could happen.

Back to the story at hand. It took four executive producers, eight potential directors, six life rights option periods, a writers' strike, and several network executives changes over seventeen years to receive that unapologetic *yes* from the powers that be to move *I Am Somebody's Child* into development and then on to production. Where does that kind of a growth mindset come from, you may wonder? To face rejection day after day for every single reason imaginable and yet have the boldness to keep on keeping on isn't child's play. Repeatedly, I was told there were no actors to play the character of Regina Louise, a poor, abandoned, and illegitimate Black girl who happens to be the lead of the story. Not since *The Color Purple* had a character with similar impediments been represented or explored.

I was determined to wait it out until an actor was born who could play the role. I heard that there was no audience for such a story, and that little Black girls were the last to be considered for carrying an entire film for a hundred minutes. The millions of dollars needed for such an investment was a climb too far out on that proverbial limb. Nevertheless, to believe, to endure one setback after the next only motivated me to calculate my comeback. I understood that there were gatekeepers in place everywhere to weed me out of the pack as I pursued my dreams. It wasn't personal. It's like that for many people. And many give up, throw in the towel, so to speak. However, we all need to remember that the strength of spirit and character it takes to resist the invitation to deny our heart's desire to blossom is grace, the great fortifier of effort taken on behalf of our own essence.

The late Rev. Alice Bandy, minister of Seaside Center for Spiritual Living, defines grace as "knowing that the Universe is unfolding exactly so at all times and that it is all God and all Good."

Since grace wouldn't have it any other way, on September 6, 2018, Howard informed me that he had hired Lisbeth Scott as the official composer of our film. Three days later I sat in the third row, center stage, at an event where she gave a musical performance. Afterward, I approached Lisbeth and extended her the thank-you my spirit had promised to give her for her rendition of "Amazing Grace." During our conversation, she told me this:

My mom won a piano over the radio when I was six. That was my first piano. Because my mother was a fervent believer in the power of the arts, and how necessary they are in the lives of children in particular, she found me a wonderful French piano teacher who came to the house. She was very tiny, and always wore purple and lots of jewelry. She gave me the bones to understand how to create sounds on the piano; I used to love to make things up. And that was the key for me.

I would practice all the classics, but I loved that hour when I would give myself over to just improvising. Back then, I did not know that meant I was actually writing music. I thought it was just what everyone did. Ever since I have been in love with music. It has been my saving grace, my home. I have traveled a great deal throughout my life, and wherever I am, it is the music that makes me feel at home. It's constantly playing in my head, and reinventing itself every few minutes. I rarely listen to the radio because of that: there is one inside me.

Whenever hardships or challenges arose, I always kept the music very close; it was my safe place. Ever since I could remember, I had one dream, and as soon as I got out of college I just picked up and left and headed straight for it. I had no money. I had a car that was on its last legs.

I spent most of the time by the side of the road waiting for help, which eventually came because I have undying faith. I've been tested millions of times. I curl up and cry, and then I get up and say, "You are not going to destroy me and you are not going to stop me." My one dream was to move to California and live by the ocean, preferably in Venice Beach, where musicians from all over the world live.

I moved to LA and got a job playing for a modern dance class. My sister was a beautiful dancer, so I had experience. I used to experiment with singing, and someone who was playing in the next studio where I was recording heard me, and that someone just happened to be interning for Hans Zimmer (think *Lion King*, *The Amazing Spider-Man 2*, and *Inception*, just to name a few of Zimmer's film scores). He approached me one day and said, "You have a great voice." I did not even know I could sing.

Yep, no idea. Life is a series of discovering our gifts, one by one. The intern said, "Hans Zimmer is working on a film, and we need a voice just like yours. Would you be interested in recording with us?" The next day I was recording for Hans Zimmer in my first film session ever. The film was called *Toys*, starring Robin Williams, a Christmas story. I jumped in with the top composer in Hollywood for three weeks, doing all these magical multivocal things, experimenting with my voice, finding out what it could do. It was really like being thrown into the deep end and having someone scream, "Swim!"

Through all the hardship — this industry I am now in can be challenging — you hold fast to the faith you have in yourself because it is always getting tested. We need to just accept this moment and all the moments that have come before us as the building blocks of where we are now. Every day I wake up and I say, "Thank you, thank you, and thank you again," because I am learning to accept myself, and to accept that I absolutely love what I do, and that I am good at it, and that I have my own way of doing it that is not like other people's ways, and that is okay. And I am so lucky that I have been surrounded by an incredible support team in the industry, and I have been able to write for several films now, two for Universal, that have just been a dream. Sometimes we find that our dreams have actually morphed into different dreams even better suited for us. And that is where I find myself right now. It is mind-blowing for me.

My whole life as an artist, I have written songs about love. I always intend, when I am writing music, for the message to be one of love and being included and belonging and light. And when I first started out, people would make fun of me for it, and I would think, "So? This is who I am." It took a while for me to say to people, "You know what? This is why I am here. This is what I create, and this is what I am going to continue to create. I accept that about myself, and it does not matter what you think of me."

Dream the "I'm Possible" Dream, Part 3

Ms. Lisbeth Scott said what she said, and I love it! As a Black, creative woman, one of the deepest-held dreams I have ever had is to one day stand onstage at the NAACP Image Awards, not only as a presenter but as a nominee. Oh, and make no mistake, I am one of those people who have a scrapbook of my acceptance speeches already written out. Uh-huh. That's right, you heard me. I am never quite sure when success is going to come around the corner and meet me head-on, so I must stay prepared. There is an old axiom that success is 80 percent preparation and 20 percent opportunity. Well, I try to stay 160 percent prepared for that 20 percent opportunity. I know what you're probably thinking: *Who on earth does this child think she is?* Like I said, *I know.* But I can't help myself. Some girls dream of Cinderella weddings, having huge families, making tons of money. I've always dreamed of supporting humans to become all of who they are, making a lasting impression on the world and walking red carpets with women who, like me, love all things glamorous, lots of bling-bling, and leaning into a microphone like a queen, in order to have our say.

Sure, many of us have heard the tales that our skin color, socioeconomic background, gender, and social status dictate whether or not our dreams will come true. Nevertheless, like so many other women, I've always been determined to chart my own path by any means necessary. I've always turned my envy into action. Sure, it's been one heck of a journey, but in the words of the late, great American poet, activist, writer, and cable car conductor Maya Angelou, "I wouldn't take nothing for my journey now."

On July 26, 2010, I received notice that my one-woman show had been nominated for two NAACP Theatre Awards for Best Playwright and Best One-Person Show. Walking that red carpet with family and friends was everything you might imagine: exciting, scary, intimidating, and fantastic all rolled up into one marvelous evening! Standing next to or brushing shoulders with some of my favorite actors, Sharon Leal, Nia Long, Meagan Good, Monique Coleman, and Tamera Mowry, was jaw-dropping. Although my play did not take home a trophy, I heard my name and the name of my play announced in the presence of seriously talented peers. The win was in being nominated in the first place. The win was in having at least some aspect of my dream come true: I was invited to the awards show. That motivated me to continue to believe in myself.

I have heard people say suspicious things such as, "I know she could not have been raised by Black people." Oh, I thought y'all knew: I was raised by Spirit! Laugh. Out. Loud. All I know is this: I am Black enough to dream of making my Black-enough dreams come true. And to the ones with unsolicited commentary, know this: I ain't mad at you. I appreciate you because you help to remind me of the importance of going for what I know. You motivate me to give myself permission to transform my devastation into my motivation. You encourage me to keep taking a stand for the hopes and dreams of every little Black child, no matter their social status, the hue of their Black skin, the "properness" of their sentence structure, or whatever it is they have had to do to survive this life in the skin they are in. Let's go!

On February 22, 2020, I walked that red carpet into the fifty-first annual NAACP Image Awards at the Pasadena Convention Center, as I believed I would. Did you all hear me? I said, I once again walked that red carpet as if it were made just for me. Because fashion is everything to me (if only I had five lives to be all the things I feel in my soul), I'd be absolutely and unforgivably remiss if I didn't mention that, like our very own Madam Vice President, I too strutted through the crowd shrouded in an all-white suit (tuxedo) and a quadruple wreath of pearls finished off with that all-too-fabulous prodigious organza pussy bow. Head on over to my Instagram page and feast your eyes. The photo is on my profile! That moment was all things stupendous. I had never felt so elegant and ladylike and permitted to be where I was in all my glamour.

This time, though, I walked that carpet with the beautiful Black girl who played the younger version of me in the Lifetime film. Remember when I said I was willing to wait for a Black girl to be born in order to play that role? Well, dadgummit, there we both were. Do y'all hear me? High heel to high heel, my black Valentino Rockstuds to her pink patent-leather Steve Maddens, we bootstrapped our Black-enough selves all the way to those sparkling glasses of champagne (served by some fine AF hosts), and once more brushed shoulders with people I revere. Tamera Mowry called out to my girl Angela "I love your hair." Epic shout-out from one vision of Black Girl Magic to the next! Lord have mercy, Morgan Freeman was there with his sexy, soothing, and commanding voice that nearly hypnotized me into believing I could just walk up onto that stage and wave hello to the crowd and let it be known that I was available to attend any after-parties. Rihanna wore Givenchy in deep purple. Oh, Lord, try to stop me if you can. Cynthia Erivo was in the house, as was Jill Scott, along with BeBe Winans (the night before) and Octavia Butler. I sat at the same table as Tiffany Haddish and her entourage as we all ate the mess of tempura shrimp, collard greens, and corn bread heaped on our plates. Y'all have to know that I felt like the luckiest human on the planet. Hey, Niecy Nash, I saw you too (the night before at the Kodak Theatre just before the awards dinner), looking all fly like that! I saw you too, Merle Dandridge, on that 360-video booth. You better quit it, serving us all that glamorousity like it ain't no thang but a chicken wang.

Deborah Joy Winans, I know you remember me. You put the *p* in *pretty*, baby girl! I'm the one who promised your handler I'd send him a link for you to watch the Lifetime movie about my life. I know, I lost his card. And Lynn Whitfield, that red sequin suit and fedora you were flossing was on flames! And while my little film, which was nominated for Best Director, did not make the cut, I did move over to the side so that Adrienne Banfield-Norris and her PR person could cut in front of me on that red carpet. I'd always imagined Jada Pinkett Smith playing the older version of the Regina character, and Willow the younger. And there I was, making side-mouth small talk with *the* mama and grandmother. Don't even try to tell me I had not arrived at my dream.

And just for the record, as if I need to clarify this for the record, which of course I don't but it just feels right to say it because it wants to be said and I am going to give myself permission to do it: I was as Black as anyone else in that room that night. I may not have ever truly belonged to a Black family of my own, within a specific community, but that night I belonged to every person in that room in a Black excellence kind of way. We all, each in our own way, had worked our Black asses off to get to where we were. We have, many of us, bootstrapped our way out of bumper-to-bumper tight spots one back-and-forth turn at a time and withstood unconscionable levels of indignation from people who did not believe there was an audience for our stories, for our literary or musical offerings.

In my opinion, those of us who dare to dream the "I'm Possible" dream are the definition of a growth mindset, always moving the dial of our possibility forward, always in it to win it, to give possibility another chance, proving us right that we are worth our own heart's desires, no matter how long they may take to come to fruition. And if I'd been any closer to the stage when Rihanna stood at the lectern after accepting the NAACP President's Award and asking folks to invite their friends of all races to "pull up," her spit might've smeared my shaded-in eyebrows till they were dripping down the side of my face into the pocket of my jacket. In other words, I did not miss a word of what she said. So I hereby give myself permission to take a page from RiRi's speech. Now hear this: I invite you all to pull up to your lives, pull up to your dreams, and pull up on yourselves and grant yourself the permission needed to dream the "I'm Possible" dream, in your own way, in your own time, and of course, on your own terms. And so it is!

Before You Go…

First, I'd like to thank you for your reading time. It's an honor and a privilege to hang out with you. I hope you have not only witnessed but also in some way large or small experienced all the good that lies in accomplishing a dream, and I encourage you to turn toward the inclinations that lie awaiting in your heart. They need you to coax them into existence with affection.

Take some time now, and using your permission slip, pick one of the bootstrapping takeaways below, and write expressively in response to it. Use whatever implement turns you on. After all, it's your dreamscape you're interested in. Your dreams aren't picky: they welcome computers, pencils, pens, crayons, and braille machines to wake them from their slumber and assist them in dancing toward their full expression. Once you've completed this task, go ahead and fill out the Dream the "I'm Possible" Dream Questionnaire below. Have as much fun as possible. Good luck!

Bootstrapping Takeaways

- Your dreams rely on your momentum.
- Your efforts can cut through the dense lawn of your imagination.
- Give your dream a set of wheels.
- Write expressively.
- Build a rendering.
- Take your dreams to bed.
- Visualize until you materialize.
- Hold steadfast to your goals.
- Connect with grace.
- Hold fast to your solemn vows.
- Remain vigilant.
- Practice your dreams.
- Cultivate undying faith.
- Dream of red-carpet events and walk them like you mean it.
- Rebuke lesser invitations to engage universal intelligence.

Dream the "I'm Possible" Dream Questionnaire

To dream the dream of your possibility is to take a step toward fostering unconditional love. And just like love, your dreams lie within your grasp. The commitment we make and the time we give ourselves is what our dreams require. As the strategy in this chapter suggests, if you remain steadfast and accepting, your dreams will manifest. Answer the questions below to gain a better understanding of your relationship with your dreams, goals, and desires.

1. What is my personal definition of *possibility*?
2. How has my lack of commitment to my purpose impacted my relationship to my dreams and aspirations?
3. What is the first dream I remember having for my future self? What happened to it?
4. What am I not willing to accept regarding my dreams?
5. Do I have any self-sabotaging traits? What are they? Is it possible that I am afraid of my success?
6. What are my needs concerning my dreams? What am I willing to do each day to meet these needs?
7. What am I willing to give up in order to meet these needs? Who do I need to become? Am I willing? If not, why?
8. What are the greatest obstacles to dreaming unconditionally? What can I do to address them?

Conclusion

Permission to Walk the Red Carpet of Your Dreams

Our time together is finally coming to an end, and I would be remiss if I didn't leave you with a sweet and loving way to have a proper closure. So let's venture into a bedtime visualization, which you should feel free to record, or you can go to my website (www.iamreginalouise.com) and have a listen. Now, I can already foresee some concerns over the fact that some of the images in the visualizations are biased toward one shoe designer over another, but not to worry. Although I have a penchant for Sophia Webster's all things butterfly stacks, you can replace them with whatever you'd like in your viz, okay? Great.

A half hour before turning in, slowly and intentionally begin the process of winding down, whatever that means to you. Here are a few suggestions:

- Begin disconnecting from technology.
- Choose a playlist that is timed to go off at bedtime.
- Take a shower or bath, whatever is most relaxing for you.
- Spray your pillow with your favorite soothing essence (optional, of course).

- Place your journal and writing implement, or your recorder, within reach.

When you're ready, get cozy in bed.

Now that you've settled in, take a deep breath, and upon exhalation softly close your eyes. Turn your attention to your breathing. Follow your inhalation and now the exhalation. Again, take a deep breath in, and release it. And again. Allow your breath to settle you into the moment.

Now, imagine you've been invited to an event where you are to be the guest of honor. Everything is set. All you need do is plan your attire, which of course is evening formal. What will you wear? A skirt, a shirt, a string of Chanel pearls? Bring to mind the high-heeled or kitten-heeled shoe of your dreams. What's your favorite color? Take your time; have fun with this. Allow whatever shows up to do so. How are you feeling? Name the feelings as they arise, one after the other. Stay with your feelings for as long as you want. Refrain from pushing; there's no need to apply pressure — just allow what is to be.

You're in a limo now. You are moving through your favorite city in the world — how fortunate that the event planners took this into consideration. The limo stops and you step onto the red carpet and look down at your shoes. Do they sparkle, dazzle? Are they smooth like butter? Take your time. This is your moment. It is whatever you want it to be. Revel in your uniqueness. Now start walking down the carpet. Are there lights, cameras, and action on both sides of the carpet? Are there people around you? What are they doing? Are they screaming out your name in celebration? What are they saying? How does it make you feel? You're on your way to receive an award for all the hard work you've done, and many people are there to celebrate you and your contributions to humankind. Feel the confidence you've earned, and quietly, to yourself, whisper, "I'm so proud of you." Allow the energy from your own acknowledgment to dissolve into your being. You are encircled in an energetic field of joy and gratitude.

Continue walking toward the auditorium entrance. As you step across the threshold, your hands are in the pockets of your A-line skirt, your French cuffs covering your wrists. What material is your skirt made of? How does the fabric of your skirt feel in your hands as you lift it? What color is it? What perfume are you wearing? What's the scent?

You are offered an hors d'oeuvre. What is it? Bite into it. Identify the flavors. Take your time and chew it, slowly. Swallow. You are offered a glass, something to drink. Take a sip. What is it? Place the small plate and glass on a nearby waiter's tray.

Now you're standing at the entrance of the grand ballroom. Take it all in, the rows of tables, the decorations. What's the theme of the evening? How do you feel being here in this place that was prepared especially for you? Don't overthink it; simply allow whatever arises to do so in its own time. The lovely lady at the registration table smiles and appears delighted to meet you: she's heard so much about you and the humanitarian work you've done on behalf of women and children. You greet her with an equally warm smile and thank her for the kind acknowledgment.

After you happily sign her program, she hands you your table number, and you take your auction booklet and placard and the evening's program. A tall, well-groomed courtesy host in a tux and tails grabs your hand in their white-gloved one. My, this person is quite charming and uncommonly attractive. What do you like best about this person? How do you feel while with them?

Before you can ask for a name, you are seated at your table. What are you thinking? You are in the front row, stage left. You lift your skirt to sit, and as you do, you get a glimpse of your dazzling shoes, and you await the beginning of the evening's festivities....

And so, dear reader, here we are once more, but this time we've reached the end of our time together. However, I suspect our journey is just beginning, and should that be the case for you as well, I look forward to connecting with you. In the meantime: I wish you the best of everything that is good. I am so delighted we had this time together. I'd like nothing better than to stay in touch with you. Check in from time to time. Let me know how the strategies are working for you. Share with me any other life circumstances you're interested in delving into more deeply. I am so excited to walk this journey with you, to laugh, to have fun, and to find an endless array of opportunities to discover our own permission!

Here is my contact information:

Instagram: @therealreginalouise
Facebook: www.facebook.com/regina.louise.5
Twitter: @iamreginalouise
Website: www.iamreginalouise.com

Much love,

Acknowledgments

Thank you, Elise Cannon, my homey from way back, my client, champion, and friend. How in the world did you get to be so kick-ass, and how did I get to benefit in all the best ways? Your heart is a cleared-out space for your juggernaut goddess energy to show up again and again in order to show the f**k out! Never stop doing that thang that you do the way that only you can do it.

And thank you to all the brave humans who gave of your time and energy and shared your stories so generously in the interest of luminous souls seeking to heal themselves with kick-ass strategies and bootstrapping gusto. May your lovingkindness lead the way to forever transformations.

Georgia Hughes, thank you for granting this project permission to exist on its own terms: you have truly been an ally in my desire to level up and make this contribution to personal-growth work. You are the best editor a manuscript could ever hope for, so loving and supportive. Our book is such a fun and festive contribution to the space of healing, and I am so grateful to have taken the journey with you: I wouldn't have wanted to do it with anyone else.

Mimi Kusch, your attention to detail made the difference in how each sentence moves. I appreciate the effort you took to collaborate and engage with the text, ensuring that the message of permission and unconditional self-love remain at the helm of this invitation.

To my family and friends, I look forward to all of you purchasing this book and gifting it to everyone you know! LOL! We're not done. The best part is yet to come, and that happens when we sell the hell outta this book and pay healing ourselves with our own love forward. Please, let's have a reason to hire a taco truck even if it is six feet apart. I love all of you.

Thanks, Jay Z, for including my father's song in the backdrop of "Girls, Girls, Girls." Not only do the sweet little royalty checks support several foster children's dreams, but I also get to hear my father's voice forever. Hug. Kiss. Hug. Kiss!

And finally, thank you, Red, for hanging with me, encouraging me. You'll always be my Day One!

Notes

Introduction

p. 2   *This is the task of anyone who carries the burden*: Regina Louise, *Someone Has Led This Child to Believe: A Memoir* (Evanston, IL: Agate Bolden, 2018), prologue.

p. 12   *adults view young Black girls*: Rebecca Epstein, Jamilia J. Blake, and Thalia González, "Girlhood Interrupted: The Erasure of Black Girls' Childhood," Georgetown Law Center on Poverty and Inequality, September 2017, https://www.law.georgetown.edu/poverty-inequality -center/wp-content/uploads/sites/14/2017/08/girlhood-interrupted .pdf.

Kick-Ass Strategy #1

p. 48   *self-kindness involves more*: Kristin Neff, *Self-Compassion: The Proven Power of Being Kind to Yourself* (2011; repr., New York: HarperCollins, 2012), 42.

Kick-Ass Strategy #3

p. 77   *I have cherished the ideal*: Nelson Mandela, "I Am Prepared to Die," April 20, 1964, The full transcript of Mandela's speech is available at http://db.nelsonmandela.org/speeches/pub_view.asp?pg=item& ItemID=NMS010&txtstr=prepared%20to%20die.

Kick-Ass Strategy #7

p. 148   *that if we hear only a single story*: Chimamanda Ngozi Adichie, "The Danger of a Single Story," TED Talk, July 2009, https://www .ted.com/talks/chimamanda_ngozi_adichie_the_danger_of_a _single_story.

Kick-Ass Stategy #8

p. 171   *Fifty-three percent of Americans*: National Women's Law Centre, "The Lifetime Wage Gap, State by State" (March 2020), https://nwlc .org/resources/the-lifetime-wage-gap-state-by-state.

p. 172   *Black women are just as ambitious*: LeanIn.Org, "The Pay Gap Is the Tip of the Iceberg for Black Women," *PR Newswire*, August 22, 2019, https://www.prnewswire.com/news-releases/the-pay-gap-is-the-tip -of-the-iceberg-for-black-women-300905708.html.

Kick-Ass Strategy #9

p. 189   *With a spiritual mind treatment*: "Spiritual Mind Treatment," Center for Spiritual Living, accessed February 5, 2021, http://www .scienceofminduk.org/what_spiritual_mind_treatment.html.

Kick-Ass Strategy #11

p. 217   *this running or turning away from feelings*: Drew Horning, conversation with the author, October 2020.

Kick-Ass Strategy #14

p. 259   *speaking is a form of writing*: Pat Schneider, *Writing Alone and with Others* (New York: Oxford University Press, 2003).

p. 270   *knowing that the Universe is unfolding*: Rev. Alice Bandy, "Grace: Being a Transparency of the Divine," in Rev. Christian Sorensen, *Foundations of the Science of the Mind — Student Workbook* (Los Angeles: United Centers for Spiritual Living, 2007).

Index

About the Author

Regina Louise is a sought-after speaker, teacher, coach, and author. Recently she was the recipient of the prestigious Christopher Award, given to producers for stories that "affirm the highest values of the human spirit." In 2019 she received the Jordan Award for service in transforming foster care through advocacy and the arts; the Community Service Award for Children and Families from the Seneca Foundation; and the NAMIC Vision Award for original programming that "reflects the lives, spirit, and contributions of people of color and represents the ethnic and cultural diversity of the viewing audience." She is the author of the bestselling memoirs *Somebody's Someone* and *Someone Has Led This Child to Believe*. A Lifetime movie, *I Am Somebody's Child: The Regina Louise Story*, is based on her life and was nominated for a 2020 NAACP Award for Best Director.

In 2011, wanting to honor a pledge she made to herself as a young foster child and to support her son who was struggling in college, Regina returned to college. She graduated summa cum laude from the California Institute of Integral Studies and then went on to University of California, Riverside, to earn an MFA in creative writing and writing for the performing arts.

Regina's work in the theater was nominated for two NAACP Theatre Awards. Currently a Hoffman Process teacher, she also leads workshops and has speaking engagements around the country. She is often featured in magazines and on news outlets, including *Good Morning America*, PBS, BBC, NBC, CNN, NPR, HLN, and many others.

www.iamreginalouise.com